First Edition

A RAISING UP
Memories of a North Carolina Childhood

R. C. Fowler

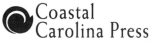

Coastal
Carolina Press

Wilmington, North Carolina

A Raising Up—Memories of a North Carolina Childhood
R. C. Fowler

Coastal
Carolina Press

Coastal Carolina Press
4709 College Acres Drive, Suite 1
Wilmington, NC 28403 U.S.A.
www.coastalcarolinapress.org

First Edition

Cover artwork and book illustrations by Ruth Marie McCurry
Book designed by Maximum Design, Inc.

Printed in the United States of America
Library of Congress Cataloging - in - Publication Data

Fowler, R.C., 1927-
    A raising up : memories of a North Carolina childhood / R.C. Fowler. -- 1st ed.
      p. cm.
    ISBN 1-928556-06-X (trade) -- ISBN 1-928556-07-8 (casebound)
    1. Fowler, R.C., 1927---Childhood and youth. 2. Rural life--North Carolina. 3.Farm
    life--North Carolina--Pender County 4. North Carolina--Biography. I. Title.

CT275.F68716 A3 2000
975.6'625043'092--dc21
[B]

ISBN 1-928556-06-X

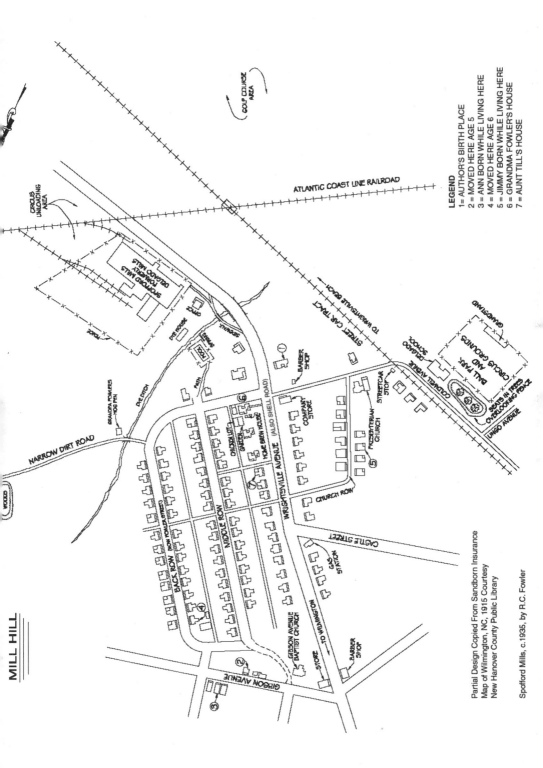

MILL HILL

LEGEND
1 = AUTHOR'S BIRTH PLACE
2 = MOVED HERE AGE 5
3 = ANN BORN WHILE LIVING HERE
4 = MOVED HERE AGE 6
5 = JIMMY BORN WHILE LIVING HERE
6 = GRANDMA FOWLER'S HOUSE
7 = AUNT TILL'S HOUSE

ATLANTIC COAST LINE RAILROAD

CIRCUS UNLOADING AREA

GOLF COURSE AREA

SPOFFORD MILLS FORMERLY DELGADO MILLS

DYE HOUSE
OFFICE
TOWER
DYE DITCH
SPRING
SPILLWAY
STREET CAR TRACT
TO WRIGHTSVILLE BEACH

NARROW DIRT ROAD
WOODS

GRANDPA FOWLERS HOG PEN

BARBER SHOP

PATH

CHICKEN LOT
GARDEN
HOME BARN HOUSE

BACK ROW (NOW FOWLER STREET)
MIDDLE ROW
WRIGHTSVILLE AVENUE (ALSO SHELL ROAD)

COMPANY STORE

STREETCAR STOP

COLGROVE AVENUE
DELGADO SCHOOL
BALL PARK AND CIRCUS GROUNDS
GRANDSTAND
SEATS IN TREES OVERLOOKING FENCE
LINGO AVENUE

PRESBYTERIAN CHURCH

CHURCH ROW

CASTLE STREET

GAS STATION
TO WILMINGTON
STORE

GIBSON AVENUE BAPTIST CHURCH

BARBER SHOP

GIBSON AVENUE

Partial Design Copied From Sandborn Insurance
Map of Wilmington, NC, 1915 Courtesy
New Hanover County Public Library

Spofford Mills, c.1935, by R.C. Fowler

The names of all of the relatives mentioned in the story are real. Most of the other characters' names have been changed.

Due to the passage of time, some of the dialogue and events included in the story may not be stated precisely as they happened, but the threads that weave the story are true.

Acknowledgements

In the late evenings, I would slip away to a small cabin at the back of our property and write. I thank my wife, Lee, for putting up with my blank stares during the day and my absence during the late night hours. Thank you for your patience and understanding; somehow you knew I had to write this story.

My daughter Connie will never know how much her quiet patience and devotion in translating my longhand scribbling into the printed word meant to me. Connie, I thank you so much. You were—and still are—a blessing to me.

I am most thankful to Virginia (Ginger) Dunlap, not only for her invaluable help in editing my story but also for her encouragement along the way. Ginger, I am truly grateful for all of your help.

Finally, to Sherrie Hurlee, who helped me with the final wrap-up— thank you for your help and patience.

The author at 11 years of age.

Prologue

To some, my story *A Raising Up* may not be special, but it's special to me. It's a story of one family's struggle during a difficult time—the period from 1932 until the fall of 1945—the years of the Great Depression and World War II. It was a time when life was hard, but we were not alone in our struggle. Many families had similar experiences.

A Raising Up tells of our family's life in a cotton mill village. It was there, on a cold December afternoon in 1927, that I came into this world. I was born in the front corner bedroom of one of the many company-owned houses that lined the row streets. I was the first of six children.

In the spring of 1937 we moved about twenty-five miles to a farm in rural Pender County, where I was quickly introduced to the mule and plow. Our farm home was a small, unpainted frame house with a tin roof. In this humble home, I was taught the value of hard work, truthfulness, and responsibility. Here, through good times and bad, our family grew ever closer.

In this book I write of the Owl. Sometimes in my mind I picture his view as he made his flight through the night over a small farmhouse, its tin roof brightened by the moonlight.

From time to time in the story, I also speak of angels. Could have been after the Owl passed over our home and flew on through the night that a guardian angel came, hovered, and lingered a while. Who's to say?

There in the house below, in a small bedroom, four brothers lay in one bed and two sisters in another, all trying to stay warm, each with his or her own special dreams. In another room lay the father and the mother, the father with his dreams of making it good on the farm and giving up the long ride back and forth each day to his job at the cotton mill. The mother's dreams were of seeing her children fed, clothed, and brought up the right way.

I spent eight and a half years in that little house and on that farm. In the fall of 1945, I left home to seek my fortune. It's been more than half a century since I left, but memories of my childhood and the old homeplace still creep into my mind.

My story may seem insignificant. But as the number of us plowboys dwindle, I thought I would write it—in tribute to my mother, and to all the families who lived through those times.

R. C. Fowler

December 1999

One

Some of my first recollections are of living in Mount Tabor, a small town in Columbus County, North Carolina. I must have been around four years old, and my sister Doris was a year and a half younger than me. These memories have grown dim over the years, and about all I can remember of that place is living in a house on a lane leading off the main road.

I do remember climbing a peach tree in the front yard, getting my foot caught in a fork of the tree and hanging there upside down, cussing. I'd picked up cussing early from my daddy. Mama came out, helped me down, and switched me real good for cussing. My excuse was that you're supposed to cuss when you're hanging upside down in a peach tree.

My next memories are of living in an old house on a highway just north of Wilmington, North Carolina. One evening when I was about four and a half years old, some people brought Mama home from the hospital. She had a baby boy with her. She said his name was Bobby Lee. It didn't take me but a few days to see that a baby took up too much time. I talked to Mama about it. She said we'd have to keep him.

One day Mama said we were going to visit some of her distant relatives who lived down a narrow dirt road that ran alongside our house. We started out, Mama carrying Bobby and me and Doris walking. Well, at least I was walking, but Doris was wobbling and staggering along. Mama said, Doris, what on earth is the matter with you? Doris just stood over a big pine root in the road and said, Look at that pretty chicken.

Mama smelled Doris' breath and said, Doris, you're drunk. I didn't know what drunk was, but I found out that night when Mama and Daddy were talking about what had happened. Drunk was what happened when a little girl found where her daddy kept the homemade wine and helped herself to it. Daddy hid the wine.

We moved again, this time just a little ways south along the highway. Daddy wanted to hurry and get settled in 'cause it was coon-hunting season and he was a big coon hunter. Sometimes he'd bring them home for Mama to cook. At first I didn't want to eat raccoon meat, but then Mama and Daddy said that anybody that ate coon meat could climb real good.

One day after eating coon meat, I started to show off by climbing a small tree next to our side porch. It must have been true about eating coon meat and climbing 'cause everybody on the porch said they'd never seen anyone climb a tree like that.

One day my first cousin, Sam Wells, came to visit us. His mama, Aunt Ruth, was Mama's sister. Me and Sam had a good time playing with a little toy airplane that he'd brought with him. We talked about what a good thing it would be if we could fly. There was an old barn behind the house, so we climbed to the roof, held out our arms like airplane wings, and jumped. We hit the ground real hard. We lay on the ground a while wondering why we couldn't fly. Sam gave me his toy airplane. I knew me and Sam would be friends for life.

We moved again, not very far, just to a little farm back off in the woods like. Our new house was on what was called the Morgan farm. It was an old house with wood siding and high wooden steps going to the front porch. We could sit on the porch and look over the fields. They were sandy and lonesome-looking.

Daddy was sharecropping with Mr. Morgan, who must've been real rich 'cause he owned his own house as well as the farm where we lived. Our new home was grey-looking inside and out. Mama, Daddy, and Bobby, who was still a baby, slept in one room, and me and Doris slept in another. I'd lay there at night thinking how quiet and dark it was, and would feel a little scared. Doris would be asleep and I'd think how bare the room was and watch the window curtains moving in the breeze.

One night after I drifted off to sleep, a terrible screeching sound woke me up. I ran to Mama's room screaming, Mama, Mama, what is that? Mama opened the door and said, What's the matter, son? I told her about the awful screeching sound.

That's a screech owl, son.

What's he make that noise for?

Well, when he does that it means somebody's going to die soon. But we can stop him from screeching.

How, Mama?

By turning a man's shoe upside down in the corner of the room.

Mama, can you turn that shoe upside down in my room?

She did and went back to bed. I was still scared. There was just enough moonlight coming through the window that I could make out that shoe upside down in the corner. I hoped it would work. Doris was still asleep, and I finally fell asleep too. I woke up the next morning and the sun was shining. We were all still alive. It looked like that shoe in the corner had saved us.

Daddy had an uncle who owned a dairy nearby. Some days he'd go over and work part-time. One morning after breakfast, Daddy told Mama he was going to work at the dairy that day. After Daddy left, Mama said, Children, we're going out today and look for brierberries. Mama carried Bobby. It looked like we'd done decided to keep him after all. Me and Doris ran along beside her, every now and then running off in all directions if we thought we saw anything that looked like a brierberry bush. We had pretty good luck and after a while Mama said we had enough berries for supper. On the way home me and Doris ate some of the berries.

When Daddy got home, he had some milk and butter he'd brought from the dairy. Mama said, We're going to cook biscuits to go with our milk, butter and berries. She kept the flour in what was called a fifty-pound lard stand, a kind of large can with a lid. When Mama opened the lid, she said, Well, we're almost scraping the bottom of the barrel. There was enough flour for biscuits, though, and we had a good supper.

Sometimes, late in the evening after supper and before bedtime, folks would come by to visit. Usually they were about Mama and Daddy's age and were sharecroppers too. They talked about different things, but mostly they talked about the Depression, the hard times and all. It just seemed like nobody knew what to do to make things better.

Mama said she'd got a letter from Aunt Maybelle and Uncle Rudolph, who were living in Fayetteville, and they thought there was a job coming up at the cotton mill there. Daddy said he'd go to Fayetteville after the crop was in. I went to bed. The last thing I remembered before going to sleep was seeing the red glow of a cigarette in the dark and hearing them still talking about the Depression thing.

One day Daddy brought a cow home. I heard some neighbors say it was a Holstein heifer. The cow was black and white and she licked her sides a lot. I'd never seen such a big tongue. I wanted to pet the cow, but Mama said, No, you see that big tongue she's got? If she licks you on your forehead, it'll give you a cowlick. That means your hair will stand straight up in front for the rest of your life. I didn't want that 'cause I was having big hair trouble already. It was starting to go around and around. Mama said it was beginning to curl.

Daddy had three younger brothers who'd come sometimes to help out on the farm. Their names were Ralph, Robert and Otto. I liked for them to come 'cause they were always laughing and joking. One day when they were helping with the tobacco crop, Daddy let me go to the barn to watch them put in tobacco. When they came from the field up to the barn, they were really laughing. I heard them say that Robert had bit the head off a tobacco worm. I didn't see anything funny about that, but I laughed anyway. Otto said, R.C., I can spell my name backwards. I said, Let me hear. He spelled his name and it was the same frontwards and backwards. He thought that was real funny.

One evening when I came in from playing, Mama said we were all going over to a neighbor's house. I asked her what for. She said we were going to pay our respects. When we walked into the neighbor's house, some people were crying and others just looked real sad. There was a big box in their front room that was raised up higher than my head. A man picked me up so I could see in the box. There was a big man laying in the box with his hands across his chest. I asked, What's he in that box for? The man said, Because he's dead.

Well, I wasn't sure what dead was, but I'd heard that when you died, you couldn't play or do anything anymore. It was very serious. I didn't think that even Daddy's brothers could see anything funny about being dead. I didn't know why that man died, but I thought maybe it was 'cause he didn't put a shoe upside down in the corner of his room the night we heard the screech owl.

🔉

One morning Mama said, R.C., today we're going for a walk down the railroad tracks. I liked that 'cause maybe I'd see a train. We walked down the little dirt road towards the main highway. We crossed the main road and started walking down the tracks. There were plenty of rocks to throw and I walked on the rail, seeing how far I could go without falling off. Before long we came to a shed-type building. Mama said it was a depot. There were lots of women there with small children. At first I thought, Oh boy, we can all play. But as soon as we got there we had to stand in a line. The children up front started crying and screaming. Before long I was at the front of the line, and a woman in a white dress stuck a needle in my arm. It hurt a lot. After that, me and Mama left and started back down the railroad tracks towards home. I was glad to get away from that old depot.

On the way home my arm began to hurt. I didn't try to balance myself on the rail or throw any rocks. I walked along with my head down and my hands in my pockets. I didn't care if I never went down those old railroad tracks again. We left the tracks and crossed the main highway and turned down the dirt road towards home. When we got home, my arm was hurting real bad. Mama said I must've had a reaction to the shot. I went to bed and fell asleep.

A few days later, Daddy's brothers came back to help put in tobacco. Everybody was at the barn or in the tobacco field except Mama, me, Doris and Bobby. I wanted to go to the tobacco barn and hear Daddy's brothers laugh and talk. I couldn't wait for them to come home for dinner, so I slipped away and walked to the barn. When Daddy saw me, he asked what I was doing there. I knew I'd done wrong, slipping away, and knew I was in a lot of trouble. The only thing I could think to say was, Mama said dinner's ready. Daddy said it seemed a little early for dinner to be ready, but he told everybody, Let's go eat.

They put the mules in the stable, closed the barn doors and walked back to our house. Everything was okay until we got to our front yard. Mama came out on the front porch and asked Daddy, Why is everybody coming home so early? Daddy told Mama, R.C. said dinner was ready. I was standing at the bottom of the front porch steps looking up at Mama, and Daddy was standing behind me. Mama said, Dinner's not ready and I didn't tell him that.

Daddy must've thought something was wrong, 'cause on the way home he'd broke a switch off a bush and started hitting it on his leg. Well, I knew he still had that switch so I started walking up those steps. When I got on the first step, I felt that switch on my backside. I ran for the top step as quick as I could, but Daddy was faster and he switched me all the way up the steps. I thought, I'll never tell a lie again. Laughing and having fun ain't worth all these problems. My little behind felt like it was on fire!

A few days after the whipping I was sitting on the porch step, watching some men working out in the field. They had a small thing the mules were pulling that looked like a wheelbarrow turned upside down. Daddy said it was a sand pan and that the men were making that big pile of sand so that the fertilizer company could use it for filler in their fertilizer.

As I watched, the sky began to get dark and the wind began to blow. The men quit working and left. I sat there on the top step with both hands under my chin and watched as the wind blew around a rusty piece of tin on the barn roof. How lonesome it seemed when it blew up and fell back down. It sounded like *squeak* and *squonk*, and the swirling sand made it seem even more lonesome. I thought with all that was happening, like my hair beginning to curl, hearing the screech owl, getting a needle stuck in my arm, Daddy whipping me all the way up them high steps to the porch, and the lonesome squeaking and squonking of that tin roof, I was ready to leave that place. I hoped we'd go to Fayetteville soon. I didn't even care if we took Bobby.

That night Daddy went hunting. He really liked dogs and hunting. He said, If I catch anything, I'll bring it home so you can see it. He was gone a long time, and I went to sleep. Later Daddy came home and woke me up. Mama said, Alton, leave the child alone.

Carrie, I want him to see this possum.

I said, get that thing out of this house.

Daddy turned the possum loose and it ran under their bed. He shined the flashlight under the bed and told me to look under there. When I looked, I saw two big shining eyes. I said, Damn, what eyes! Mama said, Alton, you see what you've done. You've taught the boy to cuss. I hope you're satisfied. Now get that stinking possum out of here. Daddy grumbled, but he put the possum in the yard.

Next day I heard Mama and Daddy talking about the farming season coming to an end. They were saying it was time to close things down and go to Aunt Maybelle and Uncle Rudolph's in Fayetteville. That night Daddy said, R.C. let's wrestle. We played on the floor and had a good time. Daddy began to sing a song,

Me and my wife live all alone
In a little log hut we call our own;
She loves gin and I love rum,
And don't we have a lot of fun!

Ha, ha, ha, you and me,
Little brown jug, don't I love thee!
Ha, ha, ha, you and me,
Little brown jug, don't I love thee!

When I go toiling on the farm
I take the little jug under my arm;
Place it under a shady tree,
Little brown jug, 'tis you and me.

He couldn't sing, but I liked the wrestling part anyway. After a while, Daddy said, R.C., let's go check on the barn one last time and close things down. I asked Daddy if I could carry the lantern and he said okay. I had to hold the lantern with both hands up high in front of me. It was heavy, but I liked to hold it anyway. We checked the barn, closed the doors and went back home.

The next morning, Daddy caught the train to Fayetteville. A few days later, Mama got a letter from him saying to come on up. Me, Mama,

Doris and Bobby caught the train and went to Aunt Maybelle's house in Fayetteville. Aunt Maybelle had three boys. I slept with them.

Next morning, Aunt Maybelle told Uncle Rudolph something had to be done, it was just too cold in the house and the children were freezing. Mama said there was a man who sold wood about a block away and you could get all the wood a man could carry for twenty-five cents. Mama and Aunt Maybelle got the twenty-five cents together. It was decided that Uncle Rudolph would carry the wood because he was taller and had the longest arms. When Daddy and Uncle Rudolph got to the wood yard, Uncle Rudolph held out his arms and Daddy loaded him down. Daddy said the man selling the wood told him he'd never seen one man carry so much wood. We were warm for the next few nights.

On Christmas morning when I woke up, I went into the kitchen. On the table were three wooden toy pistols. Daddy had carved them out of the stove wood they'd brought home. Me and Aunt Maybelle's two oldest boys had a lot of fun pretending to shoot each other with the toy pistols.

One day after we'd been in Fayetteville a few weeks, Daddy got home from work early. Mama said, Alton, what are you doing home so early?

Well, Carrie, I lost my job.

What happened?

They just said there was no more work, and they were sorry because I was a good worker. Do you think we have enough money to catch the train back to Wilmington?

I think so, Alton.

Maybe I can get work in the cotton mill there. Pa's still the dye house boss man at Spofford Mills. Maybe he can help me get on.

I hope so, Alton. I'd like to go back to Wilmington. All my folks are there, except Maybelle here in Fayetteville.

I wanted to go back too because Mama said that's where I was born, in the front corner bedroom of Grandma and Grandpa Fowler's house. We left Fayetteville and took the train back to Wilmington.

We moved into a cotton mill village house on Gibson Avenue. It had a narrow front porch looking over the sidewalk. The porch floor was high off the ground and me and Doris would lean over the porch rail and watch people go by. She'd get me in trouble sometimes, telling me to spit on the children when they walked by. Sometimes I would. Mama didn't think much of that.

It was real cold in that house. We had a wood heater in the front room. One day Bobby was playing close by the heater and tripped and fell. His head hit the damper on the front of the heater and the damper handle punched him in the eye. When we picked him up and looked at his eye, all you could see was white, no blue eyeball. Mama took him to the doctor and when she brought him home, he had a patch over his eye like a pirate. He looked funny with the eye patch and his hair sticking straight up in front. Mama said he had a cowlick. That heifer cow we had on the Morgan farm must've licked him in the face.

Daddy got a job at the mill as night watchman. He said the pay wasn't much, about ten dollars a week, and that the workers were talking about going on strike. He said it sounded good, though, to hear the roar of the cotton machines again, even if they did run all day and night. Mama said that her daddy, my Grandpa Harrell, was the water boy when they built the cotton mill and my Grandpa Fowler was now the dye house boss. He mixed the dyes that colored the cloth. Daddy used to work in the mill when he was a little boy. He said he was so small he had to stand on a box to reach the machine.

Living there wasn't any better than living in Fayetteville. It was cold and drafty, and there wasn't a lot to eat. We had running water, but the toilet was an outhouse. We were used to the outhouse, though. That's all we'd ever had. The county tried to help us. Sometimes they'd send someone around with cans of dried milk. It had a sweet taste when you ate it dry.

One night we were sitting around the wood heater and there was a loud noise on our front porch, like someone was hitting it with a rock. We all looked at one another and Doris said, What was that? Mama said, You know it's Valentine's Day and I bet that somebody has left us a valentine. Usually when someone leaves a valentine, they'll make a noise like that. We all ran out on the front porch and sure enough, there was a pretty valentine laying there. We heard someone laughing and we could see the shadows of three or four young men among the bushes. I could tell that they were Daddy's brothers and Aunt Til's boy, Carl, who was Daddy's first cousin.

Bobby took the valentine, ran into the house and gave it to Mama. Mama opened it up and said, You all stand around the heater now and I'll read it to you. We backed up to the warm heater and Mama read the valentine. Sure enough, it was from Daddy's brothers and Carl.

The next morning, I heard Mama and Daddy talking about our house and how they didn't like it. They said it was just too hard to heat and it was so small. Mama said, I think there's a house down the street that's going to be vacant soon. It's a little larger and it's not as high off the ground. If we could move into it, I think we'd be better off.

A few days later, our house caught on fire. I saw the smoke and hollered for Mama. She told me to run down to the little store on the corner and tell the store man to call the fire department. I ran down to the corner and told the man our house was on fire. He had a telephone and called the fire department. The fire trucks came real quick and put the fire out.

That night Daddy said, Carrie, y'know that house down the street that you were talking about moving to? Well, that family moved out today and I've already talked to the cotton mill folks. They said we could move there. I think it's time to leave this house. Mama said, I think so too, it smells like smoke. It reminds me of the house we lived in in Tabor City. You know when it caught fire and burned, we lost everything we had. I'm ready to move.

We moved again, this time about one block down and across the street. The house we moved into was still a mill village house. It wasn't as high off the ground as the last house, but the yard was real small. The front yard was about ten feet, and the side yards were about five feet on either side of the house.

One day my mama's aunt on her mother's side came to see us. She lived on Mercer Avenue, which was about a mile from where we were living. Mama said, This is my Aunt Lanie, your great-aunt. She's going to stay with us a few days. She'll be taking care of you children because I have to go away for a little while.

I asked Mama, Why do you have to go away? She said, I just do, that's all.

The next day Mama left and Aunt Lanie took care of us. She was a real religious woman. She talked to us about Jesus and read the Bible a lot. In a few days Mama came home and brought a little baby with her. It was a pretty little girl. Mama said her name was Ann.

Mama and Daddy were talking about how our family was growing and how we needed more room. Daddy said there was a house on the back row of the mill village that was vacant, and that it had more side and front yards and a big back yard where we could have a vegetable garden. You could tell that Daddy wanted a garden to work in real bad. We moved to the house on the back row.

The yard was bigger and there were some big trees. It was early September and Daddy got busy planting a fall garden. Our house was on a corner lot. On one side was a street and on the other side was another mill house. A little boy who was about seven years old lived there, and he hollered and screamed a lot. Mama said he was real sick. One day a big black car came and took him away. Mama said he had died and that he was better off.

❧

One evening Daddy came home from the mill and told Mama that the mill workers were all on strike and that nobody would be getting any pay until it was over. That night Mama and Daddy and some of the other mill workers sat around our front room and talked about the strike. It sounded like things were just going to get worse. After the neighbors left, Mama put us children to bed and said, Just hush now and go to sleep, everything's gonna be all right. Before I went to sleep, I could hear Mama working in the kitchen and singing,

> *As a mother stills her child,*
> *Thou canst hush the ocean wild;*
> *Boisterous waves obey Thy will*
> *When Thou sayest to them "Be still!"*
> *Wondrous Sovereign of the sea,*
> *Jesus, Savior, pilot me.*

The next morning a man came to our house and talked to Daddy. He said, Alton, all the mill workers are on strike and no one's working, but you're the night watchman and we still need someone to look out for things at the mill. You'll have to keep on working. Daddy said, If I do, the strikers will beat me up for sure. The man told Daddy that wouldn't happen. He said, We've already met with the strike leaders, and everybody knows that the mill must be protected from vandalism so when things are settled, they'll have a place to work. Daddy told the man, Okay. If that's the way it is, I'll be there tonight to look after the mill. Daddy said he wasn't real happy about the situation, but he knew it was the right thing to do and that we could sure use the money.

One day, a few weeks later, Daddy came home from the mill and said the strike was over and all the mill workers could go back to work. They were even hiring more workers. Daddy and Mama talked it over and it was decided that Mama would go to work at the cotton mill too. She got hired, all right, only thing was her and Daddy worked on different shifts. Sometimes they'd both be away from home. When that happened, Mama always had some lady lined up to stay with us children. Mama said sometimes when her and Daddy were going back and forth to work, they'd pass one another like two strangers in the night.

&

One day Mama said, R.C., you need to be in school, but your birthday's December 26th. That's too late to start school this year, so you'll have to wait until next year. I wanted to go to school, but it seemed a little scary. School was about six blocks away. Mama said, Don't worry, we'll find a house on the Church Row. That's only two blocks from school. I was glad to hear that, 'cause there were a few older boys who were bullies and liked to fight us smaller boys. I was small for my age and kinda skinny. I usually hid from them when I was walking from our house to Grandma Fowler's, which was about four blocks away. It just seemed like they knew when I was going to Grandma's, and they'd chase me all the way to her house.

I hated the walk to Grandma's house, but when I got there it was worth being chased. She always hugged me and had something special for me. Mostly she knew that I liked pork-n-beans and she always had some. In the summertime, me and Grandma would sit on her front porch, talk, and watch the people going back and forth from the mill and the company store. The company store was just across the street. I liked to go there, mostly 'cause there was a big candy counter right by the front door. Another thing I liked about the store was, some nights me and Grandma could hear music coming from the big upstairs room. Everybody called it the band room. The music players all lived on the Mill Hill. Uncle Roy Potter, who married my Aunt Bessie, played the trumpet.

Seven of Daddy's brothers and sisters and Grandpa worked at the mill. They got paid on Friday, and I was always hanging around the kitchen table at payoff time. I'd done found out that was a good time to hang around, 'cause on Friday evenings Grandma had a big supper meal and all my aunts and uncles were at the table eating, talking and always laughing.

Grandma bought a high stool just for me and said that I could sit at the end of the table. It was a pretty blue stool. Every time one of my aunts or uncles finished eating and left the table, they'd always come by where I was sitting on my stool and leave me a nickel, dime, or quarter. Sometimes I'd get all quarters and when I did, Grandma'd say, That's pretty good money, R.C. I'd say, I think so, Grandma, and you know what? Mr. Mooney at the company store likes it too.

After the big supper on Friday evenings, my aunts and uncles would get ready to go out for the night. They were always excited and talking about boyfriends and girlfriends and things. When Grandma finished cleaning the kitchen, she'd say, R.C., let's go sit on the front porch. I'd sit on the porch with Grandma and we'd talk about things like what she was going to plant in her garden and how she was thinking about getting some more chickens and how it was about time for Grandpa to start making his home brew for the year.

One evening I put my hand in my pocket and felt my money. I told Grandma, If I stay with you tonight, I can get up early in the morning and go across the street to Mr. Mooney's company store and buy candy and stuff. She said I could stay. We sat on the front porch and watched the sun go down and the company store lights come on. It was band night, and the music players were warming up. I could see Uncle Roy through the upstairs window of the band room playing his trumpet.

The cotton mill machines droned on and I began to feel sleepy. I must have fallen asleep, 'cause the next thing I knew Grandma was laying me down on Uncle Ralph and Uncle Otto's bed. I raised up and she said, Everything's okay. You can sleep here tonight, and tomorrow when you wake up, you can go to Mr. Mooney's store.

The next morning Grandma cooked breakfast, and after everybody ate I asked her if I could go to the store. She said I could, but to be careful crossing that street. I looked both ways, crossed the street and looked back to see if Grandma had seen me being so careful. Sure enough, she was standing on the front porch watching me.

When I got inside the store, I walked back and forth in front of the candy counter. There was a lot to choose from. I couldn't decide whether to get the black twisted licorice sticks or the sweet pieces of candy that looked like little weenies. I got some of each. Mr. Mooney was very patient. He took my money, put my candy in a brown paper sack, gave it to me and said, Now, R.C., you go straight back to your grandma's and be careful crossing that street. I left the store, put my hand in the sack, and got the piece of candy that looked like a small weenie. If it was red inside when you broke it open you'd get a free piece of candy. It was white.

One day when I was at Grandma's, she told me my Aunt Bessie was going to start bringing her little girl, Jeanette, over on Friday nights and they'd be eating supper with us. I guessed that'd be all right. I just wondered how come they had to come over on Friday nights. I knew one thing, Jeanette wasn't going to rock in my rocking chair or sit on my stool at the kitchen table. Sometimes Jeanette's daddy, Uncle Roy Potter, would come over to Grandma and Grandpa's house and practice playing the trumpet and Aunt Helen would play the piano.

I liked playing around Grandma's house and yard. Grandpa had two raccoons that Daddy had caught when they were young and he'd made pets out of them. They were always into everything and upset Grandma a lot. One day I heard Grandma tell Grandpa, Luke, I want you to get them raccoons away from here. I'm tired of having to put up with them. He told Grandma, I'm keeping them raccoons. They're my pets.

I wanted to go to school and learn things, but it was going to be a good while before I could start. I told Mama, I want to know how to read and write and how to add and them kind of things. Mama told me I didn't have to wait to start school to learn things because she could help me. She said I ought to learn pretty fast.

Mama started helping me and I began to learn to read and write and do some adding and subtracting. We were getting the newspaper and I liked to look at the funnies.   After a while, I was able to read them a little. Nearly every night after supper I'd study my reading, writing and arithmetic.

One morning I woke up with my jaw swollen real big. Mama said that I had an abscessed tooth and I should stay in the house out of the weather until it got better. I wanted to go to Grandma's and I worried Mama until she said I could. She told me to go straight there and to be good.

When I got to Grandma's, I opened the kitchen door, and when she saw my swollen jaw, she said, R.C., you go outside and spit out that chewing tobacco now! I said, Grandma, I don't have any chewing tobacco in my mouth. Mama said I have an abscessed tooth, and it hurts real bad. Grandma said she was real sorry and she gave me a hug. Then she gave me an aspirin and a spoonful of cocoa quinine. I liked the taste of the cocoa quinine.

Grandma was baking biscuits on her wood stove and I stayed in the kitchen with her. It was nice and warm, and the heat from the stove felt good on my swollen jaw. The baking biscuits smelled real good. Grandma looked in a cabinet in the kitchen, took something out and said, Hold out your hand. When I did, she put two shiny marbles in it. She said, I found them when I was working in the garden yesterday. She knew that I liked marbles 'cause I was making friends with a lot of boys on the Mill Hill and they all loved to play marbles. It seemed like Grandma was always finding marbles in her garden. I didn't know how she did it. I looked in the garden a lot and I never found one.

I told Grandma I wanted to go outside and feed the chickens and play. She said, Your grandpa's in the home brew house, why don't you go watch him for a while. I went out to Grandpa's home brew house. He was working on putting brew in the bottles. I said, Hey, Grandpa, what you doin'? He said, Well, I'm putting the home brew in these bottles and sealing them with these bottle caps.

I watched him for a while. The bottles would go around on a little table that turned. He'd pull down on a handle and a bottle cap would seal a bottle. Grandpa hadn't looked at me yet. He was still looking at his bottle capping job. He stopped capping and took a big swallow out of one of the bottles and smacked his lips. He looked at my swollen jaw and said, Humph. Then he took some more swallows of the home brew, looked at me again and said, What happened to you? I told him that Mama said I had an abscessed tooth but that Grandma had given me some medicine and it wasn't hurting as bad.

Grandpa's pet raccoons had been sleeping in the corner of the home brew house and they were beginning to wake up and stir around. I said, Grandpa, Grandma don't like them raccoons. She says that you ought to get rid of them. They mess up her house. Grandpa didn't like that. He got upset and said, It's my house too, and them raccoons will stay until I say they go.

He threw one of the bottles into the corner of the home brew house. It scared the raccoons. They jumped up on the table and knocked over a lot of Grandpa's bottles. They fell on the floor and there was broke glass all over the place. Grandpa cussed. One of the raccoons ran between his legs and out the door. Grandpa said, You'd better git, you bastard! He threw the bottle he was drinking out of into the corner. It scared the other raccoon and he ran between Grandpa's legs too. Grandpa cussed him. Then he said, Them raccoons have got to go. I thought to myself, I know Grandma will be happy about that.

I walked over to a wooden davenport that Grandpa kept out in the yard, up close by his home brew house. One end of it was rolled up kind of like a pillow. Sometimes I'd lay on it and watch the clouds and imagine what all they was shaped like. I went over and laid down on the davenport. I hadn't been laying there long before the neighbor's cat came over, jumped up and lay down beside me.

After a while, Grandpa came out of the home brew house and walked over to where I was. He was still sipping on one of them bottles. I had my hands under my head and my knees drawed up. Grandpa said, What you doin', boy?

Oh, I'm just resting.

Humph.

Grandpa, I heard some of them mill folks say that they think you spend too much time messing around with that home brew.

They do, huh?

Yeah, and some of them say they think you like it too much.

You listen to me, boy. It's none of their damn business and if I hear any more out of you about my home brew, your little behind won't be laying on my davenport anymore.

Grandpa went back in the home brew house and slammed the door real hard. The cat jumped up, ran across the yard and went through his special hole in the hedge that divided the neighbor's house from Grandpa's.

I went into the house. Grandma was still cooking. I told her what Grandpa had said about me not laying on the davenport anymore. She said, Don't worry about it, I'll handle your grandpa.

Grandma, how come you're cooking so much?

Well, it's Friday and you know what a crowd we have for supper on Fridays.

You don't think Jeanette's coming over, do you?

She might.

I thought, well, she ain't gonna get none of my Friday night money 'cause I'm just gonna be sittin' on my blue stool when she gets here.

Two

We were still taking the paper, and Daddy said that in a few months we'd be able to buy a radio. I thought that would really be something, it played music and everything. I knew 'cause Grandpa had one. Grandpa had more things in his house than most mill workers 'cause he was a boss man. There were even inside toilets in his house. All the mill bosses had inside toilets. Everybody else on the Mill Hill had outhouses, just like us.

Grandpa really liked to listen to the news on his radio. He listened to it every night. He said that the world had better take notice of that fellow in Germany called Hitler.

Well, my jaw'd got all right, but my ears were starting to hurt a lot. Mama said I had the earache and that when I was real small, I'd had the earache nearly all the time. My ears began to hurt worse. Almost every night I'd wake up screaming, and Daddy would come over to my bed, light a cigarette and blow smoke in my ears. I didn't know if that helped or not, but after a while I'd go back to sleep.

One day when I was at Grandma's house, I climbed up on the fireplace hearth to see a fancy-looking clock that Grandpa had on the mantel. I was moving the clock around and slipped and fell on the floor. Something fell and hit me on the side of the head. Mama was there and she came running and said, What on earth's going on? I was crying, but I told her what happened. She rubbed my head and said it was going to be all right. Then she said, Look at that. She was pointing to something on the hearth. It was a big yellow and red lump. She looked at it real close and said, That's a big lump of corruption that came out of your ear when that clock hit you on the head. My head was sore a few days, but my ears stopped hurting.

&

We moved again, this time to another mill house on the Church Row. It was only a few minutes' walk to the schoolhouse. At the end of the street from our new house was a wooden church. I guessed that was where the street got its name. Nearly all the streets in Spofford Mill village were called rows. They were streets with a row of houses on either side. The names were like Back Row, Middle Row, Church Row. Then there was Wrightsville Avenue that came from Wilmington and went through Spofford Mills and on to Wrightsville Beach. Most everybody called Wrightsville Avenue the shell road. It was made out of oyster shells.

Sometimes Mama's Aunt Lanie would stop by to see us. She'd be going from house to house asking for a donation to help build a church in East Wilmington. That's where Grandma Harrell and Aunt Lanie lived. Aunt Lanie wanted everybody to go to Sunday school and church. One day when she was at our house on the Church Row, I pointed to the church on the corner and told her, That's where I go to Sunday school. She said, That's good. That's a Presbyterian church and they're good people, but I'm a Baptist, and I have faith that some day there will be a Baptist church in East Wilmington.

Aunt Lanie said she was having Sunday school class next Sunday in a house on Mercer Avenue, across the street from where her and Grandma Harrell lived. She wanted me to come. I thought that'd be good, 'cause to get there we had to walk about a mile down railroad tracks and across a big high trestle. Maybe I'd get to see a train come by.

The next Sunday, Mama took me and Doris and set off down the railroad tracks. When we started walking across the trestle, we looked down at the creek that ran underneath. It seemed like a long way down. We were glad when we got to the other side. We still had a ways to go to Aunt Lanie's

Sunday school. The creek passed under the trestle, then disappeared as it curved behind some trees. I could hear some boys splashing in the water. It sounded like they were having a good time, swimming, hollering and all. I thought, I bet I could learn to swim in that creek.

We got to the house where Aunt Lanie was having her Sunday school class. When we went into the room, there were about ten other boys and girls there and another woman to help Aunt Lanie with the teaching. I sat down in a chair next to a window. I could look out the window and see Grandma and Grandpa Harrell's house across the street.

Aunt Lanie said, Everybody bow your heads and let's pray. She prayed for us, the Sunday school class, the future church, sinners, and just about everybody. I looked out the window while she was praying and saw Grandpa cleaning up his wagon. I knew he was getting ready for the next day when he'd hook up his horse to the wagon and ride across town selling vegetables, fruits, peanuts and other stuff. It was called *huckstering*. One time he let me go with him and drive the horse. We sat up front on a board seat and you could see all around. Grandpa said I could drive a horse real good. It was a lot of fun. Ever so often he'd stop to sell his customers vegetables and stuff and he'd weigh them on a scale that hung on the back of the wagon.

Aunt Lanie finished praying and the other woman said, You know, the Baptists always take up collection. Mama had given me and Doris a penny each. We put them in the plate they passed around. The collection was ten cents. Aunt Lanie talked about Cain and Abel and said something about the first murderer. I couldn't keep my mind on what she was really saying. I kept looking at Grandpa loading up that wagon across the street. It was a pretty green wagon with a yellow stripe.

Mama said that Grandpa liked horses and wagons and really liked to sell things. She said that when they all lived in the country—up in Pender County, about twenty-five miles away—Grandpa and Grandma Harrell and all their children lived in a log cabin, and Grandpa had a one-room store.

She said he just liked selling.

Aunt Lanie said, Now, R.C., pay attention. I turned away from the window and the other woman was saying something about Sampson slaying ten thousand Philistines with the jawbone of an ass. I put my hand over my mouth like she had said a bad word. Aunt Lanie said, Now, R.C., an ass is like a donkey or a horse. I didn't understand and looked out the window again. Grandpa was still loading his wagon. I knew that meant he was definitely going out huckstering the next day. I wanted to go too, but I knew I had to start school.

Aunt Lanie said, Now everybody bow your heads again. She prayed some more and then said Amen. I got up to go and she said, R.C., wait just a minute. We're going to ask a few questions about our Sunday school lesson. It seemed like we were going to stay in that room all day. The other woman said, Okay, class, here's the first question. How did Sampson kill all them Philistines? I put up my hand. I knew I could answer that. I remembered them saying something about horses. Aunt Lanie said, Okay, R.C., tell us how Sampson killed the Philistines. I said, He slew them with the jawbone of a horse's ass. Aunt Lanie and the other woman looked at each other. The other woman kind of smiled. Aunt Lanie said, R.C., you mean the jawbone of an ass.

The other woman said, Okay, class, who was the first murderer? Well, I was sure I could answer that because it was on Grandpa Fowler's radio nearly every night. I raised my hand again and the other woman said, Okay, R.C., who was it? I said, It was John Dillinger. The woman said, Class dismissed!

I ran out the door and across the street to Grandpa Harrell's house. I watched him finish loading his wagon. I told him that I'd just left Aunt Lanie's Sunday school class, and he asked me, How did things go?

I think pretty good, 'cause I knew all the answers to the questions Aunt Lanie and that other woman asked the class.

R.C., do you want to go huckstering with me tomorrow?

I want to go, but I can't 'cause I've got to start school.

Grandpa acted like he was surprised and said, Are you old enough to go to school?

Yeah, I'm past old enough, and I want to go so I can learn a lot of stuff.

That's a real good way to feel about starting school.

I noticed Grandpa was coughing a lot. He always coughed, but it seemed like he was coughing more than ever.

Grandpa, I have to go now. Mama's calling me.

Well, you be good in school. It just don't seem like you ought to be starting school already.

I'm beginning to grow pretty good now. See, I can stand flat on the ground and look over the tailgate of the wagon.

Well, I guess anybody that can stand flat-footed and look over the tailgate of my wagon is for certain ready to start school.

The next morning, Mama took me to the schoolhouse. She talked with the teacher a few minutes and left. There were a lot of other boys and girls in the class. It seemed like we were all standing around looking at one another. The teacher told us her name and said, Now let's all settle down and be seated. Everybody scrambled for a desk. Sometimes two students would get in the same seat, but after a while everybody got a seat to themselves.

The teacher had all of us stand up and tell our names. Then she wrote some things on the blackboard. It looked like we were going to start learning on our first day.

After school was out, I started walking towards Grandma Fowler's house. On the way, I passed by the Presbyterian church. I thought the Presbyterians must've had a lot of money; they already had their church, and they had a regular preacher. One time when I was in their Sunday school class, the teacher said that the next summer the whole Sunday school was going to take the trolley to Wrightsville Beach. She said we could go swimming and have a picnic. I'd been thinking about becoming a Presbyterian, maybe before the next summer. I hoped Aunt Lanie didn't get mad.

When I got to Grandma's house, she was sitting on the front porch. I pulled up a rocking chair next to her and sat down. She asked me, How did things go on your first day in school? I said, It went good, we're already studying and learning things.

After a while Grandma asked me if I wanted a mayonnaise sandwich. I said that I did. She knew that I liked mayonnaise sandwiches. After I ate the sandwich, Grandma said, Your grandpa bought two more roosters today. He's out in the chicken lot now. Why don't you go out and see what they look like. I ran out to the chicken lot where Grandpa was feeding the chickens.

Hi, Grandpa, what kind of roosters have you got?

Hey, R.C. These are game roosters. Sometimes they're called *game-cocks.*

Why do you call them that?

Well, I think it's because they like to fight.

Do you think they'll fight people?

I don't think so, but be careful around them.

I watched the game roosters walk around the chicken lot, and they looked like they were ready to fight. I thought Grandpa was right, I wasn't going to get too close to them roosters.

🐿

Some of the boys that had chased me before I started school started teasing me and calling me teacher's pet. I was tired of them chasing and teasing me and I thought, I ain't going to take it anymore. Besides, I believe I can whip them anyway. I flew into one of the boys and put him on the ground. I held him down a while and then let him up. He came at me again and I put him down again. Before I let him get up, I hit him in the face a few times. When he got up, he ran off and left me alone. I thought, that's what I should have done the first time he chased me. It felt good.

When I got to Grandma's that evening, I told her what happened at school, about the fighting and all. She said, Now, R.C., I don't want you fighting in school.

Grandma, I won't start any fights, but I'm not going to let anybody run over me any more. I'll fight them first. Besides, I found out I'm pretty good at it.

My word, I hope you don't start doing like my boys did.

What did they do, Grandma?

Just about everything you can think of.

Tell me something they did.

I don't know where to start.

Just tell me one thing.

Well, one evening after school was out, I was over at the company store doing some shopping and the school principal was there buying some things. I spoke to her and she said, Mrs. Fowler, I was sure sorry to hear about your husband. I asked her what she meant. She said that Ralph, Robert and Otto had come to her with their heads down, acted real sad, and said that they had to talk with her. She asked them what the trouble was and they told her that their daddy was dying.

Grandma, Grandpa's still living.

I know that, son.

What did you tell the principal?

I told her, Just you wait until I see them boys. They're going to get it. She asked what I meant and I told her that their daddy dyed every day. He was the dye house boss man for the cotton mill and it was his job to oversee the dyeing of all the cloth.

What did she say?

She said, Well, I do declare. I told them boys I was real sorry and that I felt that they should be home with the family. I gave them permission to go home.

Grandma, did they come home?

No, they didn't.

Where you think they went?

I know where they went. They went straight to that golf course.

I know, Grandma. They talk about caddying at that golf course a lot. What happened when they got home?

Luke beat their asses.

Oh.

♣

One day Ralph did something that made Grandpa Fowler mad and he told Ralph, Boy, I'm going to give you a good whipping. Ralph said, There ain't no such thing as a good whipping. Grandpa started trying to catch Ralph. Ralph started running, trying to get away. He ran to Grandpa's home brew house and tried to crawl in a hole that was under the log foundation, but he got stuck halfway under the log. Ralph had a big behind and it was sticking out. Grandpa used his belt on Ralph and tore his butt up. Some folks was coming by from the mill and saw what was going on. They laughed and said, Look at Ralph, he looks like a rat trying to get under that log. From then on, everybody on the Mill Hill called Uncle Ralph Squeaky.

One Friday evening I was in Grandma's house sitting on my stool at the kitchen table and everybody was eating and talking about the latest thing on the Mill Hill. This time they were talking about something called the Squeezer. I asked Grandpa, What's a Squeezer? He said, Well, these young boys here on the Mill Hill have been staying out late at night, just roaming around and getting into mischief. The talk is, some of the boys have been attacked by a huge, hairy, ugly-looking thing and it nearly squeezed them to death. It seemed nobody knew what it was, but just about everybody was staying home.

Uncle Otto said, I hope they catch that thing soon. The other night when I was coming from the mill, I saw a shadowy figure following me.

Grandma said, Yeah, when he got home he was white as a ghost and scared to death, and he had a drink bottle in his hand. Otto said, Yeah, I was scared. If that Squeezer had caught me, I was going to try and hit him with the bottle. Robert said, I ain't scared of no damn Squeezer. I'm going out at night when I want to. Grandma said, You'd better be careful, boy. Ralph said, To hell with the Squeezer. Grandpa said, You boys shut up.

I was afraid they might forget to give me my money. After all, it was Friday evening and I needed the money to buy candy and stuff at the company store. Besides, I was expecting Aunt Bessie's little girl, Jeanette, to start coming over on Friday nights before long. I thought, If she does come, I'm not going to let her sit on my stool at the table. I just don't want her getting any of my money.

One evening, when I got home from school, Daddy was feeding his chickens. One of the hens had some little biddies. I asked him if I could have one. He said yeah and handed me one of the biddies. I told him I'd take good care of it. Daddy said, That's right, son, you have to make sure it has plenty of food and water. I held the little biddy close to me and thought, now I have three things: my stool, the marbles that Grandma gave me, and this little biddy.

I heard Mama and Daddy talking about our president. They said that he was a good man and it seemed like he was trying to do the right thing. Everybody felt like things were going to get better soon. The year was 1934 and our president was Franklin Delano Roosevelt.

Daddy got us a radio. It was a black box with a round speaker on top and dials and lights and things. The night after we got the radio, some neighbors came over and we all sat around the radio and listened to the president talk. Daddy said he sure was glad that we had a Democrat for president. That last president we had, that fellow Hoover, just about caused us all to starve to death. He said he'd never vote for a Republican again as long as he lived.

When the school year ended, I was promoted to second grade. The cotton mill owners were building a swimming pool for the mill workers. I wanted to learn to swim and couldn't wait for the pool to be finished. When it was, I wanted to be the first one in.

Spofford Mills

Three

My chicken had grown a lot and I told Daddy I was thinking about selling him. He asked why I wanted to do that. I said, I want to get some money so I can buy things from the company store.

What kind of things?

Candy and stuff.

Well, he's your chicken. It's up to you.

I think I'll see what Mr. Mooney will give me for him.

Good luck.

That night I lay in bed and wondered how I was going to get the chicken from our house to Mr. Mooney's company store. I remembered the last time we moved, I'd seen Daddy catch the chickens and tie their legs together. I'd asked him why he did that and he said so they'd stay still. The next morning, I caught my chicken and tied his legs together. Daddy was right—the chicken couldn't go anywhere, he just lay there.

Mama came out to the chicken lot.

R.C., what in the world are you doing?

I'm going to sell my chicken to Mr. Mooney.

What on earth for?

So I can buy candy and stuff.

Son, you get money from your grandpa's house every Friday.

Yeah, but it don't last a whole week.

Well, I guess it's all right.

I took the chicken and started walking to Mr. Mooney's store. On the way the chicken messed on me. It looked like he could've at least waited until I got to the store and got my money. I put the chicken down on the sidewalk and took some grass and wiped my hands. By then, I was ready for sure to get my chicken sold and get out of the chicken business.

Mr. Mooney was busy waiting on some other people, so I just stood over by the candy counter with my chicken and waited. After a while, he came over and said, R.C., what in the world have you got there?

Mr. Mooney, I've got a real nice chicken here.

What are you doing with him here in the store?

I thought you might want to buy him.

I just might. Let me see him.

I gave the chicken to Mr. Mooney. He took him and walked around holding him in both hands, raising him up and down, like he was trying to see how much he weighed. He walked over to some of his customers and asked them what they thought. They smiled and said, Looks like a nice chicken to me. Mr. Mooney came over, looked straight at me and said, R.C., I'll tell you what. Seeing as you're a regular customer, I'm willing to offer you twenty-five cents for this chicken. I said, I'll take it, and thought, I hope I get the money before the chicken messes on Mr. Mooney like he did on me. I spent all the money on candy.

🐝

One evening after school, me and Grandma Fowler were sitting on the front porch in our rocking chairs. I said, Grandma, the other evening, just after dark, I went to the company store with Ralph to get an orange drink. Some of the fellows were hanging around outside the store looking at the Freeman house. You know they have some daughters, and you could see the shadows of them changing clothes through the upstairs window shade. Grandma said, I can guess what happened.

Well, them boys acted real strange. They were howling, slapping their legs, and whistling and stuff like that. Why'd they do that?

Young men do weird things like that.

Ralph, Robert, and Otto were doing it too.

Grandma got up to go inside and said, Yeah, they're all just foolish young men.

Grandma, where you going?

Well, son, it's time for my shot.

What kind of shot?

I know you've noticed all these bandages on my legs, son. I have what's called diabetes.

What's that?

It's a disease that can keep sores from healing like they should.

I'm sorry, Grandma.

Now don't you worry about me. I've had this for a good while now.

Who sticks the needle in you?

I do.

I thought, I hope I don't get no diabetes. I hate needles.

❧

One day after school, I started running towards Grandma's house. When I got to the company store, I could see her sitting in her rocking chair. I hoped she'd ask me if I wanted a sandwich. I was real hungry.

Hi, Grandma. I thought I'd come by to see you.

I was expecting you, seeing as how you come by every day. Guess what I found today?

What?

When I was working in the garden, I found two more marbles. See?

They look like new marbles.

Well, I found them in the garden.

Grandma, it looks like your leg bandages are soaked with blood.

Yeah, I was feeding the chickens today, and one of those game roosters jumped on me and scratched my leg.

I hate them roosters.

They're mean, all right. I told Luke that he was going to have to feed the chickens from now on.

Grandma started into the house to fix me a sandwich. She turned and said, Why don't you go out and play and I'll call you when it's ready.

That's what I wanted to do anyway. I was planning on making me a slingshot. I needed one so I could shoot at things. I'd done got me a piece of rubber from an inner tube and some leather from an old shoe and I'd got a knife from Grandma's kitchen. When I started making a hole in the leather with the knife, my hand slipped and I cut my finger. When Grandma brought my sandwich, I showed her where I'd cut myself. She said, That's pretty deep, I'll put a bandage on it. She bandaged my finger and gave it a kiss.

I went back in the house and all of Daddy's brothers and sisters and some of their cousins were in the parlor. I asked Grandma what they were doing. She said, Aw, they're just playing around. They say they're having a meeting. I went in the parlor to see what the meeting was all about. Everybody was sitting around laughing and talking. Aunt Helen started playing the piano and Carl, Aunt Til's boy, stood up and said, Quiet, everybody, I'm calling this meeting to order. Everybody sat down. I did too. Carl said, Okay now. For our first order of business, I want all the ladies to cross their legs. Everybody laughed. I laughed too, but I didn't know what was funny. I just wasn't interested in their meeting.

I got up and went to the fireplace room, where I'd fallen and hit my head. There was a picture of a big ship over the fireplace mantel. The name of the ship was *Titanic.* Grandpa Fowler liked that picture a lot. He said that the *Titanic* had sunk in 1912 and that it was an historic event, whatever that was.

Grandpa liked his books, too. He had a lot of them in the fireplace room. There was one whole set of books called encyclopedias. Sometimes I'd get one off the shelf, lay down on the floor and look through the pages. I could read some of the words. After all, I'd done been promoted to the second grade. I went to the kitchen where Grandma was cooking.

Grandma, I'm not interested in their meeting.

I don't blame you.

Carl told all them ladies what was in the meeting to cross their legs.

That sounds like Carl. I don't know what Til's going to do with that young man.

What'd he tell 'em to cross their legs for?

Who knows. You know, Til's my sister and she's your great aunt.

Yeah, I know. She knows that I like the funny papers, and she saves them for me. I go to her house every week, and she gives me all the funnies she's saved up. I like Aunt Til a lot. I'm glad she lives here on the Mill Hill. Grandma, I'm still wondering why Carl asked all them ladies to cross their legs.

Now, R.C., you just can't ever tell what's on Carl's mind. Just forget about it.

❧

One evening when I got home, Mama's sister, Aunt Roxie, was there crying. I asked her what was the matter.

R.C., Papa died.

Grandpa Harrell?

Yes, son, he died this morning.

The last time I went huckstering with Grandpa Harrell he was coughing a lot.

I know, son, he'd been sick for a long time.

I hate he died.

I know, son.

Aunt Roxie, where's Mama and Daddy?

They're helping with the funeral arrangements.

Well, I thought, I didn't want anything to do with a funeral 'cause I remembered seeing the dead man at that house when we lived on the Morgan farm, how still he was, and everybody crying and real sad, and how that big black car came and carried the little boy away when we was living on the Back Row. I didn't want to see any more dead people. I wondered what was going to happen to Grandpa Harrell's horse and wagon.

The day they were going to have Grandpa Harrell's funeral, I told Mama, I don't want to go. I don't like to see dead people, especially my grandpa. Mama said, I know, son. You can stay here with the rest of the children. I've got somebody coming over to look out for you while we're gone.

Mama and Daddy went to Grandpa's funeral. I stayed at home with Doris, Bobby and Ann. It bothered me that they were going to bury Grandpa without me being there. I decided to go to the cemetery and wait for the funeral to get over. I told the lady that was looking out for us that I was going to the cemetery. She asked if I knew the way.

Yeah, I do. It's about two blocks behind Grandpa Fowler's hog pen.

Well, I guess it's okay, if you're sure you know how to get there.

I know the way real good. You go past the company store and Grandma Fowler's house, past the dye ditch and the hog pen. The cemetery's close to Forest Hills schoolhouse, it's before you get to the railroad trestle and the swimming hole. I know 'cause that's the way I went to Grandpa Harrell's house to go huckstering with him.

It sounds like you know the way all right, but be careful.

I will.

I left our house and started to the cemetery. I stopped when I got to Grandpa Fowler's hog pen and watched the hogs for a while. Grandpa had a small pipe with a piece of metal welded on the end that he used to clean out the hog troughs. It looked like a real spear. Sometimes I'd slip down to the hog pen and just throw it around. I knew I had plenty of time before everybody'd get to the cemetery, so I threw the spear a few times. I was careful to put it back in its place before I left. Grandpa Fowler would get real mad if it wasn't where he'd left it.

I got to the cemetery before anybody else and waited at the edge of the woods. Pretty soon they came and had the service. Before long, everybody left but the family and some of their friends. They were all standing around looking at the flowers. I got to thinking about Grandpa, the horse and wagon and huckstering and things, and I started crying. Daddy's sister, Aunt Helen, heard me and came over. She said, Well, R.C., I didn't know you were here. I didn't think you were coming. I told her I'd decided to come anyway. She said, Well now, don't cry. Come on with me, and let's go home.

Aunt Helen put her arm around me and we walked to Grandma Fowler's house. I felt better after I got there, and I took my slingshot and went out in the yard to play. I tried not to think about Grandpa Harrell. I thought, I'm only eight years old and done already seen three dead people. I think that Depression thing has something to do with it. It was getting late and I knew I'd better hurry home.

Grandma, I'm going home now.

I think you'd better, it'll be getting dark soon. Now, you go straight home and don't stop by Willie's house. I know you and him like to play every chance you get.

I know. I'm going straight home.

I started for home at a trot. That way I'd get there before dark. When I passed Willie's house, I thought about how he liked to go to the moving picture show and see the cowboys and horses. Every time he got home from the picture show, he'd tell me all about it. He didn't leave anything out. He even clicked his tongue to make a sound like the horses did when they was running. I liked Willie. I saw him, his little brother, and his mama and daddy sitting around their kitchen table eating supper.

I could see the light on in our house, which was about four houses down from Willie's. I knew Mama would be feeling bad about Grandpa. I thought, I just bet she'll be singing, *Jesus, Savior, Pilot Me*. I opened the front door. Mama said, R.C., is that you? She always asked me that. I said, Yeah, it's me, I'm home. She said, Come on into the kitchen, we're getting ready to eat supper. While we were eating, Mama and Daddy were talking about the funeral and everything. Mama said, It's bad about Papa dying, but we've been expecting it. He's been sick for a long time.

A few days later, Daddy brought a little dog home. His name was Dizz. Daddy said that he was named after a famous baseball pitcher. He was a pretty little thing. He was grey with black spots and had a little brown on his ears. Daddy said that he was a bird dog, but he was going to teach him to hunt raccoons. He said, When we move to Pender County, we'll have plenty of room to hunt. Mama said, Alton, you know I don't want to move back to no Pender County.

Well, I don't see why not, Carrie.

I was born and raised on that farm, Alton. I plowed the fields with oxen and mules along with my sisters. All I can remember is hard work from daylight to dark.

I'm tired of public work. I'm working nearly all the time, and we're just barely gettin' by. I believe I can make a go of it farming.

Well, you know, that old log cabin I was born and raised in is still there, but my sister Ruth, her husband Jessie, and their children are living in it now.

We'll build our house on the old farm on your part of the inheritance.

My part is only twenty-five acres. When Mama's ancestors came over to America from Scotland, they had two thousand acres of land in Pender County. Over the years, it's dwindled down to two hundred and Mama's dividing that up between us eight children. That gives us only twenty-five acres apiece.

I know, but I think we can make a better living on that twenty-five acres of land than I can make at this cotton mill.

Alton, I have bad memories of the farm—hard work, loneliness, few neighbors, no electricity, no water except a well. Besides that, the nearest store is five miles away.

Carrie, I really want to get off this Mill Hill. I started working in the mill when I was ten years old and I'm just tired of the cotton mill and the roar of them machines twenty-four hours a day.

I know, but times are hard and at least you have a job.

I'm just so tired of the mill. I want to get away from here, get out on my own and have our own piece of land. I want to farm for a living.

We'll talk about it another time.

❦

I was in the third grade and things seemed to be going along okay. I did mess up a few times, like when I made a C in school and Mama was real upset. One evening when I got home from school, she said, R.C., where's your aviator hat?

Mama, I forgot and left it at school.

Well, young man, you and me are going back to the schoolhouse right now and get that aviator hat. I want to talk to your teacher anyway about that C you made.

It was only one C.

Yes, but you can do better than that.

When we got to the schoolhouse, the teacher was still there. Her and Mama talked for a while. They decided to move me to another desk. Seemed like they'd figured me and another boy were rolling toy cars back and forth to each other, and moving me across the room would put a stop to that.

On the way home Mama said, Now, R.C., you'd better not make any more C's. You can do better.

I'm gonna try to do better. Besides, since my desk got moved, me and my friend can't roll them little cars down the aisle anymore.

Another thing, R.C., you got to keep up with your aviator hat. It keeps your ears warm. You know you've always had ear problems.

I just can't keep up with it, Mama.

Well, son, you know Charles Lindbergh was the first man to fly an airplane across the Atlantic Ocean by himself, and he wore an aviator hat just like yours.

He did?

Yes, he made that flight in 1927, the year you were born. He was trying to be the first man to fly across the Atlantic Ocean solo.

What's solo?

That means you go right by yourself.

If I keep wearing this aviator hat, I bet when I get big I can fly an airplane, too.

Maybe.

Mama, if I learn to fly an airplane, I'll fly all over the place.

Boy, you got big dreams.

Daddy kept talking about moving to the country and farming. He said we'd have chickens, hogs, a cow and a garden with lots of vegetables. It sounded like we'd have plenty to eat and milk to drink, all right. When Daddy talked about living on a farm in the country, he made it sound real good. Mama still didn't want to go. She told Daddy, If you're dead set on going, I guess we can try it for a while. Maybe two years. If things haven't worked out like you expected by that time, we'll move back to town.

Carrie, I don't think that'll happen. As far as making a living, I'm planning on planting tobacco for a money crop. When I lived with Ma and Pa on our farm in Columbus County, we raised tobacco and did real good.

Yeah, but that was before the Depression. It's different now. Besides, Alton, you know that raising tobacco is hard work. You have to work tobacco nine months out of the year.

I know it's going to be hard work, but you'll have to say that I'm not afraid of work.

You do work hard, Alton.

Seemed like Daddy felt good about moving to the country and all. When he wasn't working at the mill, he was working on an old truck in our back yard. It wasn't really a truck, just a motor sitting on a frame. Mama asked Daddy, What in the world is that contraption?

Well, Carrie, that's going to be our transportation.

I can't see how.

Wait until I finish with it.

Daddy worked hard on making a truck out of the contraption. Him and Uncle Rudolph built a wooden bottom for the truck bed and a wooden seat to sit on up front. Daddy said him and Mama would sit up front and that me, Doris, and Bobby could sit on the wooden floor in the back of the truck. Daddy told Mama maybe she could hold Ann up front with her.

Alton, I'll be holding another baby by spring.

Oh yeah, that's right, Carrie. I guess Ann can sit in the back with the rest of the children.

I guess, but we'll have to keep a close eye on her, and Bobby too.

Mama and Daddy were worried about Bobby 'cause it seemed like he was always getting into trouble, like the time he fell on the heater and messed up his eye. One time he heard me and Doris talking about a puppet show at school and he ran away to the schoolhouse so he could see it, too. I found him in the schoolyard and took him home. Then one day the woods between our house and the schoolhouse caught on fire. It seemed like everything was burning. School let out and we all ran home. Smoke was everywhere, and the fire trucks were all over with their sirens screaming.

People were gathered around the back of our house all excited and wondering how it got started. Mama hollered out, Do you children know where Bobby is? We said, No, we just got home from school. She yelled, Well, help me look for him! After a little while, Doris said, Mama, I found Bobby. Mama said, For God's sake, where is he? Doris told Mama he was under her bed. Mama looked under the bed and Bobby was there all right, all rolled up in a ball. Mama said, Bobby, come out from under that bed.

I don't want to, Mama, I'm scared.

Well, the fire trucks are here and they're putting the fire out.

I hear them.

Well, come on out now.

Bobby crawled out from under the bed. Mama picked him up and patted him on the back and said, Don't worry, honey, everything's going to be all right. She asked him why he was so scared and if he knew how the fire started.

I had some matches and I was playing in the woods in back of our house.

Oh my God, what did you do?

I just struck one match.

Jesus, Savior. Well, it's all over now. Don't ever do anything like that again.

I ain't.

🐿

Daddy worked on the truck contraption every chance he got. He told Mama that it'd be ready by spring, when school was out, and that he was planning on us moving to the farm in Pender County then. Mama still wasn't happy about moving. She said, Alton, you know how you teased me about how me and my sisters used to roost in that big old oak tree like chickens?

You know I was just teasing.

Well, we didn't sleep in that tree, but it's about big enough for somebody to live in.

Yeah, I know. That's the biggest oak tree I've ever seen.

That tree's got a history behind it.

Like what?

When my great Uncle Jimmy was in the Confederate Army, he was wounded in the battle at Fort Fisher, about fifteen miles south of here.

I know where Fort Fisher is.

Well, they sent him home to the farm, and he brought an acorn and planted it in the front yard of the log cabin. So, that's an old tree.

I bet if that oak tree could talk, it could tell some tales. Like all them generations that lived in that log cabin, and like how the farm went from two thousand acres down to two hundred.

Yeah, and just think, the cabin's older than the tree. Our family don't talk about it much, but I heard that somebody in the family along the line was a gambler and he gambled some of the land away.

❧

I didn't know what to think about moving to the country. I had a lot of friends on the Mill Hill and I liked the Presbyterian church on the corner of our street. One summer our whole Sunday school took the trolley to Wrightsville Beach and had a picnic. We swam and played and had a lot of fun. Then we took the trolley back home. It stopped right by the church that was only one block from our house. I really liked them Presbyterians. I hadn't even joined the church and they still let me go on the Sunday school trip, and it didn't cost me anything. Them Presbyterians were good people.

Sometimes I'd think about how I learned to swim in the mill village pool and to skate on the sidewalks, and how Grandma Fowler was always finding marbles for me in her garden. Grandma said that maybe before long her and Grandpa would leave the mill village and move back to their farm in Tabor City. I didn't want them to go back. I wished they'd stay on the Mill Hill and I could too, until I got grown.

Another thing, I just knew I was going to miss my Great-Aunt Til. She had a special place for me to read in her attic and she always brought me cookies and soft drinks. Sometimes I'd read for hours just laying there on the floor. I tried to keep up with all the funnies. I thought about them things and wondered about moving to that farm in Pender County.

&

One good thing about the farm was that my first cousin Sam Wells lived in the log cabin with his brother, James Kenneth, his sister, Goldie, and their mama and daddy, my Aunt Ruth and Uncle Jessie. I'd be glad to see Sam again. I thought about him a lot, how he gave me his toy airplane after we jumped off that old barn roof. I thought about seeing all those animals on the farm. I wasn't so sure about the cow, though. I didn't want no cow licking me on my face and giving me a cowlick like Bobby had. Having curly hair was bad enough. People were already starting to call me Curly.

It seemed like there was always something to do on the Mill Hill, like checking out the candy counter at Mr. Mooney's store, watching them young men shoot pool and listening to them old men that hung around the store. They were always talking about how they'd marched on Washington in 1932. They'd fought in the Great War, and they wanted a bonus. They said they deserved it. And if they didn't get it, they were going to get together and march on Washington again. I told Grandpa what the men said. He said, Yeah, son, I think they deserve it. What worries me, though, is that fellow Hitler in Germany.

Grandpa, if war does come like you think, or if you move back to Tabor City, can I have your encyclopedias and that picture of the *Titanic* that's hanging over the fireplace?

Grandpa just shook his head and walked away.

Four

It looked like we were going to move to the country sure enough 'cause Daddy had the truck runnin' and he was going to the country every chance he got to work on our new house. He said it would be the first house of our own. It sounded real good, having our own house and truck and twenty-five acres of land.

Sometimes on Saturdays Daddy would let me go with him to the farm. I'd play and watch him and Uncle Jessie and Uncle Rudolph work on the house. I'd hand them boards and things like that. I liked to drive nails, but it seemed like I bent them a lot.

Daddy said our house was twenty-four feet wide and twenty-four feet long with a porch on the front that went out six feet. It was a nice front porch, but it wasn't as big as the one we had when we lived on the Morgan farm. It was only about three steps up before you got to the floor. I thought if Daddy gave me a whipping while I was going up them steps like he did on the Morgan farm, it wouldn't last too long.

I'd only had two whippings in the past month, one when I left my aviator hat at school and made that C. The other one was when I fought the school bully for picking on my sister Doris. I didn't know why Mama whipped me for doing that. It didn't do any good 'cause if he bothered her anymore, I was going to fight him again.

One day when I was sitting on the porch with Grandma, she said, R.C., I know you're gonna miss this old Mill Hill.

I'm gonna miss sitting here rocking with you on the porch. Another thing I'm gonna miss is being here when the circus comes to town.

I know you're going to miss that. I've seen you running along beside them elephants.

Yeah, they unload the animals and everything at the railroad tracks beside the mill. I always meet the train, watch them unload, and then follow them all the way to the ballpark that's in back of the schoolhouse. They have lots of things in the parade, like animals and clowns. And they have something that looks sort of like a big piano with a lot of colors, and it sits on a cart pulled by a horse. The music is real loud and they play it all the way to the ballpark.

Yeah, I know, I hear it when it comes by. But it's not a piano. I think it's called a calliope.

I like them circus people. Most times they give me a free pass to the circus.

I hope you don't worry them circus people to death.

Aw, I don't. But one time they asked me to leave them alone until they could get set up for the show.

Well, I can understand that.

Grandma, I left them alone all right. But I did stand across the street and watch them set up their tent and things. I got to talk to the cowboy star. I told him that I had a friend who could click his tongue so it sounded just like when a horse was running. He thought that was real funny and told me to be sure and watch his show.

Did you?

Uh-huh. You know what else I'm gonna miss, Grandma?

What, son?

Well, I like to play ball with the big boys. You know Grandma, in the park, when they're not having the circus or them ball games where you have to pay to get in, Daddy's brothers and all them other young men play ball over there. I follow them around and they always choose me on one of their teams.

They do?

Yep. 'Course I'm always the last one they pick, but at least they choose me. Sometimes I think they wish I wouldn't follow them everywhere.

Well, I don't think that.

I don't know, Grandma. When I hit the ball, all them young men on my side say, Run. All them young men on the other side say, Foul ball, or, You're out! I just run back and forth between home plate and first base. I tell you, Grandma, most times I don't know whether I'm safe or out.

Don't worry about it, son.

If they don't quit laughing at me, I just might quit following them around everywhere.

That'd teach them a lesson.

I'll tell you something else, Grandma.

What?

Promise not to tell?

I promise.

You know when they have the circus and them pay baseball games? Well, all your boys and them others climb up in the trees and look over the ballpark fence and see everything for free.

That don't surprise me.

But it's not right, is it, Grandma?

No, it's not.

I know Aunt Lanie wouldn't like it.

No, she wouldn't, son.

❦

School would be out in a few days, and we'd be leaving the Mill Hill for the farm in Pender County. Sometimes I'd wonder about things like who was going to cut my hair and things like that. Since we'd been living on the

Mill Hill, Mr. Walter had been cutting my hair. His barbershop was a little building behind the house where I was born. It had a striped barber pole out front. Everybody on the Mill Hill got their hair cut at Mr. Walter's barbershop.

All the grown men got their hair cut and a shave for twenty-five cents. I'd hear them say around the Mill Hill, Shave and a haircut, two bits. I asked Daddy what two bits was. He said it was the twenty-five cents they paid for a haircut. I didn't know why, but it seemed like when everybody around the Mill Hill sang or played a song, they'd always finish it by saying, Shave and a haircut, two bits.

Things had gotten busier around our house. Daddy and Uncle Rudolph were hauling our furniture to that house in Pender County, and it looked like we'd be moving for sure in just a few days. I started putting some of my stuff in a box. Mama came over, looked down in the box, and said, Now, R.C., you know we can't take everything.

Why not?

Well, you know them skates you got in that box—there's no place to skate on the farm.

There's not?

No, but don't feel bad. Your daddy's going to have to leave some things behind, too.

Like what?

For one thing, you know how he loves to listen to the radio, like the news and championship fights and things like that?

Yeah, I've heard him talking about them famous fighters. He really likes that stuff.

Well, he's going to have to sell the radio.

How come?

There's no electricity where we're moving to.

How's he gonna hear the news?

He'll figure out something. He's talking about saving up and buying a radio that's run by battery.

&

Daddy took Mama to the hospital, but they didn't seem to be too worried 'cause they said she'd be back home in just a few days. Well, they were right, 'cause in about two days they brought Mama back home. She was on a stretcher, just like when she brought Bobby and Ann home. I looked on the stretcher, and Mama had a little baby with her. I asked her, Where'd you get that baby?

I got him at the hospital. He's your new brother. His name is James Gilbert Fowler.

How old is he? He looks real little.

Well, he's only two days old.

That seems like a lot of name for somebody just two days old.

For goodness' sake, R.C., sometimes you say the strangest things.

Do we have to call our new brother James Gilbert Fowler?

We'll just call him Jimmy.

That sounds better.

&

School was out. The next morning, we all started getting ready to move to the farm. I decided to go see Grandma one more time. I got my skates out of that box where I'd been putting things to take to the country and headed for Grandma's. When I got there, she was sitting on her porch.

Hey, Grandma.

Hey, son.

I can't stay long. I've got to hurry back home. We're leaving for the farm in Pender County this morning.

Yeah, I know, son.

Grandma, tell Jeanette that she can have my place at the table and my blue stool, and I might as well give her these roller skates. Mama says I can't use them up in the country.

She's right about that. I know Jeanette will be glad to get these skates.

Grandma, I've got to go now. Tell everybody I said bye and tell Grandpa if war does come or if y'all move back to that farm in Tabor City, don't forget about giving me them encyclopedias and that picture of the *Titanic*. And I'd like to have that davenport, too.

I'll tell him, all right. Now come here and give me a hug.

Grandma gave me a hug and I started back to our house on the Church Row. When I got ready to cross the street in front of her house, I looked both ways real good and then ran across. I looked back to see if Grandma was looking. I liked for her to see me cross the street, especially when I'd looked both ways real good. She was looking, all right. She waved and I waved back. I knew I had to hurry, but seeing as how I was right in front of Mr. Mooney's store, I thought I'd just go in and tell him bye and while I was in there, I'd just walk by the candy counter one more time.

Hey, Mr. Mooney.

Hi, R.C.

Mr. Mooney, we're leaving the Mill Hill this morning. We're going to be living on a tobacco farm in Pender County.

I know. Your daddy's been telling me about it.

Well, I've got to go.

Just a minute, son. Let me give you something to take with you.

I ain't got any money.

This don't cost anything. I've just got too many sweets on hand right now. You take this bag of candy with you, and all you children can eat it on your way to the farm.

Thank you, Mr. Mooney. We all love candy, but our baby brother Jimmy can't eat it yet.

Well, you'll figure out something to do with his share.

Goodbye, Mr. Mooney.

When I came out of the company store, Grandma Fowler was still sitting on the front porch. I waved to her with my hand that was holding the bag of candy. I bet she just knew what I had in the bag 'cause when she waved back, she was laughing. All the way from across the street, I could see her stomach jiggling around like it did when she laughed.

I started for our house on the Church Row at a trot. I liked to trot anyway, and when I did, it only took about ten minutes from Grandma's to our house. As I trotted past Mr. Walter's barbershop, I thought about all the times that he'd cut my hair and how sometimes he'd tease me about it being curly.

I liked Mr. Walter, but I couldn't stop to say goodbye. I had to hurry. Anyway, he knew that we were leaving the Mill Hill. Besides, I was kind of ashamed ever since that evening when everybody on the Church Row was sitting out on their front porch passing the time. Seemed like everybody on the Mill Hill liked to sit out on the porch in the evenings. Sometimes they'd holler out to whoever was sitting on the porch across the street.

What made me feel ashamed was one evening when Mr. Walter came walking down the street. I think he'd finished cutting hair for the day and had closed up the barbershop. As he passed by the houses, the people would say, Hi, Walt. When he got to our porch, I said, Hi, Walt, and the next thing I knew, I was laying out in the front yard.

What happened was when I said, Hi, Walt, Daddy reached over and slapped me real hard on the back of my head and knocked me off the porch. I got up and said, Daddy, why'd you hit me like that? He said he did it 'cause I said, Hi, Walt to Mr. Walter. I told him everybody else on the street said it. He said, Well, to you, it's *Mr. Walter.*

Well, that taught me a lesson all right, but it seemed to me that Daddy could've just told me not to say, Hi, Walt. The worst thing about getting slapped off the porch was that just about everybody on the Church Row and

Mr. Walter saw it. It made me feel real bad. I tried to forget about it, but I found out when you tried to forget about something, it just made you think about it more.

When I got to Willie's house, he was playing in his front yard. I told him that we were leaving for that farm in the country and I didn't know when I'd see him again. But I just wasn't going to forget about him. He said he wasn't going to forget about me either and that he sure was going to miss us playing together and climbing up in that old sycamore tree and spitting tobacco juice.

I left Willie's and started on down the street. I could see the truck in front of our house. It had some things on it, but mostly our family. When I got up to it, Mama and Ann were sitting on the seat up front. Mama was holding the baby and Daddy was trying to crank the truck. He was having a hard time getting it started. Dizz was sitting on the ground just looking like he didn't know what was going on. I picked him up and put him on the back beside Bobby and Doris. He was real big and heavy. He must've been all the way grown.

I went around to the front of the truck and watched Daddy trying to crank the motor. It just didn't want to crank. He'd put the crank in the slot and turn the handle over and over. Sometimes it would kick back and hit his wrist. After a while Daddy took the crank and threw it way down the street. Then he went to get it and cussed a whole lot. After a while, he got the truck started and I ran and got on the back beside Doris and Bobby.

Daddy jumped on the seat behind the steering wheel and we started down the street, sputtering and jerking along. I grabbed Dizz so he wouldn't fall off. By the time we got to the street corner, the truck started running better and it was easier to hold on. I looked back down the street and watched the Presbyterian church disappear as we rounded the curve at the end of the Church Row. We were on our way. I thought, Goodbye, old Mill Hill.

Five

We got to our new home in Pender County around dinnertime. That was what we always called the meal in the middle of the day. Some people called it lunch, but we always called our meals breakfast, dinner and supper. Some people called suppertime dinner, but I liked suppertime better.

My cousin Sam Wells heard us drive up and came running from the log cabin where they were living. It was the same cabin that Mama was born and raised in. Aunt Ruth and her family were living there, but they were building a new house about a quarter of a mile on down the road. They'd be moving before long 'cause the cabin was on Uncle Buddy's part of the inheritance. Uncle Buddy was one of Mama's brothers.

I grabbed one of the biscuit sandwiches Mama had brought and told her I was going to play with Sam. She said okay and that I could eat more later. Sam said that he'd show me around. It didn't look like there was a whole lot to see, but we started out. First, we stopped at the pump in our new back yard and got a drink of water.

Sam, this water tastes funny.

Yeah, it does. Uncle Rudolph said it's 'cause it has a lot of iron in it.

Does the water at the log cabin taste like this?

I think it tastes a little better. We get our water out of a well, you know, a big hole in the ground.

Let's go see.

We went to the log cabin. Aunt Ruth and Uncle Jessie came to the front door. Sam's sister Goldie and his brother James Kenneth were playing in the yard around the big oak tree. I told Aunt Ruth that we were moving into our new house. She said that was good. Aunt Ruth didn't talk much.

Sam showed me the well. It was a big hole in the ground all right, with boards around what was called a well curb. We looked down in the hole, and way down you could see water. There were weeds growing on the side of the well all the way down to the water. We drew up a bucket of water and tasted it. It tasted better than the water that came out of our pump.

Me and Sam ran all over the place. He showed me their hogs that they kept in a pen and their mule that lived in a building called a stable. He said their mule's name was Bill and that most he-mules were named Bill. The top part of the stable door was open. Bill stuck his head out the door. Sam petted him on the head and pulled one of his ears. He said I could pet him, too. I told him, Yeah, I'll pet him later.

There were a lot of fruit trees and grapevines. There were apple, pear, peach, plum and mulberry trees. There was even an old walnut tree way down in the back of the field. Sam said they were all real old, especially the three mulberries and that walnut tree, and they were at least as old as the big oak tree in front of the log cabin. I told Sam, I'm going to eat some of the fruit off them trees.

It's better to wait until they're ripe.

I'll just try one of each kind.

All right, if you want to, but I've got to go now. It's time to feed up.

What do you mean feed up?

Well, I have to feed all of the animals every morning and evening, except the chickens. We just feed them in the mornings.

Why don't you feed them in the evening?

We let them out of the chicken lot in the morning after we feed them. Then they just scratch around all day and feed themselves. Besides, they go to sleep real early.

Daddy had some chickens. I used to be in the chicken business, too.

You was?

Yeah, but I sold out to Mr. Mooney who owns the company store.

Gosh! Well, I got to go now. Mama's done lit the kerosene lamp.

❦

Our house had four rooms—a kitchen, living room and two bed-rooms. There weren't any walls between the rooms, just framing. Mama and Daddy had hung some sheets around their bedroom. Jimmy slept with them 'cause he was a baby. The rest of us children slept in another room, me and Bobby in one bed and Doris and Ann in another. The only furniture in our living room was a trash-burning stove, three high-back chairs and a little round table that held a battery-set radio.

The kitchen had a long table with a chair at each end and a bench on each side. There was a wood cook-stove on one wall with a little table beside it that held a water bucket with a dipper. There was an oak box lined with metal called an icebox.

It was real dark inside our house at night. We had two kerosene lamps, but Mama said we could only keep one burning because kerosene cost money. The one we kept burning was in the kitchen. Mama said that way if any of us wanted a drink of water in the night, we could see how to get to the water bucket.

We all went to bed. Bobby went to sleep right off, but I just lay there with my hands behind my head. My eyes were wide open, but all I could see was the dim light of the kerosene lamp in the kitchen. I didn't know what to think, it just seemed so quiet. I missed the hum of the cotton mill.

I wondered what Grandma Fowler was doing. I bet that Jeanette had already taken over my stool, and I just knew all of them young men were at the company store, laughing, shooting pool and looking up at the Freemans' upstairs window.

Mama, it sure is quiet.

I know, but you'll get used to it.

All I can hear is them crickets and frogs.

You'll get used to that, too. That's about all you're going to hear at night from now on.

I lay there thinking how lonesome it seemed. It reminded me of when we lived on the Morgan farm. 'Course, we had closer neighbors there and Daddy's brothers and sisters came to see us. I thought, Nobody's going to come and see us way up here in these woods. I wished when I woke up in the morning I could hear the cotton mill humming and look out the window and see people going back and forth to the mill, and that I could run to Grandma's house and rock with her on the porch, and she'd fix me a mayonnaise sandwich and give me some marbles that she'd found in her garden. I could go play with Willie, and climb up in that sycamore tree and watch him spit tobacco juice.

I didn't know what I was going to do when I woke up in the morning. I hoped me and Sam could play. It was fun playing with him our first day on the farm. I liked seeing the chickens and them hogs, but I didn't know about that mule Bill. Maybe he was all right, but he sure was big and he had real big teeth.

Mama.

What, son?

My stomach hurts real bad.

What's it feel like?

It just hurts real bad and it's swelling up.

What did you eat today?

I ate some apples, pears and plums off them trees.

Well, that's what's causing your stomach to hurt. You're not supposed to eat fruit until it's ripe.

I ate a lot. Sam didn't eat any.

Sam knows better.

Mama, I think I'm dying.

You're not dying. You'll be all right in the morning.

I don't think I'll live 'til morning.

You will.

I got to throw up. What do I do?

Well, you know what we did when we lived on the Morgan farm?

You mean that slop jar bucket?

Yes. There's one in you children's room. Use it.

It was dark and I couldn't see the slop jar bucket. I got the lamp from the kitchen table and ran back to our bedroom. When I did, the lamp went out. I put it down and ran to where I thought the slop jar was and threw up.

I feel better now.

That's good. Now go back to bed.

Mama.

What now?

Well, when I ran with the lamp, it went out.

Yeah, I could tell. In the morning I'll show you how to hold your hand in front of the chimney when you walk.

I'm not sure I threw up exactly in the slop jar.

Don't worry. That's going to be one of your jobs every morning from now on, to clean up around the bucket and make sure it gets emptied.

Where do I empty it?

Way out in the woods. I'll show you. Now be quiet and go to sleep.

I couldn't go to sleep. I decided to get up and light the kerosene lamp. I thought I'd just put it in our bedroom and turn the wick down low. That way it wouldn't use much kerosene and we could see how to get to the slop jar.

I got up, lit the lamp, and put it in our bedroom. I went through the kitchen to the back door, opened it and looked out. It was not as dark outside. The stars were out and the moon was shining. I wished that we had windows with glass in them. That way we could at least have some moonlight come in.

I remembered when we lived in that old house on the Morgan farm, how it had them big glass windows and the moonlight would just light up the room. I thought back to our first night in that house, with that old screech owl and all. I wondered if there were screech owls around our new house. I hoped not.

Doris started groaning and moaning. I asked her what was the matter. She said her stomach hurt real bad and she felt like she was dying.

Doris, did you eat fruit off them trees today?

Yes.

I did, too. But I threw up a lot and I'm okay now.

I got to throw up, too.

You have to use the slop jar.

Doris jumped off the bed and started running. She threw up a lot and went back to bed.

Morning finally came. The first thing I heard was Mama saying, Everybody up, I won't call you again. Then she said, R.C., first thing I want you to do is empty the slop jar and clean up that mess. I picked up the slop jar with both hands and held it as far away from me as I could. I emptied the bucket in the woods, cleaned up the bedroom floor, and then went in the kitchen. I sat on one of the benches and watched Mama cook breakfast.

Everything smells real good, Mama.

All cooking smells good to you.

Mama, do you think someday we can get windows with glass in them? It's real dark in our house at night, and there's not much light in the daytime, either. What do you call them boards with them leather hinges on them that cover our window holes now?

They're called shutters.

I'll be glad when we get windows with glass in them.

We're doing the best we can. The Depression's still on and everybody's having a hard time.

I think the Depression is worse here in the country.

It's the same all over. Now, bring in a bucket of water and open up the shutters.

I brought the water in, set the bucket on the little table next to the cook-stove, and opened the shutters.

Mama, is that all?

No, son. The chickens, the hogs and the mule have to be fed.

I don't mind feeding them chickens and hogs, but I don't know about that mule. He's got them real big teeth.

Well, he's got to eat too.

What do I feed him?

Right now, you give him about eight ears of corn.

Can I just throw it to him?

No. That mule's not going to hurt you. You've got to put the corn in that box under the tree where he's tied.

Well, I guess I can do that. But is that where that mule's going to live, tied up to that tree? Or is he going to have a stable?

He's gonna have a stable and you can help your daddy build it.

I don't know how to build no stable.

Don't worry, your daddy will show you what to do. Now eat your breakfast. You've got to help your daddy and Uncle Rudolph today.

After we ate, Daddy said, R.C., come on, let's go hook up the mule.

What do you mean *hook up the mule*? He's already tied to that tree.

Boy, you got a lot to learn. When we say hook up the mule, we mean put all that harness and gear on him. You know, the bridle, collar, trace chains and things like that. That way, you can hook up plows, planters, drag logs or whatever. Today we're going to be cutting logs for our new tobacco barn and we'll use the mule to pull the logs. Come on, now. Let's get the mule hooked up. Your Uncle Rudolph and his oldest boy, Lewis, are coming over to help us with the log cutting.

I looked across our field and saw Uncle Rudolph and Lewis. They had just come out of the woods and were headed across the field towards our house. Aunt Maybelle, Uncle Rudolph and their four boys had moved into their house the same time we moved into ours. From our house to theirs was about a five-minute walk across a small field through a patch of woods. The woods had a little stream running through it called a branch. The narrow dirt road that ran through the woods to their house was just wide enough for a mule and cart. Daddy called it a cart path.

We went into a patch of woods on our piece of land and Daddy and Uncle Rudolph started cutting down trees with a crosscut saw. They got down on their knees up close to the tree and pulled the saw back and forth through the tree until it fell. Then they took an axe and trimmed off the limbs. Me and Lewis started putting the limbs in a pile. Daddy said he'd burn them when they were dried out.

It wasn't too long before we had some logs cut and ready to be moved to where we were going to build our barn. Daddy showed me and Lewis how to back the mule up to the ends of the logs and wrap them with a chain. Then he drove the mule, pulling the logs for the first trip so me and Lewis could see how it was done. It wasn't too hard to learn. Me and Lewis pulled logs while Daddy and Uncle Rudolph cut down more trees. It was hard work and we were glad when dinnertime came.

Mama had the table set, and we all ate and listened to the battery radio. It was playing country music on the WPTF Raleigh radio station. Everybody was talking about how good we were getting along cutting the logs. It looked like in a few days we'd have enough to build our tobacco barn. Daddy said we had to have the barn ready for next year's tobacco crop. After that, we'd start on the stables and the corn crib. I asked Daddy, What are we going to build them with?

We're going to build everything out of logs.

That's a lot of logs.

We got a lot of trees.

Daddy, I thought when we moved up here it was already a tobacco farm.

No, we'll plant our first tobacco crop next year. Right now we've got to get everything ready. Next year we'll have three acres of tobacco. That's all the government will let us plant. It's called an allotment. But we've got plenty to do this year, tending these twelve acres of corn, sweet potatoes, sugar cane, soybeans and that big vegetable garden.

It sure sounds like it, Daddy. I'm ready to go back to dragging them logs now. I kind of like doing that.

Mama said, R.C., you be careful around that mule. You know he's a little bit wild anyway. Your daddy got him real cheap from Mr. Worley. He's that gentleman that lives back down the road between here and the sawmill.

Yeah, you've already told me who all lives on this road.

Maybe so, but listen to what I'm saying now. One day Mr. Worley had that mule hooked up to his cart and was riding along down the road when something scared the mule and he started running so fast the cart turned over and almost killed poor old Mr. Worley. That's why we got him so cheap. You just can't tell about that mule.

I know, Mama, but he's strong and he's a lot bigger than Uncle Jessie's mule. Sometimes he can pull two logs at a time.

Maybe so, but you be careful around that mule's heels. You know my Grandpa Harrell got killed by a mule.

How?

The mule kicked him in the stomach and he died right off.

Did he bite him too?

No, he didn't bite him, for goodness' sake.

When our mule eats corn, he wraps his lips around the ear of corn and when he bites down, you can hear a real loud crunch. Sometimes while we're unhooking them logs, he'll lean his head down and eat grass. And when he gets briars in his mouth he'll roll his top lip way up and his bottom lip way down, and all you can see is real big teeth.

Son, he just does that to keep the briars out of his lips.

It seems like he looks right at me when he does it.

We went back to work cutting and hauling logs. Me and Lewis were learning pretty good already. We'd found out that sometimes we had to dig a trench under the logs so we could get the chain underneath and sometimes we had to use a pry pole to move the logs around.

Uncle Rudolph showed us some things about working around mules. Like you didn't just walk up to a mule's heels and hook up something 'cause that's how people got kicked. Uncle Rudolph said, Just watch me, I'll show you how it's done. He walked up to the mule's head and started talking real low. He said, Hey, Bill, old boy. Then he started humming and petting him real easy. He petted his neck, side and back. All the time he was doing that, he was mumbling something.

By the time he got to the mule's heels, old Bill seemed real relaxed. Uncle Rudolph said, Now you see how relaxed he is. You can tell he is because all his back weight's on one foot. The other foot's just touching the ground with the front of his hoof. It's hard for him to kick when he's standing like that. He's sort of letting you know that everything's okay.

Uncle Rudolph, what were you saying when you was mumbling like that?

Well, nothing in particular, you just keep talking kind of low and sort of run your words together like an auctioneer. You can just say, Uh huh, uh huh, hey there, Bill, uh huh, uh huh, oh yeah, let's go now, uh huh, uh huh, 'at a boy, oh yeah, let's go now, uh huh. You say things like that. You just make it up as you go along.

Uncle Rudolph, I know you say *gee* when you want him to go right and *haw* when you want him to go left and *giddy-up* when you want him to go frontwards and *back up* when you want him to go backwards, but what do you say when you really want him to do something and you're humming and mumbling like that?

Well, you say it kind of like this. Oh, well, yeah now, um, hack-up here now, I say hey, yeah, hack-up here now. You see what you do is, when you say *hack-up*, you say it a little louder than all that humming and mumbling. The mule knows all that humming and mumbling don't mean nothing, except it helps pass the day and it lightens the load a bit.

Does everybody talk to mules and horses like that?

No. Most generally, the loggers talk to mules and horses like that. Sometimes they'll just plum add gospel to it.

How do they do that?

I've heard them say, like, Well now, mule, hack-up here, oh yeah, sweet Jesus, oh now we's hooked up, and let's giddy-up, oh Lordy, yes, come on now, mule, let's pull just a little bit, oh Lordy have mercy, yes. You see, it just helps the day go by and when you work ten hours a day in the log woods with a short break for dinner, which is usually a can of sardines and crackers, you have to do something to make the day pass.

Uncle Rudolph, can I tell you a joke?

Yeah, go ahead.

You know there's mules, horses and donkeys and sometimes them donkeys is called asses.

Yeah, I know.

Do you know what the stretchingest thing in the world is?

What?

Well, there was this man that had an ass.

What's the joke?

The man tied his ass to a tree and walked a mile.

Uncle Rudolph laughed and said, Where'd you hear that?

I told him one of the young men at the Mill Hill told me and I hoped he wouldn't tell Aunt Maybelle or Mama I'd told it. He said he wouldn't tell.

It was getting late in the evening. Aunt Maybelle had already come over to our house because it was time for her and Daddy to get in the truck and head for town and their jobs at the cotton mill. Daddy said he just hated to think about going to work at the mill, but he knew we needed the twelve dollars a week. Especially since we were trying to get things going on the farm and all. Aunt Maybelle said there was no way her family could do without the ten dollars a week she was making.

Daddy tried cranking the truck. It wouldn't start, so we pushed it out on the dirt road in front of our house. He headed the truck towards Wilmington, and him and Aunt Maybelle got on the seat. Daddy said, When I holler ready, everybody push us down the hill. That's the only way this thing's going to start.

It wasn't much of a hill. It went down a little ways before it started back up again, just before the road disappeared around a curve. The *everybody* that Daddy was talking about pushing was me, Mama, Doris, Uncle Rudolph, Lewis, and another cousin who'd come up by that time. We all put our hands on the back of the truck and waited for Daddy to holler *ready*. When he did, we all started pushing. The truck started moving real slow. It was hard pushing on the muddy dirt road, but we got it moving pretty good. Just before we got to the bottom of the hill, Daddy tried to start it. It jerked and sputtered, jerked some more, and then quit. Daddy said, It sounded like it wanted to start, let's push the damn thing back up the hill and try it again.

It was harder pushing back up the hill and we were getting tired. Aunt Maybelle and Daddy got out of the truck and helped us push. Daddy held on to the steering wheel with one hand and pushed with the other. When we got about halfway back up the hill, Daddy slipped and fell in the mud. He got up, cussed and wiped his muddy hands off on his pants, grabbed the steering wheel and started pushing again. Me and Lewis was pushing side-by-side. We didn't say anything, but when Daddy fell, we looked at each other and grinned.

When we got back to the top of the hill, we rested a little and pushed it back down the hill again. Same thing—sputter, jerk, sputter, jerk, but no start. We pushed it back up the hill. Everybody was real tired and Doris couldn't push anymore. We rested a while, then we pushed again. By the time we got to the bottom of the hill, Daddy had the truck started. He raced the engine—whoom, whoom. Then they started off down the road. Daddy and Aunt Maybelle didn't look back, but Aunt Maybelle waved before they disappeared around the curve.

All us pushers just stayed there in the road for a while. We were all leaning over with our hands resting on our knees. Everybody was breathing hard. After a while Mama said, All right, everybody, let's go. We all got things to do.

Uncle Rudolph and his boys left to go to their house across the branch. Mama said, R.C., you get busy with your feeding up and all. You know what to do?

I feed and water the mule, the cow, and the hogs, and gather the eggs. That's right, son.

I finished my jobs and washed the mud and chicken manure off my feet. I'd already found out that when you walked around in our yard, you had to keep your britches legs rolled up 'cause the yard just seemed to be muddy a lot and there was chicken manure everywhere.

Mama and Doris got the food on the table. We had a plate of hot biscuits, and a big pot in the middle of the table with some stewed tomatoes, a bowl of rice and some slices of fried meat. Mama said the blessings. After we finished eating, Jimmy started crying. Mama told Bobby and Ann it was their bedtime and for me and Doris to clean up the kitchen while she fed Jimmy. Me and Doris took the other lamp and put Bobby and Ann to bed.

Then we cleaned up the kitchen. I told Doris, I don't think I'm going to listen to the radio tonight. I'm just going to bed. She said, Me too. We put the lamp on the kitchen table, turned it down low and went to bed.

Doris, it sure is quiet, ain't it?

It sure is.

Are you scared?

Some. Are you?

I'm some too. I think I'll see if Mama's awake.

Mama?

What, R.C.?

It sure is dark up here in the country.

I know, son.

Mama, do you think anything'll get us tonight while Daddy's off working at the cotton mill?

No, son.

It was Doris what wanted to know.

Uh-huh.

Mama?

What now?

You know them big birds that come in late in the evening and start flying higher and higher, and every time they flap their wings they go cheep, cheep, and when they get real high, they dive down and go whoomp. Then they go right back up and do the same thing again. What are they, and why do they do that?

They're called bull bats, and they do fly real high. When they see insects, they dive down and get them. That's when they make that *whoomp* noise.

Can I sit on the front porch and watch them tomorrow evening?

Tomorrow's Sunday. All you do is your regular jobs and you can play the rest of the day. Now go to sleep.

I slept good. I only woke up one time. That's when I heard Mama moving around in the living room. I got up to see what was going on. Mama had the front door open a little and was looking outside. She was holding Jimmy. I said, Mama, is everything all right?

Yes, now go back to bed. It'll be daylight in a couple of hours and your daddy will be home soon.

Mama, looks like the kitchen lamp's going out.

I know. Tomorrow night make sure it's full of kerosene. Then it'll last all night.

I went back to bed.

At daybreak, Daddy and Aunt Maybelle drove up in the truck contraption. Mama had breakfast ready and Aunt Maybelle ate with us before she went across the branch to her house. Daddy went to bed and I did my jobs. I was ready to play. I hoped Sam would hurry up and come on to our house. I walked out and looked down the road. I saw him trotting towards our house. I started trotting to meet him.

Hey, Sam, can you play today?

Yeah. Can you?

Yeah. All I have to do today is them regular jobs, and I done finished this morning's part.

Me too.

Sam, let's go back to my house and we can start playing there. What you want to play?

I brought my marbles.

Sam stuck out his leg and put his hands on his pants pocket. It was full of marbles. I told Sam, I got marbles, too. My Grandma Fowler gave me a bunch. We walked down the road towards my house and talked about shooting marbles, about good shooters and things. We said we were just going to play for fun, not for keeps. We both said when school got started back we'd play our classmates for keeps at recess time and that we just bet we'd win their marbles.

Sam didn't talk as much as me, and he kinda looked down a little when he talked. Everybody said he took after his mama, my Aunt Ruth. She didn't talk much either, and when she did, she talked real low and looked down a little. I liked Sam and Aunt Ruth.

I noticed every few minutes Sam would stick his chin out and down. I asked him why he kept doing that. He said ever since he started school he had to wear an aviator hat all winter, and it felt like he still had it on all the time. It seemed like the strap was always under his neck, and he did that to try to make the feeling go away.

Does it go away?

No. It seems like it's always under my neck.

I been having to wear an aviator hat, too. I don't like them, but I've always had ear trouble and Mama says I just got to wear it in the wintertime.

I don't think I'm going to wear mine to school next year.

Well, I know I'm not going to wear mine anymore. Besides, I can't keep up with no hat. I lost mine a whole lot, and I got some whippings for it. But I'd rather get a whipping than wear a doggone aviator hat. I just ain't wearing one no more.

Me neither then.

Sam, let's go to the house and get a drink of water. We got a water bucket inside the house.

We do, too.

When we walked through the living room, Sam said, Y'all got a picture on the wall.

It's not a real picture. It's just a big calendar with a picture on top with two angels in it.

It looks good. I like a picture on the wall.

I do too, but have you looked at that picture real close?

What you mean?

Well, it's them two angels. One of them's standing in the clouds with one hand down and kind of held open, and the other hand is held up with a finger pointing towards heaven. And the other angel's holding on to a big stick, sort of like a walking cane, in one hand, and the other hand's pointing towards heaven. You see, them clouds are dark and the sun is barely shining through. I know them angels is good and all, but it just seems like they're looking right at you all the time.

Yeah, it sure does.

I'll tell you something else, Sam.

What?

Well, you just can't say anything bad around Mama and Aunt Maybelle, and especially Aunt Lanie. You know like when you hit your finger or hurt yourself and it seems like you just got to cuss? If Mama hears you, she just rolls her eyes back in her head and says, Jesus, Savior and Aunt Maybelle'll go around singing, Rock of ages, cleft for me. And there's no way you can say anything in front of Aunt Lanie. You just have to hold your finger real tight and bear it or cuss under your breath.

R.C., what you think cleft means?

I don't know, but Aunt Maybelle likes to say it. I think it means like that's the way the rock was carved out or something. I ain't sure. But if you want to hear some cussing, you just come to our house when Daddy's trying to start our truck contraption. I think Aunt Maybelle just goes in a trance, and you ought to see how far Daddy can throw that truck crank.

Let's get our drink of water.

That sounds good, Sam. You know the best thing I like about religion so far?

What?

You don't have to work on Sunday.

Yeah. That's the best part.

Me and Sam hadn't been playing marbles very long before Aunt

Maybelle's three oldest boys came up. They were old enough to play all right, but their younger brother, Billy, couldn't play 'cause he was only four. Pretty soon Sam's younger brother, James Kenneth, came to play. James was eight, so he could play all right.

Pretty soon all six of us were shooting marbles in our front yard. We could all shoot pretty good, so we decided to draw a bigger ring to shoot across. We were getting along pretty good until Billy and Bobby came up and wanted to play. We told them they were just too little to shoot, but they could chase our marbles for us. They liked that all right, and that way we didn't have to chase our own marbles.

It wasn't too long before Sam's sister, Goldie, came up. She went in the house and her and Doris started playing girl stuff. By then, Aunt Maybelle and Uncle Rudolph had come over. Uncle Rudolph sat in a rocking chair on the front porch, smoked his pipe and watched us play.

Mama and Aunt Maybelle came out on the porch. Mama said, Do y'all realize that there are twelve of you children here now and you're all first cousins? Everybody's playing except Jimmy, and one of these days he'll be right out there too. Now, y'all play good. Me and Maybelle's going to cook a good Sunday dinner with chicken, hot biscuits and all. We're all going to eat here today.

That night, after we went to bed, I lay awake thinking how all us cousins played nearly all day and what a good time we'd had. Me and Sam had done a lot of exploring. We walked all over Aunt Maybelle's, Aunt Ruth's and our farm. Looked like it was going to take a good while to explore all two hundred acres of what was left of the old Larkins place. Me and Sam were going to explore the log cabin next. They'd already moved everything from there and into their new house.

We had both kerosene lamps lit, but they were turned down so low you could hardly see. I went to the kitchen, got a drink of water, turned the lamp on the kitchen table up a little and went back to bed. I wondered what

Mama meant when she said that me and Doris would be doing different jobs tomorrow.

I began to drift off to sleep. It felt good except them doggone mosquitoes were still biting. I could hear Doris slapping at them, and there was something else biting under them covers. I wondered what it was.

When I woke up, Mama was cooking breakfast. I went in the kitchen and she told me to get a bucket of water, then run do my other jobs. She said we had a lot to do that day. After breakfast Daddy and Uncle Rudolph and the Cottle boys went back to cutting and hauling logs. I asked Mama, How come them Cottles help us with our barn and all?

They're going to help us with our barns and outbuildings, and we're going to help them with theirs. But today me and you younguns are going to have to chop corn.

What do you mean *chop corn*?

You know your daddy and your Uncle Rudolph planted the crop this year while you and Doris were still in school at Spofford Mills.

That corn's about two feet tall now.

Well, we still have to plow it about two more times. But before we do, we have to take hoes, thin it and chop out the grass and weeds. Me, you and Doris are going to start that today.

What about Bobby, Ann, and Jimmy?

Bobby can help us. He can pick up the corn that we thin out. And Ann can help look out for Jimmy.

I don't think Bobby's going to work a lot. Sometimes he feeds the chickens in the morning, but that's just 'cause he likes to see them eat and scratch. I don't think he's that good of a worker. Besides, he's only five.

That's old enough to start working. Everybody's got to do his part.

What about Ann and Jimmy?

We'll put Jimmy in a washtub under one of them mulberry trees and Ann can watch him.

Ann's just three years old.

Ann's a good child, and she'll look out for Jimmy.

I know, Mama. She don't hardly ever cry. She just walks around sucking a bottle and twirling her hair with her fingers.

That's enough talking. The sun's already over the top of them trees. Now you take one of them washtubs, put a quilt in it, and take it to that first mulberry tree out in the cornfield.

There were three mulberry trees in the first field in the back of our house. They were about one hundred fifty feet apart and about halfway down the corn rows. I took the washtub and quilt and put it under the shade of the first mulberry tree. When I got back to the house, Mama had Jimmy in her arms and Doris had a hoe. I got two more hoes, and we set out for the cornfield with Bobby and Ann tagging along.

Mama put Jimmy in the washtub, placed the quilt around him, and told Bobby and Ann to look out for him. Then Mama, me and Doris started thinning the corn and chopping out the weeds. I could tell that I wasn't going to like chopping corn. Doris didn't like it either.

Mama, I'd rather haul logs and help build the tobacco barn and them other buildings.

You can help with that after we get all the hoeing done.

How long is that going to take?

That depends on how hard you work. We've got about eight acres to hoe.

Is this the last time we have to hoe the crops this year?

Yes. They've already been hoed twice. Now go check on Ann and Jimmy and tell Bobby to come help us.

I went to the mulberry tree, checked on Jimmy, and told Bobby what Mama said. He came back with me, but I didn't think he was going to be much help. Mama asked me how Jimmy and Ann was doing. I told Mama that Jimmy's tub was in the sun, but I'd pulled it back in the shade of the tree and that Ann was just sitting there beside the tub twirling her hair.

What was Bobby doing?

He was throwing dirt clods.

I figured that.

Mama, Jimmy was sucking his bottle, but I think his diaper needs changing.

Mama told Doris to go change Jimmy's diaper. I was glad I didn't have to change no diapers. That slop jar was bad enough.

Mama, how come them mulberry trees are spaced out like the same distance apart? I wonder why they're the only trees in this field.

Well, it's not good to have too many trees growing in a field. If you do, it just makes it harder to grow crops. And I'm not sure, but I think they're spaced like that so's whoever's working in these fields in the hot summertime can stop and rest in the shade.

Yeah, Mama, and so you can put babies under the tree in a tub while you're working, too.

I guess so, son. Now chop that corn.

Mama told Bobby to gather up the corn that we'd thinned out. She said we could feed it to the mule and the cow that night. I told Mama, them mulberry trees are real big. Me and Sam together can just barely reach around them. I wonder how old they are.

I don't know, but my great Uncle Jimmy Larkins planted an acorn in front of the log cabin. That's where that big oak tree comes from.

I wonder who planted them mulberry trees.

I don't know. They were here when I was born, and they were big then.

Mama, how old are you?

I'll be twenty-nine in November.

How old is Daddy?

He'll be thirty-two in November.

I guessed that wasn't really old, because there were people living on our road that were all the way up to eighty-five.

Me and Doris were getting hungry. I asked Mama, How long before we get to eat dinner?

We'll go eat at twelve o'clock.

We don't have a clock out here, Mama.

Don't worry. The sawmill whistle will blow when it's twelve o'clock.

My stomach says it's twelve o'clock now.

Doris said, Mine too.

It wasn't long before the mill whistle blew and we headed towards the house. Mama took Bobby and Ann on ahead so she could start cooking. I took hold of the handle on one side of the tub, Doris took the other, and we carried Jimmy. I liked dinnertime on a farm. We always had plenty to eat. There was always one big pot in the middle of the table. Most times it was filled with vegetable soup, and we had plenty of hot biscuits and fatback meat.

When Daddy was home, he'd sit at one end of the table and every time he got a biscuit, he'd pinch off a little piece and put it beside his plate. You could always tell how many biscuits he'd ate. Mama said it was a stupid habit.

We played the battery radio at dinnertime and listened to country music. On real hot days we'd take an hour or more off for dinner. We called it the heat of the day. We did that so all of us and the mule could rest up. That way we could work better in the evening. I liked the time we had off in the heat of the day. When they said *heat of the day*, it was sure enough right 'cause even though we were inside the house and out of the sun, it was still real hot. Our house didn't have any ceilings, just a hot tin roof. When it rained it cooled down some, but the best thing about the rain was the sound of it beating on the tin roof.

Another bad thing about the hot weather was them flies. During the day the shutters were open and the flies just swarmed in. There was just no way to keep them out. Mama said they were bad because of all them animals we had. Every day after dinner, before we went back to the fields, we'd chase the flies out the door. Somebody would hold the door open, and the rest of us would take towels and fan the flies out. When we got most of the flies out, we'd take down the old fly tapes that were hanging from the ceiling and put up new ones. The tapes hung down about three feet and the flies got stuck all over them. It was the same thing every day. I hoped one day we'd get glass windows and screen doors.

Most days were about the same. After we ate breakfast, I'd either help Mama and Doris in the fields or help with the cutting and hauling of the logs. Sometimes in the evening after supper, we'd sit on the front porch steps and watch the bull bats and the fireflies. Then we'd go in and listen to the battery radio before we went to bed.

❧

Daddy said we had a good crop going and the barn and other out-buildings were coming along real good. I liked working on the buildings. Daddy showed me how to take the bark off the pine logs. I used a drawing knife that was made special to get the bark off. It took a lot of work with that old drawing knife because we took the bark off all the logs we used except the ones we built the tobacco barn with.

❧

One day Mama said, R.C., take the cow to that grassy spot past the cornfield and let her graze. She'll like that nice green grass, and we can save on corn. Just make sure you hold on to that cow chain until her sides look like they're good and full.

It sounded like an easy job. While I was leading the cow down the path to the grassy spot, I thought to myself, I'll just tie her to that old walnut tree and while she's helping herself to the grass, I'll get one of them water-melons out of our patch and help myself.

I tied the cow to the tree, started eating on the watermelon, and watched the cow eat. Looked like she was getting real full. Pretty soon I finished my watermelon and untied the cow. I took her back up to the house so Mama could see what a good job I'd done. She looked at one side of the cow and said, Well, that looks good. Then she walked around and looked at the other side and said, Son, take this cow right back to the grassy spot. She's not full.

What do you mean not full?

She's nice and full on one side, but you just look at the other side. I looked at the other side of the cow. She looked like she was starving to death.

Mama, what's wrong with the cow?

There's nothing wrong with the cow. She's just not full.

She's full on the other side.

Son, what you don't realize is that cows have more than one stomach.

How many they got?

I don't know for sure, but you take this cow back and let her eat until she's full on both sides.

Good Lord, Mama.

Don't good Lord me, boy. Now git. Just remember this—when you don't do the job right the first time, you just have to lick that calf over.

What's that mean?

That's just my saying for if you don't do it right the first time, you just have to do it again.

Mama, how'd you come up with a saying like that?

Well, when a cow has a calf, she always licks him real clean, and then she looks him over real good. If she don't think he's clean enough, she'll just lick him again. Now, what you got to do is lick that calf over.

Mama, I think you've got a saying for just about everything.

The days were getting longer and hotter. Me, Mama and Doris were still chopping corn and weeding the sweet potatoes and peanuts. We worked in our big vegetable garden nearly every day. Mama and Doris had started putting up pickles, making relish and canning whatever vegetables were ready. Mama said she was going to can about fifteen hundred quarts of vegetables and berries for the winter. She said that way we'd have plenty to eat during the cold winter months. It looked like we were going to have plenty of meat to eat too. Some of our sow hogs had some little pigs, and Daddy said they'd be just about the right size come hog-killing time. I asked Daddy, When's hog-killing time?

Son, it's after the first hard freeze.

How come you have to wait for freezing weather?

If you kill hogs before cold weather, the meat will spoil.

How do you keep it from spoiling?

Well, we put plenty of salt on it, and then we hang it in the smokehouse and cure it.

How do you cure it?

We hang it on hooks from the smokehouse joists, build a fire out of hickory wood and smoke the meat. I'll show you all about how to do it when hog-killing time comes. Now go help your mama in the fields.

Daddy, I want to work on the buildings some more. I'm tired of chopping with that doggone hoe.

Yeah, I know. But you go on back to them fields now and work hard. Maybe in a few days you can start back helping me on the buildings.

Can I help build the smokehouse?

Yeah. You can start by skinning the pine bark off the logs.

But I'd rather be the one that helps put the logs together and put the top on and all.

I know son, but somebody's got to skin the bark off all them logs, and you've got pretty good at it.

Me, Mama and Doris went back to the fields. We got Jimmy, Ann and Bobby settled in the shade of one of them mulberry trees and started hoeing corn. It was the same thing over and over. Mama chopped two rows, and me and Doris did one row at a time. That way we could stay along together and talk.

Mama was always talking about being honest, having honor, how we should do this and how we should do that, and how everybody had to do his share and there was always something that needed to be done. I just knew Aunt Lanie would say Amen to that. Even if there wasn't anything to do, Mama would find something in a hurry. I wished she'd talk about something besides work and responsibility. I decided to change the subject.

Mama, I've noticed Dizz is acting different. He don't run and play as much as he used to.

Well, son, he's not as young as he used to be. You know before your daddy brought him home, he kept Dizz at the cotton mill for a long time. Your daddy's been night watchman at the mill for a good while now and sometimes he'd sleep on the concrete floor while he was waiting to make his rounds. He had to walk around the mill, inside and out, once every hour and punch clocks so the mill owners would know he was making his rounds. Old Dizz just seemed to know when it was time to make the rounds. He'd always wake your daddy up.

I know, Mama. Daddy let me stay with him a few nights and old Dizz would wake us up. I think Dizz misses the cotton mill.

I guess he does, son. He was always around a lot of people.

I'll tell you what else.

What?

You know Daddy keeps catching them raccoons and possums, and he'll drag one of them possums by the tail all around the edge of the woods and up the side of a tree and he'll put a raccoon in a sack and do the same thing. Then he tries to get Dizz to follow their trail. I don't think Dizz likes it.

Well, son, I'm sure he'd like bird hunting better. After all, he is a bird dog.

Sometimes when me and him are just walking along, he'll stop, point his nose and stretch his tail out. And you know what?

What, son?

When he does that, I just run ahead and partridge birds fly up all over the place.

Yeah?

Uh-huh.

Fowler House in Pender County, North Carolina

 Six

I didn't know much about farming, but I could already see that it was just work, work, work. Me, Mama and Doris were out in the fields early every morning and worked all day except for dinnertime. I was always glad when night came and it was time to go home, feed up and wash dishes. At least we could put them hoes down for a while.

One day when we were hoeing sweet potatoes, I asked Mama, What are we going to do with all these sweet potatoes?

We're going to take some to town and sell them. Then we'll bank the rest and eat them through the year.

How do you bank sweet potatoes?

Well, it's not like a bank in town where you put your money. What you do is after you get the potatoes dug, you make a layer of dirt about a foot thick. Then you put about a foot of pine straw on that. Next you pile the sweet potatoes on the straw until it's about four or five feet high. Then you put a foot of pine straw on top of the potatoes.

That sounds like a lot of work.

Next you cut some hardwood saplings and lay them on top of the straw. Then you nail two boards together so they're in an upside down V shape and put that on top. That's what gives ventilation to the potatoes and keeps them from rotting.

That sounds complicated, Mama.

It's really not.

Then what do you do?

Next you pile dirt about a foot thick all over the straw, and that's what keeps the potatoes from freezing. You know, if a potato freezes it's not fit to eat.

How do you get to the potatoes when you want some to cook?

You just leave a small opening at the bottom, about two foot square, and put an empty fertilizer sack over it. That way the potatoes stay warm and you can get to them anytime we want to.

Mama, it sounds like it's shaped like an Indian teepee.

Yeah, except it's smaller.

I bet I can play in that potato bank when it gets empty.

Maybe so.

Mama, who's that boy coming down the path?

Oh my. That's Lester, Mr. Worley's grandson. Now that boy's a talker.

What you think he's coming here for?

I suppose he just wants to talk.

Let him talk, Mama. I like to talk, too.

Now y'all can talk, but just keep on working.

Lester came up to where we was working and said, Hey, Miss Carrie.

Hey, Lester, what you doing over this way?

Well, I was just passing and saw y'all out here working, and just thought I'd stop by.

Mama looked at me and Doris, winked and said, Lester, how's everything?

Everything's fine, but I tell you one thing, Miss Carrie, Grandpa Worley sure was glad y'all bought that mule from him. He said that old Bill was one wild mule. You know he almost killed Grandpa.

Yeah, I know, Lester, he is kind of wild, but he's strong and we've got a lot of work out of him.

Maybe so, but Grandpa was sure glad to get rid of him.

I guess so.

Miss Carrie, you know them three mulberry trees out there in that field? Well, folks around here talk as how there's money buried under 'em.

Now, Lester, I doubt that.

Well now, I don't know, Miss Carrie. Folks around here say that when them Yankees come through here in the Civil War, them folks what lived here had money, and they buried it under them three mulberry trees before them Yankees got here.

Yeah, Lester, I heard that too, but I doubt it. As far as I can remember, there's never been any money around here.

I was glad Lester had come by because every once in a while we'd all stop hoeing and just prop up on our hoe handles and listen to him talk. But it wasn't long before Mama told Lester, You know, it's getting kind of late. Don't you think you ought to be getting on your way? R.C., you better go check on them children.

Me and Lester walked over to the mulberry tree.

R.C., look at that baby in the tub. He's just laying there looking up in that tree.

That's all he does—lay in that tub, suck his bottle, look up in that tree and mess in his diapers.

I believe his diapers done got mess in 'em now.

I think you're right, Lester.

R.C., like Miss Carrie said, I got to hurry home before it gets dark. I sure don't want to be walking down that lonely dirt road at night, not with them sinikin bears out and about.

What do you mean sinikin bears?

Well, you know, there's regular bears and then there's them real big bad bears. I calls them sinikin bears.

Yeah, I guess you better hurry home.

Pretty soon Mama said it was time to go in. Me and Doris picked up the tub with Jimmy in it and walked towards the house.

I asked Mama, What's a sinikin bear?

Well now, son, that's just a name some of these folks made up. There's no such thing as a real sinikin bear.

Lester talked like there was.

Well, there are bears, but you don't have to worry about no sinikin bears. That's kind of like the people on the Mill Hill making up that tale about the Squeezer.

I remember that. I didn't think there was no such thing as a Squeezer, but if there was one, I don't think he'd come way up here in these woods.

Maybe not. But I'll tell you what you younguns do have to watch out for, and that's them mad foxes. There's a lot of them up here, especially in the hot summertime.

Mama, what's them foxes mad about?

Son, it's not that kind of mad. Folks just call them mad. What's really wrong with them is they get rabies. Then they foam at the mouth and run all over the place and bite people. If they bite you, you'll die if you don't get a bunch of shots.

I thought, it seems like there's always something. On the Mill Hill, it was the Squeezer, now up here in the country it's them mad foxes. Looked like I was going to have to keep a sharp lookout for them foxes. I didn't want no more of them shots.

&

One Saturday afternoon, Mama said, Tomorrow's Sunday, and if you younguns want to shoot marbles in the front yard tomorrow, you're going to have to take the hoes and weed out all that grass.

Mama, there's a lot of grass and weeds in our front yard.

I know, but there's eight of you cousins that'll be playing. And if all of you get to hoeing and raking, you can get it done before dark.

Can we just weed where we're going to be shooting marbles?

You know better than that. Now, you go get them cousins and start weeding and weed the whole yard.

Mama, if we get all them weeds and grass out of the yard, can we take the rest of the day off?

We'll see.

Me, Doris and our cousins got the front yard weeded and raked. I went in the kitchen and told Mama, Come see how good it looks. She came out on the front porch and said, Now, children, that looks real good. There's just one more thing, though.

What's that?

Well, you've got all the yard weeded and raked all right, but now you've got to sweep it.

What we gonna sweep it with?

You just make a broom out of wax myrtle branches. Sam knows how.

Can't we just use a house broom?

No, it's too soft. It's made out of broom sage. It's no good for sweeping in the yard.

I helped Sam make some brooms. Then us cousins swept the yard. Mama came out on the porch and said, Now, children, that's more like it. Y'all got a good clean yard to shoot marbles in tomorrow. I looked over at Sam and said, Thank the Lord. He just grinned.

I told Sam what Mama'd said about the mad foxes.

Sam said, I know about them mad foxes.

Sam, I don't think it's the kind of mad that Daddy gets when he's trying to start the truck contraption. It's a more dangerous kind of mad.

I know, it's real bad. It's kind of like all them rattlesnakes around here and that other thing that happens mostly in the summertime, what's called polio.

Yeah, Sam, I heard them talking about it on the battery radio. They call it infantile paralysis. Mama said President Roosevelt's working hard to find a cure.

I heard.

Mama and Daddy said President Roosevelt's good 'cause he gives them fireside chats on the radio and he tries to make you feel better during this Depression and all.

We ain't got no radio, but we got a pump organ.

What's a pump organ?

It's kind of like a piano except it's got big pedals that you keep pumping with your feet.

Oh yeah, I saw that thing. It does look a lot like a piano. You know, Grandpa Fowler has a piano. I used to go to Sunday school at a Presbyterian church, and they had a piano too. I kind of like them Presbyterians.

I don't know nothing about Presbyterians.

Well, I'll tell you, Sam. In the summer they just put all the Sunday school classes on them trolleys that go to the beach and when they get there they have picnics and go swimming and things.

That sounds good.

You know, Sam, Mama and Aunt Lanie are Baptists, but I'm leanin' toward being a Presbyterian.

There's lots of folks around here calls themselves Holiness, and they have what they call cottage prayer meetings at our house sometimes. They preach, sing and shout, and there's always somebody there to play the pump organ.

Yeah, I heard, Sam. Aunt Maybelle's a Holiness too.

I don't know why, R.C., but when they preach like that it makes me feel like I'm a big sinner.

Sam, you ain't no big sinner. Not big as me, anyway.

&

Our first spring on the farm was gone, and summer would be over before long. It would soon be time to start thinking about going to a new school. Me and Doris would have to ride the school bus. We'd never rode a bus before and we wondered what it was going to be like.

&

It was late August and still mighty hot, especially laying in bed at night. The heat from our tin roof just kept bearing down. We were always glad when it rained at night. It helped cool the tin roof and it sounded good. Sometimes after I went to bed, I'd lay there in the quiet and think about the Mill Hill, about the hum of the mill, the company store, the candy counter, and the music players practicing in the band room over the company store. I missed Grandma Fowler a lot. 'Course, I missed Aunt Til too. I just knew she was saving them funny papers for me.

It started to rain. I laid there listening to the sound of the raindrops beating on the tin roof and fell asleep.

&

It was September and school had started. I really liked my teacher and my classmates. There were a lot of pupils in my class, and all of them had been at Long Creek School for three years already. Most everybody wanted to know where I'd been to school before. I told them that I'd lived in a cotton mill village and that's where I went to school.

When we got home from school in the afternoons, Mama always had something for us to do. Just as soon as we got in the door, first thing we heard was, you children take off them school clothes, put on your work clothes, get yourself a biscuit and a sweet potato or something and hit them fields.

One afternoon when we got home, I asked Mama, What we havin' for supper?

We're having chicken and rice tonight.

I told Doris, I just bet that one of them log trucks done run over another one of our chickens. I know Mama ain't going to kill no good laying hen just so we can have chicken and rice for supper.

R.C., I don't care how it got killed just as long as we get to eat chicken tonight.

I don't either.

After I'd finished my evening jobs, I went in the house and sat down at the kitchen table. I liked sitting there with my elbows on the table and my hands propped under my chin watching Mama and Doris cook supper. Mama said, R.C., can't you find something to do besides sitting there watching us?

I could go in the living room and listen to the radio, but Daddy's in there trying to pick that old guitar and sing, and Mama, you know his pickin's terrible and his singin's worse.

You're right about that, son.

Mama, how come we keep that old cow and feed her and we don't get nothing from her after we done skinned all that bark off them logs to make her a stable? Why don't we kill her and have some cow meat?

It's not called cow meat, it's called beef. And one thing's for sure, when you only got one cow, you can't have beef and milk at the same time.

We ain't getting no milk.

The cow will give milk when she comes fresh.

What you mean *comes fresh*?

When a cow has a calf, she comes fresh. That means she'll start giving milk.

Why don't she go ahead and get a calf?

Well, some things have to happen first.

What has to happen?

That's all you need to know for now. She'll have a calf one of these days. Then she'll start giving milk.

Do we get some of the milk?

We'll get most of it, but we have to leave some for the calf. That's enough about that now. Get washed up for supper.

Mama and Doris put supper on the table and called everybody to eat. Us children got to our places. Daddy came in from the living room, sat at the head of the table and said, I believe I'm really getting the hang of that guitar playing. What do y'all think? We all looked at one another. Nobody said anything. Mama said, Y'all bow your heads right now, I'm saying the blessings.

Daddy and Aunt Maybelle left for work after supper. Me and Doris went in the living room, sat down at the radio table, and started on our homework. Mama put Bobby, Ann and Jimmy to bed and then came in the living room. She looked over at me and Doris and said, That's good, children, make sure you do all your homework.

Mama went back to her work in the kitchen. It wasn't long before she started singing. She usually sang, *Jesus, Savior, Pilot Me*, but that night she was singing, *Precious Memories, How They Linger*. Me and Doris looked at one another, smiled and went back to our homework by the kerosene lamp.

❧

Most days after school I worked by myself 'cause all the crops were in except the sweet potatoes. We'd be digging them in a few days. I didn't mind working by myself too much. Sometimes when I was cutting down dead cornstalks, I'd pretend I was Sampson in the Bible and the cornstalks were the bad Philistines, and I was slaying them like the Bible said Sampson did.

Doris had to help Mama a lot around the house. They were doing some canning and putting up preserves, and there was always clothes to be washed. Daddy and Aunt Maybelle were working the night shift at the cotton mill. We kept both lamps burning at night because me and Doris were still scared some.

❧

The days were getting cooler. We dug and banked the sweet potatoes. I liked digging sweet potatoes. You could really see the results of all that work with them bushels of potatoes piled up high, and I liked the way we built the potato bank around them.

December came, and on the first cold day we killed hogs. I didn't like to see Daddy and Uncle Rudolph kill the hogs. I liked the other things about hog-killing days, though, like having a fire around the big iron washpot, cooking small pieces of pork on a stick held over the fire, and having a lot of people around doing things like cooking cracklings, making lard, sausage, and liver pudding and cutting up hams, shoulders and side meat.

We rubbed salt, black pepper and molasses on the meat, then hung it in our new smokehouse. After it was all hung, we built a fire out of hickory wood. Then we wet the wood so it'd smoke a lot. Daddy said we had enough meat to last until hog-killing time next year.

It looked like we were going to have plenty of meat, potatoes, corn, canned vegetables and preserves to last a long time. Mama was a good cook. She could change the meals around where they seemed like they were differ-ent. She'd take sweet potatoes and make things like baked potatoes, fried potatoes, sweet potato pie and sweet potato pudding, and she'd take corn and make baked or fried cornbread, grits, mush and hominy. It was for sure we weren't gonna go hungry.

It was Christmas Eve. I cut down a small pine tree and Mama let us put it up in the kitchen next to our eating table. Me and Doris made some paper rings and pasted them together with flour paste. We strung the rings around the tree, and put a sheet around the bottom so it looked like snow. Then we wrote all our names on a piece of paper and put them under the tree so Santa Claus could see how many of us there was. I hoped he had enough for us five children and Mama and Daddy.

Mama baked a sweet potato pie and we left it on the kitchen table for Santa Claus. After we went to bed, I told Doris, I hope Santa Claus likes potato pie. If he does, I bet he'll just leave us all some toys.

He might.

Christmas morning me and Doris woke up and ran to the tree in the kitchen. Santa Claus had come all right 'cause about half of the sweet potato pie was gone. We looked under the tree and all us children got some apples, oranges, and some nuts. Santa Claus had put them right beside the pieces of paper with our names.

Seven

It was a new year, 1938. The nights were cold. Some nights our water bucket would get a skim of ice on it. Even though it was the dead of winter, there was always plenty to do. After we got home from school in the evenings and changed clothes, there was only about two hours of daylight left to work. By the time we fed all the animals and ate supper, it was most times big dark. That's what Mama called real dark.

Sometimes after Daddy got home on Saturday mornings and slept for a few hours, he'd get things lined up so that we could work at night. One night after supper he looked at me and said, Well, I think we're gonna do a little work tonight.

What we gonna do, Daddy?

Son, we're just gonna make some wood roof shingles for the tobacco barn.

How we gonna make shingles?

Well, we cut down some big straight pine trees, and cut them up in sixteen-inch long blocks. Then we take a special axe that has a real wide blade, place it on top of the block, and hit it with a wooden maul that we make out of a small oak tree. It's called riving out shingles.

That night me, Daddy, Uncle Rudolph and my cousin Lewis worked making shingles. Around ten o'clock Daddy said, Well, boys, we've done enough for one night. Let's just take the dogs and go coon hunting.

By then we had two dogs. There was Old Dizz, and Grandma Fowler had sent us another dog. His name was Toby. He was named after my Uncle

Otto, whose nickname was Toby.

We got the dogs, guns and lanterns and set off in the woods. The dogs were excited and ready to hunt. I was already tired, and I really didn't care much about hunting 'cause I knew if you caught something, then you just felt like you had to kill it. I knew we had to kill hogs and chickens. I didn't like it, but I knew you had to kill some things. I wasn't really happy about hunting an animal down just to kill it, though.

It was a cold night. We built a fire and sat around it while we were waiting for the dogs to tree. Pretty soon the dogs started barking. Daddy jumped up and said, I believe they've treed. He hollered real loud, Yey speak, yey speak. I guessed that meant for the dogs to keep on barking so we could find them and see what was up the tree. We grabbed the lanterns, guns and axc and started running towards where the dogs were barking. Every now and then Daddy and Uncle Rudolph would holler, Yey speak, yey speak.

By then we were running headlong and just splashing through the branch water. Our feet were soaking wet, but nobody seemed to mind. I was having a hard time trying to keep up. I was running behind everybody else. Every now and then somebody ahead of me would grab ahold of a sapling limb, push it out of his way, and then just turn it loose. Most times, it would swing back and slap me in the face.

Every now and then we'd run through a briar thicket. After we got through it, we'd be scratched something bad, but it didn't slow us down. We were running, hollering, splashing, making our way towards where the dogs had whatever it was treed. Daddy said, I bet that's a big coon. It might be more than one the way them dogs are barking.

When we got to the dogs, they were looking up a big sweet gum tree and barking as hard as they could. Sometimes they'd run and jump up on the tree like they wanted to climb up and get that coon or whatever was up there. Daddy started shining his flashlight up the tree, but we couldn't see much. He said, Rudolph, these batteries are so weak I just can't see anything, but I want to get that raccoon so them dogs can have a real good coon fight. That'll make them better hunting dogs.

Well, Alton, we can cut the tree down, but if that raccoon just marked the tree so's to fool them dogs, we'll be cutting that tree down for nothing.

Yeah, I know, but let's take a chance and cut it down anyway.

Daddy and Uncle Rudolph took turns chopping on that old sweet gum tree. Every once in a while they'd take a break. Daddy would smoke a cigarette and Uncle Rudolph would light up his pipe. They'd talk about dogs they used to have, and dogs they knew about, and how good a coon fighter they was. Well, I listened, but I wasn't real interested 'cause by then I was getting sleepy.

Finally the tree fell, and the dogs ran to the top end of it like they was going to drag a big coon out of that old gum tree. Daddy and Uncle Rudolph grabbed the lanterns and ran behind the dogs. They looked around the tree real good, but didn't find anything. Uncle Rudolph said, Alton, it looks like we done cut that big tree down for nothing. Daddy said, Well, it sure looks like it. That was a smart coon. He just marked that tree and left.

I asked Daddy, What do you mean marked the tree? What does the coon mark the tree with?

Well, son, he don't mark a tree like you think. He don't use chalk or anything like that. He marks it with his scent.

He does? How?

Oh, he'll climb up the tree about twenty feet and then jump back on the ground a long way from where he climbed up. Dogs like these that don't have a lot of experience will stay right at the foot of the tree and just keep barking, but that coon'll be long gone.

Uncle Rudolph said, Yeah, but experienced dogs know better. When they smell where a coon's gone up a tree they'll circle the tree and keep making wider circles, and if that coon's jumped down, they'll find his scent and trail him off again. They won't just stay at the foot of the tree and keep barking like these dogs did.

Daddy said, We might as well head for the house.

Well, I was glad to hear that. I was ready to get home and get in my bed. When we got out of the woods and started walking through the fields, the ground was froze and hard to walk on. The sky was clear. The moon was shining bright, and you could see the frost sparkling-like on the grass. Everything was quiet and it seemed real peaceful, except once when I thought I heard a screech owl.

When we got home, we got by our heater to warm up a little before going to bed. I said, Daddy, guess what?

What, son?

Them dogs are already here laying 'side the heater.

Them sorry rascals.

Mama called out from her bedroom and said, They got here before you and started whining at the back door, and I let them in. If you ask me, them dogs got more sense than y'all got. They know it's too cold to be tromping about in them woods at night. I thought, Mama's right.

The next day was Sunday. I ate breakfast, fed the animals, then walked out and looked down the road. Sam, James and Goldie were coming towards our house. When they got there, we sat on our front porch and wondered what we could play. Sam said, You know, R.C., on cold days like this, me, James, and Goldie play fox and the dog.

How do you play?

You just choose one person to be the fox, and everybody else is a dog. You give the one that's playing the fox about a five-minute head start and let him run through the woods. He tries to keep ahead of us dogs. Sometimes he'll try to hide from us in the woods. If we catch him he has to be one of the dogs, and the one that catches him gets to be the fox. When us dogs are chasing the fox, we can bark like dogs and all.

Sam, we don't have to cut down no big trees, do we?

No, we don't play cutting down trees like when you go coon hunting at night. Besides, R.C., foxes don't climb trees.

That sounds like a good game. Let's play it.

We played fox and the dog nearly all day and had a lot of fun. Mama said there were so many of us dogs, the poor fox didn't have a chance.

❧

Spring wasn't far off, but the weather was still cold. No matter how cold it was, Mama always had something for us to do. She said just because there was no plowing or hoeing to do didn't mean we could just sit around. I'd already found out that when you lived on a farm there was always something to do, especially if you had a mama like ours.

In the evening after school she kept us busy feeding, shelling corn and cutting next season's wood for the tobacco barn. There was always wood for the heater and cook-stove to be cut, and if we had time, we'd just clear more land. We'd sowed the seed for our tobacco plants back in December, and we kept the frost off the plants with a thin cloth we kept stretched over them. It was called a tobacco canvas. We kept the weeds pulled out so the little plants could grow. Daddy said they had to be ready for planting in the fields by spring.

❧

One night when we were all sitting around the supper table, Daddy said, Carrie, we need to clear more land.

Why?

So we can plant more crops. I'd like to buy out all your brothers' and sisters' shares of the inheritance land.

Alton, you've got big ideas, but there's no way Ruth's going to sell her share.

You don't think so?

She was born here in that log cabin and she's never going to sell her piece of land.

Maybe not. But if we can buy everybody else out, that'll give us a hundred and seventy-five acres.

I wondered how we were going to buy all that land. We didn't have any money. Besides, if we did get some money and I had any say, the first thing I'd buy would be some real glass windows. That way, when it rained in the daytime we wouldn't have to close them wooden shutters that always made it so dark inside. One good thing, though, our rooms had done got divided off with pine paneling boards that Daddy'd got from the saw mill. He'd traded logs for the boards and Uncle Rudolph helped put them up.

After supper I went in the living room where Daddy was trying to pick that old guitar. It was just like I thought. He was reared back in that rocking chair with his eyes all rolled back singing, *I'm the man that rode the mule around the world,* and I just knew the next song he'd sing would be about that lonely hobo riding on a train.

🐾

Spring finally came and I was glad. I'd done found out that winter just wasn't a good time of year for me. I thought the best time of year was spring 'cause it started getting warmer and the grass turned green and the flowers started blooming. You could go barefooted and feel the soft warm dirt squash up between your toes. When your shirt was off and your pant legs were rolled up, you could feel the warm spring winds blowing over you. Besides that, the days were longer and brighter and best of all, school was out.

I made my grade all right. I had gotten along pretty good my first year in school in Pender County.

🐾

We worked through the winter all right, but it seemed like since spring came we had to get up earlier and work later. Mama and Daddy were both saying how important it was to get all the crops planted on time, especially the tobacco 'cause that's what we'd get most of our money from in the fall.

Daddy was still working nights at the cotton mill and what time he had to spend working on the farm was mostly spent plowing. He let me plow some. I could plow a little, but the plow was heavy to handle, especially at the end of the rows. Most of the time, though, Daddy did the plowing and I dipped fertilizer for him. I'd take fertilizer out of the two hundred-pound bags and put it in a peck bucket. Daddy would take the bucket in one hand and spread the fertilizer with the other. I liked dipping fertilizer 'cause you had time to rest, and I liked the smell of the fertilizer and the fresh ground after it was turned up.

It was a good time of year, all right, going barefooted with my overall legs rolled up and most times no shirt on. One good thing was that when summertime came, we were going to have all them fresh vegetables to eat. We planted a real big garden that year. Mama said she was planning on putting up another fifteen hundred quarts of vegetables and preserves. Sometimes she called it *putting up* and sometimes she called it *canning*.

We got our crops planted on time, then got busy finishing all the outbuildings and the tobacco barn. It seemed the most important thing was to get the barn finished and ready for the tobacco crop. Mama had us children dig a hole in the ground near the tobacco barn. It was about five feet square and three feet deep. There was plenty of clay, and nine of us cousins were working on that project, as Mama called it. Some of us would take the mule and a sled with a fifty-gallon barrel and haul water from our pump, and some of us would pour water in the hole. Three or four of us would get in the hole barefooted and just stomp around in the clay until it was soft. Then we'd put it in buckets and hand it out to be carried to the barn, where it was handed up to some more cousins who were already up in the barn on tier poles. That was the poles we'd be hanging the tobacco on later. Then they'd take the clay and throw it between the cracks in the logs and take three fingers and press the clay in. It had to be sealed tight so the heat would stay inside the barn when we cured the tobacco.

❦

After we got the crops planted and all the outbuildings finished, me, Doris and Mama stayed busy hoeing the crops, feeding up, washing dishes and whatever else had to be done. Mama kept us busy.

I'd been watching our cow and she seemed to be getting real fat. She wasn't just fat on one side, like when she wasn't quite full. She was real big all over her stomach. I told Mama, Our cow sure is getting big.

Now, son, you just never mind. That cow knows what's going on. I think before long she's going to have a calf and we'll start getting us some milk.

Well, I think it's time our cow started giving us something. We been feeding her a long time.

That's right, son. In just a few days we'll be getting milk and butter. Then you'll understand why we've been feeding her so long.

I wanted to ask Mama again how cows had calves and just where they came from, but she'd done told me that wasn't any of my business and I'd find out soon enough.

❦

I stayed up some nights with Daddy at the tobacco barn and he showed me how to keep the fire going in the furnace. I learned how to do it all right, but some of the pieces of wood were so big I could barely move them around. I told Daddy, I can't get them big pieces in that furnace.

Yes, you can.

No, I can't. I've tried.

Here, I'll show you how.

Daddy took a big iron bar called a railroad bar and pried the piece of wood around until he got it in the furnace. It was still hard for me to get the big logs in, so most of the time I'd pick out logs that had been split into smaller pieces and use them. Our big pile of wood was about fifteen steps away from the barn. I'd go through the pile and pick out the smaller pieces and take them to the barn shelter. That way I wouldn't have to go out to the woodpile after dark through the tall grass and weeds. I knew there were plenty of snakes around our place 'cause I'd done killed a lot of them.

Daddy took two days off from his job at the cotton mill to help with the curing of our last barn of tobacco. I stayed up with him the two nights he was home and helped him fire the furnace. After the second night he said he had to go back to his mill job and I'd have to finish curing the tobacco. I told Daddy I didn't know if I could fire the furnace all night by myself and keep the temperature right.

Oh yeah, son, you can do it all right. I've been watching you and you've been doing a pretty good job.

You think so?

Yeah, you can do it. Besides, I'll be back home by daylight to check and see if you've kept the temperature right.

That evening Daddy got the truck contraption started and him and Aunt Maybelle left for the mill. I told Mama what Daddy had said about me setting up at the barn that night. That's what everybody called it, setting up at the barn. Mama said, I know, he told me too. You'll be all right.

Think so, Mama?

I'm sure, son. After you feed up tonight you can eat a big supper and then go to the barn. Me and Doris will do the dishes and clean up the kitchen.

Mama, I might get hungry during the night.

I'll fix you some ham biscuits, and you can take a sweet potato and a jar of water. That'll keep you until morning.

Okay, Mama. I just ain't going to be running back up here to the house during the night like I'm scared or something.

You'll be all right, son.

It didn't seem like Mama and Daddy were worried about me taking care of that barn full of tobacco. Maybe they weren't, but I was. I wasn't just worried, I was scared, too.

I fed up everything and went back to the barn to check the temperature. It was one hundred seventy-five degrees, right where it was supposed to be. I thought, just more pressure on me, everything being just right when I'm taking over and all. I opened the furnace door and saw the fire was dying down. I put more wood in, closed the door, and opened the draft at the bottom a little. After the wood caught fire I adjusted the draft and checked the temperature again. Everything was still all right. I was supposed to keep the temperature between one hundred seventy and one hundred eighty degrees. I thought I could do it all right. It was just that I'd never been responsible for it all by myself before, especially at night.

I went back up to the house and ate supper. Mama said, R.C., you're mighty quiet. Now, don't worry, everything will be all right.

After supper I got the lantern and filled it with kerosene. I thought, now, I just might turn that flame up a little higher tonight. I sure don't want to run out of kerosene and be left sitting in the dark. I decided to take the kerosene can with me.

It was nearly dark by the time I got everything I needed out to the tobacco barn. I lit the lantern and sat it on the barn bench. It was just a flat wood bench that ran the length of the barn shelter, and it was wide enough so you could sit on it. There was an old quilt that we could lay on at night.

It was a dark night. The only light was the glow from the barn furnace, my lantern, and a few fireflies. Daddy had said there was nothing to be afraid of. Maybe not, but I was a little scared anyway. I didn't know what of exactly, but I kept thinking about things like them sinikin bears that Lester kept talking about and them mad foxes that Mama said roamed around at night. And I knew I had to keep my eyes open for them rattlesnakes that were always crawling around.

I knew I had to get my mind off of them things, though. I thought, I'll just go around to the barn door and check and see what the temperature is. That'll give me something to do and help keep my mind busy. I took the lantern, turned the flame up a little and walked around to the barn door that had the small glass windowpane. I felt the glass pane with the back of my hand. That way I could just about tell what the heat was. If it felt too hot, my heart would just jump up in my throat 'cause I knew if it was, the tobacco could turn out red, which meant it'd bring a lower price at market time. We had one barn of tobacco that had already turned out red during the year. Daddy got real upset about it and said, Now just look at that damn tobacco. It's as red as a fox's ass.

I kept looking at the clock that I'd brought from the house. It was ten o'clock and things were going along pretty good. I thought, well now, I might get tired during the night and I may just nod a little, but ain't no way I'm going to get no real sleep. Every now and then I'd look towards our house. I knew Doris, Bobby, Jimmy, and Ann had all gone to bed, but I just knew Mama hadn't gone to sleep. Once I thought I saw the back door open a little. It looked like I saw the light from the lamp shining out the door for just a second or two.

It was past midnight and things were going along all right. I ate one of my ham biscuits and some of my sweet potato and washed it down with some water. It was mighty quiet there underneath that old barn shelter. If I hadn't had to keep checking on that heat and putting wood in the furnace, I would've probably dozed off. About the only sounds I could hear were the frogs, crickets, and the sound of the fire burning in the furnace. After a little while, I started to hear something else. It sounded like it might be thunder way off. I checked the heat again. Everything was still all right.

The wind was beginning to blow pretty hard. It looked like there was going to be a summer storm. If it was, I hoped there wouldn't be a lot of lightning. I was afraid of lightning and, besides, it seemed like every time there was a storm close by, lightning would strike that big oak tree in front of the log cabin. You'd think as many times as that old tree had been struck, it'd be dead, but somehow it just kept on living.

It began to rain. The thunder got louder, and it started lightning real sharp. Our dogs, Old Dizz and Toby, came running out to the barn. They were soaking wet and scared. I petted them and they lay down close to the furnace. I thought, well, at least I got some company. I turned the lantern up a little more.

It was two o'clock in the morning and the rain was coming down hard. The lightning was flashing all around and sure enough, that big oak tree got struck again. The bark flew everywhere. Pieces of it flew under the barn shelter where I was, and the big flash of lightning made it seem like I was inside the lampshade of some giant kerosene lamp. Our dogs let out a yelp and ran all around under the barn shelter. I knew they were about scared to death, but right then I had to think about myself. Before I knew what I was doing, I grabbed the lantern and started running towards the house.

I couldn't see much in the darkness with the rain and all. I thought if I could just make it to our sweet potato bank, I'd dive inside. I'd hid in there before. It would be a good place to hide because about half of the potatoes were gone. The straw would seem nice and warm. I just wasn't going to go running up to our back door and start banging and hollering for them to let me in. I ran down the path that went from the barn to our house. The sweet potato bank wasn't far. It wouldn't take me long to get there.

I ran towards the potato bank with the lantern swinging back and forth in my hand. It was raining so hard I could barely see. The lightning struck again, the thunder boomed, and my heart jumped up in my throat. More lightning flashed. I slipped, fell in the mud, and dropped the lantern. I was soaking wet and covered in mud. I got up, grabbed the lantern, and made it to the potato bank, pulled back the old fertilizer sack that covered the door opening, and dived in. I was soaked and covered with mud all right, but at least I was out of the rain and lightning.

I felt safer there in the potato bank. There was enough room for me to stretch out my feet without them sticking outside. I took some of the pine straw and cleaned the mud off as best I could. The lantern went out. I guess some mud had got on the wick when I fell. I sat there in the darkness and listened to the storm outside.

It kept raining, thundering, and lightning, and the sack over the door opening was blowing all about, but I felt safe. That old potato bank was a good place to get away from everything. Sometimes it just seemed good to get in there where it was quiet and try to figure things out.

I sat in the potato bank and thought, there ought to be somebody you can go to and explain how you feel—things like how you'd rather live on the Mill Hill with your friends, Grandma, and Aunt Til, and hang around the company store by the big candy counter. I'd been trying to quit thinking about them kind of things, but it seemed like no matter how hard I tried, they just kept creeping right back in my mind. I was already figuring how long it would be 'til I finished high school and could leave the farm. I figured another seven, maybe eight more years. Then I could go back to the Mill Hill, get me a good job and make some money of my very own.

It stopped raining. I lit the lantern and headed back to the barn. It must have been nearly four o'clock. I sure hoped the heat in the barn was all right. I didn't want to mess up the first time I stayed up all night by myself watching that old barn. When I got to the barn, I checked the heat—it was still all right. I thought to myself, well, I guess I had the fire going about right when the storm started and it looks like things are going to be okay when Daddy gets back from the mill in the morning.

I wondered how our cow was doing. Mama said she thought the cow was going to have a calf during the night. If she did, I'd be the first one to see it. I hadn't told anybody, but I'd done found out where them animals come from 'cause one day when I went to feed the hogs I saw some pigs being born. I sure was surprised. When I told Daddy, he told me not to talk about things like that. Well, I hadn't told nobody else, but last year in school I heard some of the older boys talking about them kind of things.

Our dogs were still laying close to the furnace. I guessed they were trying to dry out. I didn't blame them. I backed up to the furnace and tried to dry out some myself. It was getting daylight.

After a while, I left the tobacco barn to go check on our cow. Sure enough, she had a new baby calf. She was a pretty thing, just standing there and her mama licking her all over. I thought to myself, well, old cow, you better lick that calf real good. If you don't, my mama'll make you lick her all over again.

When I got back to the tobacco barn Daddy was there. He said, Looks like everything's all right.

Yeah, Daddy, I tried to keep the heat just right.

It looks good to me.

I guess so. We had some rain last night.

Yeah, I know. Me and your Aunt Maybelle got soaked on the way home. I'm going on up to the house and get some dry clothes on and get some rest.

Daddy went on up towards the house. I knew what I was going to do. By the time they were all done eating, I'd be through feeding up. Then I'd go to the house, dry off, put some dry clothes on and eat me a good breakfast before going back out there to that old tobacco barn. I thought that when I got back to the barn I could catch me some naps between the times I had to fire the furnace and check the heat. I'd done figured out about how often to put wood in the furnace and check the thermometer.

At breakfast, I told Mama that our cow sure enough had a calf last night and it was a real pretty thing. We talked about a name for the calf, but decided to just call it *calf*, and we'd still just call the cow *cow*. That way all we'd have to say was *cow* and *calf*.

I had one more night to watch the tobacco barn and the curing season would be over for the year. It looked like we could all get busy grading

and tying the tobacco, putting it up on them special grading sticks, and getting it ready for the market.

We didn't have a packhouse. That's what you called a building that
you packed the tobacco in until it was graded and ready to take to market.
We just packed it down in us children's bedroom. That meant we had to
sleep on pallets on the floor during the two months of tobacco season. 'Course
it didn't make much difference to me 'cause most of that time I slept outside
anyway with Daddy and Uncle Rudolph at the tobacco barn.

I stayed up all the next night and fired the furnace at the tobacco
barn. I wasn't as scared as I'd been the night before, but I was still scared
some. It was the last night I'd have to sit up with that old barn until the next
season. Just thinking about it made the night pass faster.

When Daddy got home in the morning, he checked the tobacco in
the barn and said it was all cured out and everything looked good. He said I
could pull the fire. I opened the furnace door, took a long handle hoe, raked
down the coals, and left the furnace door open. Then I opened both doors to
let the barn cool down and left. We'd have to wait until the next day to take
the tobacco out and pack it down. It would take all night to get enough
moisture to keep it from crumbling.

It was a good thing that it was the last barn 'cause there was no more
room in our bedroom. Us four children just barely had room for our pallets
on the floor as it was. One good thing for Jimmy was he was still sleeping on
Mama and Daddy's bed, but Mama said when we got all the tobacco sold off
and out of our bedroom, Jimmy was going to have to start sleeping with me
and Bobby. It didn't make me no never mind, I'd just be glad to be sleeping
on a bed again. It looked like our bedroom was going to be filled up with
younguns.

Daddy showed me how to milk the cow. I thought I knew, since I'd
seen him milk cows at his uncle's dairy when we lived on the Morgan farm. I
thought all you did was pull down on them four things that hung down from

that big bag underneath the cow's stomach. But when I grabbed hold of them and pulled down, nothing came out. I told Daddy, I can't get the milk to come out and I'm pulling down as hard as I can.

Well now, son, you just don't pull down. What you do is you wrap all your fingers around them teats and then you close your fingers in, starting at the top. Then you pull down a little at the same time. If you pull down hard, it hurts the cow and she just might kick you and knock the milk bucket over at the same time. Just keep on trying.

Pretty soon I caught on how to milk the cow. Our dogs, Old Dizz and Toby, just seemed to know when I was going to milk the cow. They'd follow me to the stables and just sit and watch. Every now and then I'd squirt some milk at them and they'd open their mouths and try to catch all they could. It was kind of funny. Most of the time I got milk all over their heads, but they didn't seem to mind. That's one good thing about dogs. They just take what you give them and seem glad to get it.

We started grading the tobacco. Mama and Daddy figured it would take two, maybe three weeks to finish grading and selling it all. We children just wanted to get our room cleaned out and set our beds up so we could sleep in them again.

Every morning after breakfast we'd carry some of the tobacco out on our front porch and start grading. There was Mama, me, Doris, and two ladies that lived near us, Miss Perlie and Miss Flossie Mae. And then there was Aunt Lanie, who was staying with us during tobacco-grading time. I was hoping that with all us working on the tobacco, we'd be finished before school started. I was just tired of messing with tobacco, what with cutting wood for curing nearly all winter, sowing them seeds for the tobacco plants, and all that plowing, hoeing and raking. And then there was all that suckering, cropping and curing, and we still had all the grading to do. It was like Mama said—a tobacco crop takes about nine months out of the year.

It was the same thing every day: eat breakfast, feed up, milk the cow, empty that stinking slop jar, open the shutters and then start grading the tobacco. Grading wasn't as hard as plowing, cropping and curing and all them other things about tobacco farming. We'd just all get us a turn of tobacco, sit down on the front porch, lean back against the wall with our legs stretched out, and start grading the leaves one at a time and putting them in separate piles. We had a lot of different grades—first, second, third, light green, dark green, light red, dark red and trash. We'd take each leaf, open it up, look it over, decide which pile it went in and place it face side up. When we finished that pile, we'd get up, stretch our legs, shake the sand off us and get another turn. Every time somebody went and got another turn of tobacco, they'd say things like, Well, looks like the pile's going down pretty good, or, Looks like we might finish with this barn tomorrow.

We'd talk all day about different things while listening to the battery radio. Mama always sat on the front porch by the living room shutter opening. That way she could listen to the battery radio that sat on the little table inside. She liked to listen to them silly old stories that continued on every day. Seemed to me like it wasn't nothing but stories about people in love and mushy old stuff like that. I was always glad when it was over and the country music came on.

Mama said we'd been through the heat, the rain, and the dark and lonely nights, but we'd saved and gathered our crops. She said the biggest job left was to get the tobacco sold before it got in too high an order. That's what they called it when the tobacco got too much moisture and started to mold and rot. We had that pretty much under control because Daddy had cut a hole in us younguns' bedroom wall for a stovepipe, and we put a small trash-burning stove where us boys' bed was. The heat from the stove kept the tobacco from getting too moist.

🦌

It got real boring sitting there on the porch leaning up against the wall doing the same thing over and over. There just wasn't much to see sitting on our porch looking out over our front yard and staring up and down that dirt road. When a car or truck came by, we'd try to figure out who it was. Most times we could. There were more people who came by with mules and carts or walking than came by in cars or trucks. Every time a car or truck came by, it stirred up such a cloud of dust that it almost choked us. But we still liked to see people come by.

After a rain, the cars and trucks coming by would just splash water and mud everywhere, and they'd slip and slide around in and out of the ruts that were always in the road after a rain. We'd all stop work and watch them slip and slide. At least it gave us something to look at. 'Course, there wasn't much traffic that came by anyhow. It was mostly log trucks, mules and carts.

Once a week there was a man that came by in a car who'd stop and try to sell us things. He was what they called the Watkins Man. And then another man would come by and try to sell us about the same things. He was called the Rawleigh Man. When one of them drove up in our yard, we'd all get off the porch and go out to the car. While the man was telling Mama what all he had to sell, us children would walk up to the car windows, put our hands on either side of our eyes and press our faces against the car window so we could see better what all he had inside. Sometimes Mama would buy a bottle of vanilla flavoring or something like that.

Then there was the ice man, and once in a while a man would come by selling fish. Sometimes when we had the twenty-five cents we'd get a piece of ice to put in our icebox. Our icebox was kind of small, and we didn't keep much in there. Most of the time it was hotter in the icebox than it was outside.

Of all the people that stopped by, I liked the candy man best. Most times we didn't have money to buy candy, but the candy man would leave a small box of candy for us to try and sell. When he came back the next week, we'd have to pay him whether we sold the candy or not. We nearly always sold the candy to the ones that was helping grade the tobacco. If they didn't have the money, we'd give them credit until Friday. Daddy always paid the help on Friday because that's when he got his pay from the cotton mill.

Sometimes people walking by our house would stop to talk, and me and Doris would try to sell them candy. Most times when the candy man came back by, we were ready for another box 'cause if we hadn't sold it all, we'd just eat the rest. We always had enough money to pay the candy man, though, because we'd done been taught that when you owed somebody, you paid them no matter what.

Me and Doris kept up with the money by writing in pencil on top of the candy box about who all owed us and how much we owed the candy man. I never made much profit, because every time I thought I was ahead with the figures, I'd just eat a piece of candy. Mama said I had a sweet tooth.

Things for sure weren't like they were when I lived on the Mill Hill and went to Grandma's house every Friday evening, sat on that little blue stool and collected my money. I knew that the Depression was there too, but it just seemed like the Depression out in the country where we lived was a whole lot worse. Sometimes I'd think, I just bet Jeanette, that prissy cousin of mine, is sure enough propped up on my little blue stool every Friday now, collecting all that candy money what by all rights is mine.

Eight

We finally got all the tobacco ready for the market. The day before we took it to the warehouse where the tobacco was sold, we'd take the sticks of tobacco and spread them out in the front yard after dark. That way, when the dew fell, the tobacco would absorb the moisture. We got paid by the pound for the tobacco, and the moisture made it weigh more. You just had to be careful not to get it too moist. After we thought it was moist enough on the top side, we'd turn it over so the other side could get moist too. When we thought it had enough moisture, we'd take it all back into our bedroom and pack it down again. By then, it was almost always past midnight. We'd all be so tired we'd just fall on a pallet and sleep. We knew when daylight came we'd have to take all that tobacco right back out again and load it on our truck contraption so Daddy could take it to market at the tobacco warehouse.

After we'd loaded the tobacco on the truck, we'd cover it with a canvas and tie it down. Daddy'd get the truck started and Mama would give him last-minute instructions. The very last thing she'd say was, Now, Alton, when you get that money, you just make sure you come straight home. Mama told Daddy that every time because she knew he'd just likely as not stop at a store or someplace and brag about how much he got for his tobacco. He'd talk about how good a grade it was and how he thought the auctioneer tried to get the buyers to pay more money when they got to his pile of tobacco.

I could just hear Daddy saying, Yeah, when they got to my tobacco, I nudged the auctioneer with my elbow so he'd know it was mine and he'd tell them buyers, *Come on, boys. This here's some mighty fine tobacco, let's get up on this price a little bit.* Daddy didn't mean nothing bragging like that, he just wanted people to know he'd done something he was proud of. But I felt like Mama did—we just wanted him to get home with our hard-earned money, not mess around and get knocked in the head and robbed. Besides that, if he wanted to brag about something, he could've just said what a good hard-working family he had and how they was the ones did most of the work while he was night-watching at the mill. 'Course, he bragged about that, too, telling how he trained Old Dizz to wake him up at the right time and all. I didn't know why, but when Daddy bragged like that, he acted like it made him feel good and he'd just grin real big. He sure bragged a lot about Old Dizz. 'Course, I didn't tell Daddy, but I believed Old Dizz would've just about stood on his head to get back to town and the cotton mill.

We got all the tobacco sold and did pretty good. Daddy said he was going to get Uncle Jessie to help him put in the new glass windows the next day. I felt like shouting Hallelujah like Aunt Maybelle did sometimes. Looked like we was going to get the glass windows in before school started. I wished the school bus would come by our house. Then all the children on the bus could see our new windows.

After we got the tobacco out of the house, me and Doris swept our bedroom, put up our beds and talked about how good it felt knowing it was probably the last night we'd have to mess with them old wooden shutters.

After we went to bed, I told Doris, I don't think them bedbugs are as bad as they were before we started putting tobacco in here.

I don't think so, either, R.C., but them mosquitoes are just as bad or worse.

I know. I done found out them mosquitoes are worse in September. Doris, you know that song that Sam and Goldie taught us about them mosquitoes and the bedbugs?

Yeah, I know it good.

Let's sing it.

You sing a line and I'll sing a line.

Okay, Doris, you start.

I woke up one morning and looked up on the wall.

The mosquitoes and the bedbugs was having a game of ball.

The score was eight to nothing and the bedbugs was ahead.

Mosquitoes knocked a home run and knocked me out of bed.

We both laughed.

Doris, I think them mosquitoes are really ahead tonight.

Me too, R.C.

🐜

The next day we got our glass windows.

🐜

School started. Me, Doris and Bobby walked up to Aunt Ruth's to catch the school bus. Bobby was excited. It was going to be his first bus ride. He'd never been to school before, except the time when we lived on the Mill Hill and he'd heard about the puppet show and slipped away to the schoolhouse to see it. There were ten of us cousins that got on the bus that day. I was going to be in the fifth grade, and was looking forward to seeing my classmates again.

We had the same bus as the year before, the one with the wooden body and flat top. It was number ninety-two. All us children liked to say that we rode on old number ninety-two. That first day, after school let out, the bus driver took a shortcut after he'd let all the students off except us cousins.

It was a real narrow dirt road and the limbs from the trees on each side of the road kept hitting the bus. Sometimes they'd brush right through the windows and the leaves would fall inside. The road was so rough it was hard to hold on to our seats. The driver drove so fast that when we'd hit a big hole in the road, we'd all just fly up to the top of the bus. We were tumbling all around, but we were laughing and having a good time. The bus driver was laughing too.

It was a good thing the road was only two miles long 'cause that old bus couldn't have held together much longer. We got to the end of the short-cut road all right. It came out on the road that went by our house, right in front of Uncle Jessie and Aunt Ruth's house. It was the last stop for our bus and all ten of us cousins got off.

Me and Doris told Mama about our first day of school and about taking the shortcut on the way home. Mama asked if we'd seen an old wooden building along that road.

Yeah, I saw that building, Mama.

That's where I went to school.

Mama, that old building's just about ready to fall down.

I know, son. It was just a one-room school, and there was seven grades in that room with one teacher.

Mama, that old schoolhouse is way down in the woods. There ain't nothing on that whole road except that schoolhouse. There's just a church on one end of the road and Uncle Jessie and Aunt Ruth's house on the other end. I don't see why they'd build a schoolhouse way out in the woods like that.

Well, that's the way they did things back then. You ought to be thankful you got a nice brick school to go to that's got a paved road by it.

We are, Mama.

Me and Doris were planning on asking Mama if we could get a writing tablet that had that slick paper. The writing tablet that we were using had that real soft paper. You had to be careful how you held your pencil when you wrote on it. If you weren't, you'd punch a hole right through it. No matter how hard you tried to write good, it still looked bad. We decided not to say anything about the paper after seeing where Mama went to school. And another thing, she'd done told us before that when she went to school, all they had to write with was a piece of chalk and a slate. And when they'd written on both sides and the teacher had graded their work, they'd just wipe the slate clean and start over again.

I told Mama I'd heard people say things like *wipe the slate clean.* I guessed that was what they were talking about. Mama said, Yes, it means something like clean up what's past and start over with a clean slate. She reminded us how expensive writing paper was. We already knew that because there was a big five on the front of our tablet. That meant it cost five cents. I just knew that's why Mama always told us to write on both sides of the paper. I was glad we hadn't said anything about new writing paper.

&

Seemed like all our hard work was beginning to pay off. We'd done put in glass windows and built a two-hole outhouse. Besides that, we were buying some of Mama's brothers' and sisters' land already. Mama said we were paying them ten dollars an acre, and they had agreed to let us pay them a dollar at a time. Sometimes we'd pay as much as three dollars, and when we sold tobacco in the fall, we'd pay even more. It looked like we were going to buy all of Mama's brothers' and sisters' land except Aunt Ruth's.

We started preparing our tobacco plant beds, clearing new land, and burning the trees and limbs on the place where we were going to sow the tobacco seeds. That was supposed to kill most of the grass seeds so we wouldn't have such a hard job keeping the grass and weeds out of the tobacco plants.

It was a lot of work cutting down all the trees, digging the stumps and burning all that brush. I sure hoped it helped. I had my doubts, though, because last year we did the same thing and we still had to pick the weeds and grass out of the tobacco bed about three times. Folks around where we lived called it picking tobacco beds.

Things were going along all right in school for me and Doris, but I noticed that Bobby was getting in a lot of fights in the schoolyard. I asked him how come. He said, I don't know. It's all right, though, I kind of like fighting anyway. I told Bobby he'd better start thinking about trying to make his grade and quit fighting all the time. He didn't seem too worried about making his grade, though, 'cause every time I saw him in the schoolyard, he was at it again.

&

We were still cutting wood for the tobacco curing the next summer. It took a lot of wood, what with all the heater and stove wood to be cut. It kept us busy all winter. 'Course, I'd done found out there was always something to be done on a farm. Sometimes I wondered what if one day I got home from school and Mama said, Well, children, it looks like everything's caught up. It looks like y'all can just play this evening. But that sure wasn't nothing but a thought 'cause she always had work to last us 'til dark.

&

Christmas was coming soon, but me and Doris weren't excited too much about Christmas anymore since somebody at school had told us there weren't no such thing as Santa Claus. We didn't believe it. When we got home, we told Mama what we was told at school.

It ain't so, is it, Mama?

Well, I hate to tell you, but it's so. There ain't no Santa Claus.

Mama, are you sure?

Yes, son, it's true.

Well, I thought that was one of the worst things I'd ever heard. Me and Doris decided to put up a Christmas tree anyway. I cut the tree and we set it up in the kitchen. We decorated it like we did the last year with popcorn and paper rings, and we put that same white sheet around the bottom so it would look like snow. We stood back and looked at the tree. We thought it looked real good.

&

Christmas came and went. We were in a new year. It was January 1939. Everything at school was about the same —riding the school bus in the morning on the froze ground and every evening in the mud, slipping and sliding. When we got home it was pretty much the same thing every evening—cut wood, pick up cornstalks, shrub ditch banks, shuck corn, feed up, wash dishes and get homework. Most times at night we'd listen to the battery radio.

We all liked to listen to the radio. Daddy really liked listening to the news. I guess he got that from Grandpa Fowler. Sometimes I'd listen to the news with him. It seemed like most of it was about England and France at war with Germany, and about Hitler. Seemed he was the head man in Germany. I remembered that Grandpa Fowler had said before we left the Mill Hill that everybody had better keep an eye on Hitler. It sounded like Grandpa was right.

I knew one thing—when Daddy was listening to the news, no body had better say anything. Because if they did and he couldn't hear the news, it made him mad, and that meant everybody had just better watch out.

Our radio didn't play very loud, and when the battery got weak, you had to lay your head on the little round table that the radio sat on so you could hear. There was enough room on the radio table for me and Daddy to lay our heads. He always laid his head on his arm and closed his eyes. I laid my head on my arm, too, but I didn't close my eyes. I just kept them open and looked right over my arm at Daddy. I knew that if that radio sound got too low or there was too much static, he'd get real upset and sometimes he'd hit the table hard with his fist and cuss. One time he got so mad, he grabbed the radio, ran out on the front porch, and threw it in the yard. I guessed that's why Mama always moved the kerosene lamp off the table when she heard the radio getting weak.

One night after supper, me and Daddy was listening to the news and the radio got real weak. I could tell he was getting upset about it playing weak like that. And all that static just made things worse. We both had our heads down on our arms, but I had my eyes wide open. The radio made a lot of static and that little yellow light behind the dial went out. The radio went dead quiet. Daddy said, R.C., did you hear the last thing that newsman said?

I wiggled my chair away from the table just a little bit and said, I heard something.

Well, what was it?

I think he said there was huge fires burning in the vicinity.

In the vicinity of what?

I don't know, Daddy. That's when the radio went dead. But they was burning in the vicinity of something.

Damn!

It was March, and we'd started plowing up the fields for spring planting. Around where we lived they called it breaking up the land. I'd learned some things about plowing. I knew I had to look up ahead every once in a while so I wouldn't hit a stump. When you hit one of them underground stumps, it could break a plow point. And if it did, that was trouble 'cause you had to take it off and put a new one on, and that cost money. Daddy got upset when I broke a plow point.

Most times, though, when I was plowing I'd hold on to the plow handles and lean my head over and down-like so I could watch where the plow was cutting through the ground. You couldn't let the plow take too big a bite. If you did, it just turned up big clods, and that was bad. If you took too small a bite, it just took too long. I liked to watch the dirt turn over. It was always moist and cool, and I liked the way it smelled. Every once in a while a worm would turn up. But he didn't last long because there were always some birds following along, and they got them worms real quick.

Plowing was pretty hard work. But Old Bill, our mule, did the hardest part, pulling that plow. The hardest part for me was when I got to the end of the row and had to turn the plow around and start back. Sometimes I'd let the plow lay over and let the mule pull it around. Then I'd grab the plow handles and pick it back up. But most times we didn't have room like that because of the ditches at the end of the field.

I was just plowing in the evenings after school and on Saturdays. But school was going to be out in three more weeks, and then I'd be plowing most every day except Sunday.

&

School was out and we were all glad. We all knew we'd be working more, but eight months in school every year just seemed a long time. We got all the land broke up and ready for planting, but Mama said it was too early to plant. It was only mid-April, and we just might get some more frost.

One night at supper I told Mama, Looks like we're about caught up on work except for them regular jobs, you know, feeding up and things like that.

Well now, I wouldn't say we was caught up. I've got a little project in mind.

What you got in mind, Mama?

You know how all you children like milk, butter, and them buttermilk biscuits?

Uh-huh.

In the winter months we don't worry too much about the milk souring and the butter melting and things like that. It's different in the summer, though, with all that heat bearing down. The milk and butter just won't keep, so we're gonna dig us a well to keep it in.

I went to bed that night thinking, I just might dream about digging, that well 'cause I just bet I'm gonna be the one that digs it. Sure enough, next morning after breakfast Mama showed me where Daddy said we ought to dig the well. It was going to be off our back porch just a little ways past our pump. Mama told me to go ahead and start digging because it'd take a few days and we had to get back out in them fields before long and start the planting and all.

I started digging with a shovel, throwing the dirt as far away from the hole as I could. I knew there was going to be one big pile of dirt when I finished digging the hole. Daddy said it would be about twenty feet deep. He said that's how far they'd done drove the pipe for our pump. I could see right off I was going to be there a long time, because that clay was hard to dig and when I got it on the shovel, it didn't want to come off. I had to push it off most times with my foot. I liked to go barefooted that time of year, but that clay was too hard to push off with my bare feet. I put my shoes on, and after that the clay came off easier.

My first day of digging I got down about two feet. The second day I dug down about two more feet. I was beginning to feel proud of my well digging. The hole looked pretty good, it being round and all. I crawled out, spread all the dirt that I'd dug away from the hole and raked it down.

The next morning I found out that I had to cut the grubbing hoe and the shovel handles off some 'cause the well hole was just a little more than three feet across and I couldn't dig with them handles long like that. Another thing, I couldn't throw the dirt out the hole anymore. My cousin Sam came by, and I told him if he'd help me on the well, I'd help him back with some of his jobs. He said he would. We got us a peck bucket and tied a plow line to the bail. I got down in the hole and dug some. Sam let the bucket down and I filled it with clay. Then he pulled it up, emptied it and let it back down again.

After a few days the hole was getting pretty deep. When I had to get out, Sam would tie the plow line to the black gum tree in our yard, and I'd climb hand-over-hand until I got close to the top. Then Sam would reach down and help me out. I told him, It's getting cool and damp down there, and now when I climb up, my feet are slipping on the side of them walls. Sam said, Yeah, R.C., I think we're about finished.

Me too. Just now, before I started to climb out, there was a lot of water coming in and some small pieces of clay were starting to fall.

That sounds dangerous.

I know. I ain't going back down in that old well hole.

I wouldn't either.

I ain't. I'm just tired of messing with it. We been digging in that hole for ten days now.

I think that's long enough.

Yeah. Another thing—the whole time I was down there and you was pulling up them buckets of clay, I kept thinking what if the bail comes off and that bucket of clay falls back down and hits me on the head. I'd just be a goner.

I thought about that, too, but I checked the bail every time I pulled it up.

I'm just glad it's done, Sam.

Me too.

I'll tell you something else.

What?

You know I've heard Daddy say *cold as a well digger's ass*. You probably heard that, too.

Yeah, I have.

Well, I think I done found out why they say that.

Why?

'Cause every time I bent over to dig, my little behind rubbed against that cold, wet wall of clay, and I thought I just bet that's where that saying comes from.

Sam laughed and said he bet so, too. I looked at Sam. He had wet clay most all over him.

Sam, you got yellow clay smeared all over you.

Well, you ought to see yourself. You got clay everywhere too, except in your eyes. You even got it in your hair.

It ain't Saturday until tomorrow, but I think we're going to have to wash tonight anyway.

That's for sure, R.C. I got to go home and feed up now.

Yeah, I got to do that too. I'll see you tomorrow, Sam.

Sam started off towards home. I watched as he walked away and thought it sure was good of him to help me and I was sure enough going to help him back for it. I hollered out, Hey, Sam. Sam stopped and looked back.

What?

That thing what I said about the well digger's ass was funny, wasn't it?

Sam just grinned, swung around and headed towards home.

That night I told Mama the well was finished and there was lots of water coming in. Mama said, Tomorrow's Saturday and when your daddy gets home in the morning and gets a little sleep, you and him can build a curb around the well.

Me and Daddy built the well curb. We put a little roof over it. I told Daddy, Our well sure looks good. Daddy said, Yeah, it does. That evening, after the milking was done, we strained the milk through a cloth like we always did. But that time, after we poured the milk in the big jars, we took them to the well, tied a rope around them, and let them down into the cool water.

Next morning Mama said, Son, you know while y'all were diggin' that well, the grass come back up in the fields. I think we'd better break that land up again. If we plant like it is now, it's just going to mean a lot more hoe work. I told Mama, That'll take another two weeks of plowing.

I know, son, but it'll save us a lot of work.

We got all that extra plowing done and finished planting. It was getting late in the planting season, but Mama said we got everything planted in time all right. I was glad 'cause I hadn't been feelin' good the last few days.

Nine

The next morning when I woke up I felt kind of funny, like weak and all. Mama came in our bedroom and said, Time to get up. I told Mama I didn't feel good. She felt my face and said it seemed like I had some fever and that maybe I ought to get up and try to eat some breakfast. I got up and walked in the kitchen. My legs were wobbly and I started coughing. I didn't feel like eating. I went back to bed and fell asleep.

When I woke up, I heard Mama and Aunt Maybelle talking in our kitchen. They were talking about me. Aunt Maybelle said, I think the child's coming down with the measles. Mama said she'd better move me from the bedroom, away from the rest of the children. Mama made me a pallet on the floor in the living room.

I got moved on the pallet in the living room all right, and Aunt Maybelle told Mama she was going to have a word of prayer over me. Well, Aunt Maybelle knelt down beside me on that pallet and started praying. She prayed for me, our whole family, hers, and just about everybody up and down our dirt road.

I knew I was supposed to keep my eyes closed when somebody was praying for me, but I just kind of snuck a look at that angel picture on our wall calendar. I thought, that angel what's got one hand pointing up towards heaven and one pointing down towards me—well, I just wouldn't be surprised none if when Aunt Maybelle gets done praying, that angel hadn't done got both her arms held straight up to heaven. And if Aunt Lanie was to come by and pray for me, I just bet that other angel what's holding that big stick that looks like a walking cane would throw that stick away and just fling both her arms up towards heaven, too. Aunt Maybelle got up off her knees and her and Daddy left for their jobs at the cotton mill.

I guess my cousin Lewis, Aunt Maybelle's oldest boy, must've heard about me being sick 'cause he came over from his house across the branch to see what kind of sick it was. Mama told Lewis it was the measles and that he'd better not hang around because he just might get them, too. Lewis was standing in the doorway of our living room looking down at me laying there on the floor. I said to myself, I bet Mama's going to tell Lewis to go do my jobs, like milking and feeding up and all. Lewis turned to go back out through the kitchen. Mama said, Lewis, I want you to go do R.C.'s jobs this morning, and you better hurry because I know y'all got plenty to do on y'all's farm.

Aw, Aunt Carrie.

Don't you *Aunt Carrie* me, boy.

But I got to go home and feed up.

Lewis Richard, don't you sass me. Now git!

Lewis left to do what Mama said. I knew he didn't like it, though, 'cause when he went out the back door, he just left it wide open. I knew what that meant, 'cause I did it sometimes. Like when I wanted to sass back but I knew I'd better not, I'd just swing around-like and walk out the door and leave it wide open. And as soon as I'd get off the porch a little ways, I'd just turn and look back with both of my lips kind of stuck out. That way Mama knew I was mad all right, but it wasn't as bad as sassing back. I never got no whipping for swinging around and leaving the door open like that, but sometimes she'd make me come back and shut it. You couldn't just slam the door 'cause if you did, you'd have to close it over and over until it was closed right.

I just knew old Lewis had his lips poked out. But he knew he better not sass back at Mama 'cause if he did, Aunt Maybelle would tear his britches up when she got home. That's just the way it was around our place. You couldn't sass no grown-ups 'cause if you did, you'd get it for sure. I thought Lewis might get it anyway because when Mama told him what to do, he'd done said, Aw, Aunt Carrie, instead of him just going on and doing what she said. Another bad thing was when Mama said, Lewis Richard, 'cause when Mama and Aunt Maybelle said more than the first part of your name, it meant kind of like, you better watch it, boy.

It seemed like there was more of a breeze after Lewis left the door open. I asked Mama if she could open the front door, too. She did, and it helped some. There just wasn't much you could do about the heat there in our little house, seeing how it was sitting out in the middle of a field and had that hot tin roof and all. About all I could do right then was just lie there and sweat. There was one of them paper fans like they used in church laying beside me on the quilt, but I didn't feel like fanning myself right then. Besides, it had more angel pictures on it and it didn't make no difference how I held that fan, it seemed like them angels' eyes just kept looking at me like I was guilty of something.

Maybe it was me, but there I was laying on my quilt pallet and it just seemed like them angels in that picture on our wall were staring straight down at me. And if I did something that wasn't right, like cussing and all, they looked like they was right ready to fly straight off to heaven and tell God everything.

That little breeze that started to come in after Lewis left the back door open started moving the fly tapes around that were hanging from our ceiling. Them sticky fly tapes trapped a lot of flies all right, but every now and then some of us would forget and walk right into one and get it stuck in our hair and all.

I was thinking silly things and when I looked up at our ceiling it seemed like it was moving around-like in a circle. I didn't think I was dying, though, because I hadn't heard a screech owl in a good while.

I fell asleep and when I woke up, Daddy and Aunt Maybelle were back home. I heard Aunt Maybelle ask Mama about me. Mama told her I still had some fever but she thought I was beginning to break out. Well I knew she wasn't talking about the same kind of breaking out like when our hogs broke out of their pen, so she must've be talking about them spots I saw on me when I woke up. Aunt Maybelle felt my face and said I still had some fever. Her and Mama said I needed something to help me break out some more. Sounded like they already knew what it was going to be because Aunt Maybelle said she'd call Lewis and tell him to go get some.

Aunt Maybelle went out to our back yard and started hollering for Lewis. Everybody said she could holler louder than anybody they ever heard. She started hollering, Loouuuwisss, Loouuuwisss. She hollered like that a few times and waited for Lewis to holler back. But Lewis was way across the branch over on their farm. He could hear his mama all right, but he couldn't holler that far back 'cause he just couldn't holler that loud.

In a few minutes I heard him hollering, I'm coming, Mama, I'm coming. Aunt Maybelle came back in the house. When Lewis got there she told him to go down in the back of our field, past the tobacco patch on the other side of that walnut tree, and dig up some of them sassafras roots. I knew where they were because when I plowed close to the sassafras sapling roots, I could smell their sweet smell coming up from the ground. Mama told Lewis he better take the grubbing hoe to dig with.

Lewis started off toward the back of our field. He must've not been going as fast as Aunt Maybelle wanted him to 'cause I heard her say, Lewis Richard, now I mean you step on it, boy. I thought, I bet Lewis is going to get it. That was the second time in one day he'd done been called Lewis Richard instead of just plain Lewis.

Lewis got back with the sassafras roots. Mama and Aunt Maybelle cleaned them real good and boiled them in a pot on our wood stove. Then they strained them through a thin cloth, put some sugar in them, brought the mixture in a cup and told me to drink it. They said it was sassafras tea and it would make me break out and get well quicker. Mama said that was the same remedy that her and her ancestors had been using ever since they came over from the old country. That was why they'd never cleared that little patch of land. They just left it alone so them sassafras saplings could always have a place to grow. I drank the tea. It tasted good and made me feel warm inside.

Before I went to sleep, I heard Aunt Maybelle tell Mama that Daddy had been acting puny lately. Mama said, Yeah, he's been complaining about his neck and left shoulder being sore and hurting, and it's getting hard for him to use his left arm. Aunt Maybelle said she thought it had something to do with him laying on that concrete floor at the mill while he was waiting to make his rounds. Mama said, Yeah, that and him having to ride in that old piece of a truck all the time. Aunt Maybelle said, Yes, and every time it rains, he can't see a thing through the windshield. That old truck ain't got no wipers. He has to lean out past the windshield just so he can see a little. All that rain that's hitting him in the face, neck and shoulder is just bound to cause problems.

❧

I got over the measles all right and started back working on the farm. It wouldn't be too long before we started cropping and curing tobacco again. Daddy said all our crops and the vegetable garden looked real good. Mama said, Yes, and we just ought to be real thankful.

Mama and Aunt Maybelle got together and decided we was gonna start having cottage prayer meetings. Aunt Maybelle said she'd talk to Mr. Watson, who was a part-time preacher. Him and his wife were both what they called Holiness. Aunt Maybelle said he preached fire and brimstone. I wondered what that was. It was decided to have the prayer meetings in our house because we had four rooms, but when Uncle Jesse heard about it, he said he wanted to have some of the meetings in his house, too. He said he knew their house only had two rooms, but he thought them having a pump organ ought to make up the difference. And besides that, they had a front porch with a swing so that when somebody got overcome with joy, they could just sit in the porch swing and rest a spell. After some talking, everybody decided that'd be the right thing to do.

It was decided not to have any meetings at Aunt Maybelle's house, being you had to walk down a narrow path in the dark. It was always big dark when them prayer meetings got over. It didn't make no difference how much religion they had, they were all still afraid of them rattlesnakes that crawled around at night. Besides that, Aunt Maybelle's house just had two rooms, and she didn't have no pump organ to make up the difference.

Aunt Maybelle said she'd talked with Mr. Watson, the preacher, and he'd be glad to hold services with us all. Well, it wasn't going to be exactly with us all, because I'd heard Daddy and Uncle Rudolph say they weren't going to be able to make it. Aunt Maybelle wanted to know why. They said they already had something planned on the night of the prayer meeting. That was when they were going to get their lantern and go out in the woods and cut a bunch of stove wood. Aunt Maybelle told Daddy and Uncle Rudolph, Now, we don't know what night we're going to have the services yet. They said, We don't care. Whatever night it is, that's the night we're planning on cutting stove wood. Aunt Maybelle just walked away with her head throwed back and her eyes rolled back in her head and said, Lord, have mercy on their souls.

They started having them prayer meetings all right. The first one they had was at Aunt Ruth and Uncle Jessie's house, because they had that pump organ and could start off their first meeting with music. While all them grown-ups were inside deciding who was going to start off the preaching, us cousins were outside deciding what we was going to play. We decided on hide-and-seek. We chose up who was going to be *it* and started playing.

It was getting dark and the grown-ups must've decided who was going to preach because they had lit up them kerosene lamps and started warming up the organ. Pretty soon they were singing and preaching and playing the organ real loud. It didn't bother us children none, though, because we played hide-and-seek in the tobacco patch that was right beside the house. Everything was going along all right. We were having a good time playing and the grown-ups were having a good time singing and preaching.

It was getting late. Me, Doris and Bobby started walking back down the road towards our house. After we got down the road a good ways we could still hear the organ playing and the shouting was still going on. Last time I looked back I could see the shadows moving all around on the walls inside the house. Every now and then a shadow arm would just fling up in the air.

When we got home Daddy had his head down on the radio table trying to listen to the news, but about all you could hear was static. Daddy said he was sick and tired of that battery radio and its static and that a working man ought to at least be able to listen to the news, especially it looking like war coming on and all. I told Daddy that President Roosevelt done got people putting down poles and stringing wire all up and down the road, and I just bet it wouldn't be long before they'd get electricity by our house. Daddy said he hoped so because he was saving up to have electric lights put in as soon as they did. I hoped so, too. I was sure tired of no lights except them two kerosene lamps. Besides, Daddy needed to enjoy something. You could tell he wasn't feeling too good by the way he was walking around holding his left arm all the time.

After I went to bed it started thundering and lightning, and before long it began to rain real hard. Before I went to sleep I thought about what a good time I'd had playing with all my cousins and how all them grown-ups seemed to have such a good time too. The rain on our tin roof sounded good.

Next morning when I went outside, there was a lot of water on the ground. Sam and his brother, James Kenneth, were in our front yard. Sam said, R.C., down at the bottom of the hill there's water about three feet deep just running across the road. I told Sam, Go across the branch and tell Aunt Maybelle's boys about the water and we'll all meet back here. By then I'll be done feeding and milking, and maybe we can just all go swimming.

When I finished my jobs, I ran back to our front yard. Counting me and Bobby there was seven first cousins, all boys. It was Sunday and we decided real quick what we was going to do—go swimming. We all ran down the hill to the curve just out of sight of our house. It was the same hill we'd been pushing our truck down trying to get it started. By the time we got to where the water was going across the road, we were all naked. It didn't take long for us to get naked 'cause none of us had anything on but a pair of overalls. Before long we were all just swimming around and having a good time splashing, hollering and saying, Look at me, and things like that.

It was the first time I'd been swimming since we'd left the Mill Hill. We all wanted to swim around in that water as long as we could. We hadn't been swimming long before somebody hollered out, Lord have mercy, here comes Miss Perlie! We had to do something quick because she was coming around the bend. Lewis said, What we going to do? Sam said, We got to hide in the bushes!

We all started getting out of the water. When we got out, all we could do was run for them thick bushes beside the road. But Miss Perlie saw us before we could get hid up in them good. She hollered out, You boys ought to be ashamed of yourselves, out here in the middle of the road butt naked! By then we was all hid. We had both our hands trying to cover up our things and we was peeping through the leaves. I hollered to Miss Perlie, We was just trying to have a little fun swimming.

The middle of a public road ain't no place to go swimming, especially when you're butt naked.

Well, there ain't no place else to swim 'round here!

Don't you sass me, boy.

I ain't sassing.

Miss Perlie started walking through the water. She started off real slow-like. Then she took hold of the bottom of her dress, pulled it tight and held it down with her hand. She kept walking slow, looking down. The front of her dress stayed down all right, but the back just floated up on top of the water. We cousins just stood there in the bushes watching. The mosquitoes were eating us up. Every once in a while we had to just uncover our private parts and hit at 'em.

Pretty soon, Miss Perlie was coming out the water on the other side. She turned back and looked toward the bushes where we were hid up in and said real loud-like, You boys better get some clothes on them skinny white butts. We all just knew that our swimming was over for the day. Somebody in the bushes said real low, Damn it all. Somebody else said, Who said damn it? Everybody said, It won't me. Well, whoever said it, it wasn't loud enough for Miss Perlie to hear. She looked back one more time. Then she kind of shrugged up one of her shoulders and went, Humph. I didn't know if she was mad or just putting on, but I needed to know something.

Hey, Miss Perlie!

What, boy?

You gonna tell?

I'm gonna have to think on it.

Soon as Miss Perlie got around the bend, we ran back across the road to where we'd left our overalls hanging on some limbs and put them on real quick. We started back up towards our house. We was all wondering if Miss Perlie was going to tell on us or not.

Daddy was feeling worse and he couldn't use his left arm anymore. He had to give up his job at the cotton mill, and it got to where he had to stay in bed all the time. We moved a bed into our living room so he could be close by the kitchen. That way Mama could keep an eye on him, and he'd be where we all walked back and forth through the house during the day. Besides, he'd have the battery radio right next to him.

It was decided as long as Daddy couldn't drive anymore, we'd just take the old truck contraption and haul it off in the woods in front of our house. Daddy told me and Uncle Rudolph how to set it up so we could use it to saw wood. We chocked one back wheel up so it couldn't turn and jacked up the other back wheel so it was the only wheel that turned when the motor was running. Then we took off the tire and put a big belt on it and ran it back to a saw that was hooked to a platform. The belt made the saw turn and we could cut wood real fast.

We liked the way it cut wood, all right. But when we walked away and looked back at the old truck contraption it was kind of sad to think how it'd been our transportation for the last two and a half years. We knew we'd just use it to cut wood for a while. Then the trees and bushes would grow up around it and the old truck would be left to rust away. But we thought what we did was better than just hauling it off in the woods like it was a dead mule.

Somehow we got us an old Ford car. We were all excited about getting a new car. Well, it wasn't new, but it was new to us. Me, Doris and Bobby would get under the steering wheel and play like we were driving. We didn't know how to start it or anything, but we'd sit there on the seat and just turn the steering wheel back and forth and make noises with our lips like a motor running. We had us a car all right, but there wasn't anybody in our family that could drive it. Uncle Rudolph used it to take Aunt Maybelle back and forth to work at the mill.

Daddy laid in his bed in our living room day and night. It was a lot of work for Mama and Doris, cooking and cleaning for all of us and looking out for Bobby, Ann and Jimmy. And then they had to take care of Daddy full-time. All he could do was lay on that bed and groan. We all knew he was hurting bad all the time. Things were different in our house at night, too.

Daddy wasn't able to play the guitar and sing his favorite songs like *Little Brown Jug, May I sleep in your barn tonight, mister?* and that one he didn't hardly know any of the words to. It went something like, *I'm the man that rode the mule around the world.* He used to sit in our living room and sing them kind of songs, mostly about hard times, about the Depression and all. Sometimes he'd sing a real sad song like, *I'm just a lonely hobo, riding on a train.*

Daddy couldn't sing good, but we missed him sitting around trying to pick and sing anyway. And we missed him talking about how good we were going to do farming and how before too many more years we were going to own all the inheritance land except Aunt Ruth's. Without Daddy to help pass the time, we did the best we could at night. Me and Doris would draw and color pictures, and sometimes we'd read. Bobby couldn't read yet, and Ann, she'd just sit around kind of quiet and play with her doll.

It was decided by Mama and Aunt Maybelle that Aunt Lanie would come help out while we were having our special troubles. Seemed like all Aunt Lanie did was just help out all the time. She wasn't married and didn't have children. She helped Grandma Harrell, who was her sister, raise all eight of her children, and she helped out every time one of the grandchildren was born. When somebody in the family got sick, Aunt Lanie always came to help out.

She didn't charge anything. All she needed was a place to sleep and something to eat. If she ever did get any money, she put it in a can or a little box and saved it so someday she could see a church built in East Wilmington. Aunt Lanie worked hard and didn't say much, but she read a little in the Bible most every night. When she had the time, she'd help us hoe in the fields. You could tell which one of them workers was Aunt Lanie from a long ways off 'cause she did her hair up in a bun and wore a bonnet, she didn't wear a straw hat like the rest of us. We all loved Aunt Lanie. Nobody gave her no sass, that was for sure.

Mama, Doris, and Aunt Lanie seemed to be getting along pretty good with things at the house. I was glad because when I got in at night, I just didn't feel like washing dishes and things like that. Right then I had my hands full with the plowing, feeding, and milking. We were working hard and it seemed like we had things coming along good. I guessed them prayer meetings were helping, but I depended more on Aunt Lanie when it came to things like that.

It didn't take much for me to get ready in the mornings. Soon as I got my regular jobs done, I was on my way to hook up that old mule. Our mule Bill was an ornery cuss. I didn't blame Mr. Worley for selling him because every once in a while he'd take spells like he just wasn't going to work. When he got like that, he'd just walk all over the rows stomping down the crop. He knew better, but he just had that mean streak, and that's when me and him had to have an understanding.

Most times I made sure he knew who was boss. After all, we was the ones that done peeled all that bark off them pine poles and built him a nice stable, and we was the ones that fed him every day. And every winter I was usually the one that took that heavy grubbing hoe and chopped up all that old manure he'd dropped in the mule lot, and kept all that warm straw in his stable. It was for dang sure he was going to pull that old plow like I wanted it pulled.

Sometimes I'd think about that old mule like that, and then I'd think about how hard he worked pulling that old plow and how hot it was out in them open fields. Most times when I got to thinking like that, we'd just stop plowing so he could rest a little. I could tell he liked it because he'd prop one of his hind legs up on the front of his hoof and hold his head down low-like. 'Course, that old mule didn't know or care that all that corn and hay he was eating was a lot of what all the plowing was about.

Most times late in the evening, I'd pull the plow lines towards the house and tell Old Bill, Let's go home, boy. I always had to be careful after I said that. It didn't make any difference how tired that old mule was, he always perked up when we headed in for the day. Sometimes he'd walk so fast I'd have a time just trying to hold on to the plow. 'Course, I was glad to head for home, too. It was always good to see them kerosene lamps shining through our glass windows. When I got to our back door, I could tell by the sounds and good smells coming from our kitchen that Mama and Doris were busy cooking. Everything smelled good 'cause I was real hungry, even though most times I'd done busted a watermelon and eaten the heart out of it while me and Bill was resting.

Some evenings, I could hear Mama singing even before I opened the back kitchen door.

> *What a friend we have in Jesus,*
> *All our sins and griefs to bear!*
> *What a privilege to carry*
> *Everything to God in prayer!*

One night after supper Mama and Aunt Lanie were talking and they decided to have Mama's youngest sister come stay with us and help out until Daddy was better. She could help out with the hoeing and all. Mama's youngest sister's name was Lanie, too. She was named after Aunt Lanie, but so we didn't get them mixed up, we just called her Sister. Everybody called her that, it didn't make her no never mind. Mama said seeing as how we got so many people in our house, she was going to see about getting two more kerosene lamps. If she did, we'd have one for each room.

Sister came to live with us and was a lot of help. Sometimes she'd help me out in the fields, turning potato vines and uncovering tobacco leaves. We got the extra kerosene lamps.

Ten

We sure missed Daddy not being able to play that old guitar and sing. Another thing we missed was how some nights he'd drag out that shoe last and work on our shoes while we listened to the radio. He'd trim a piece of leather to fit, put the shoe on the last, bottom-side-up, then put some tacks in his mouth and start nailing the leather right on that old shoe. He'd kind of wave the hammer all around like he was putting on a show. And when he wanted a tack, he'd just reach up and get one out of his mouth. Sometimes Mama would say, One of these days, Alton, you're going to swallow some of them tacks. Daddy wouldn't pay her no mind, he'd just wave the hammer around some more and keep on driving them tacks.

Another thing he'd do was sometimes when Mama was cutting our hair, he'd just sit and watch and say funny things about how our haircut looked. Most times he'd say, It looks like somebody done put a bowl over your head and throwed some clam shells at you. Mama would just laugh and say, Now, Alton, you know it don't look that bad.

Well, I guessed we could get by without the singing and the guitar playing and him making fun of our haircuts, and maybe we could repair our shoes. But I knew I wasn't putting no tacks in my mouth.

Mama and Aunt Maybelle decided it was time to have another one of them prayer meetings, and they was going to have it in our living room. It sure enough looked like Daddy was going to be there for that meeting, seeing as how he couldn't go nowhere no how. When Aunt Maybelle told Daddy they were going to be holding a prayer meeting in our living room, he just turned his head and looked out the glass window. I felt sorry for Daddy. I knew he'd rather be out cutting stove wood that night.

Everybody said that Daddy had always worked hard. Even before he was ten years old, he'd worked at the cotton mill. He just wanted to get off public work altogether and he had big dreams about us owning all the rest of the inheritance land that was part of the old Larkins place.

Well, it looked like we were going to own the land all right because we'd done made all them agreements with Mama's brothers and sisters except Aunt Ruth and Aunt Maybelle. We weren't for sure, but we thought Aunt Maybelle was going to sell us her share, too. Seemed like she just wasn't satisfied with the way things was going, what with her having to ride back and forth to the cotton mill and all. I thought, it wouldn't surprise me none if they moved back to the Mill Hill.

We'd been paying some to the rest of Mama's brothers and sisters all along. It was all right with them because it didn't look like none of them wanted any part of that old farm. It didn't make no difference about it being inheritance land.

I didn't know why, but Daddy just loved the old place. I knew he wished he could get up off that bed and walk all over it again. Before he got sick, he'd take me and walk all around the boundary line and say, This is all in our name, and one of these days it's all going to be paid for.

🐝

It came time for that prayer meeting at our house and Preacher Watson and his family got there early. It wasn't long before our living room was full and they all started singing and praying. Then the preacher started preaching real loud and there was a lot of *Amens*. Every once in a while somebody would say, Tell it, brother, and, That's right, brother.

It seemed like everybody was getting in the Spirit, and somebody started talking in tongues. That was a language that nobody but them understood. They told me it was in the Bible about talking in tongues, but I didn't know about that. When somebody fell out on the floor, Brother Watson said they had done been slain in the Spirit.

Sometimes I'd get scared and go out on the front steps, watch the bull bats flying around, and try to get the preaching off my mind. But it kept creeping back in my head what a sinner I was, what with my cussing spells and all.

We finished curing the tobacco and got it all graded up. Uncle Rudolph was taking it to the market for us. I told Mama, I sure would like to go with Uncle Rudolph one time and watch them buy our tobacco. Maybe I could get me one of them big hamburgers and a Pepsi-Cola. I ain't had one in a long time. Mama said she'd think on it.

The next morning Mama said, I'm going to let you go to the market with your Uncle Rudolph. You can help him load and unload. Just you promise you're going to be good.

I'm going to be real good, Mama, I won't cause no trouble.

We'll see.

Me and Uncle Rudolph took the back seat out of our car and put in all the tobacco we could. We had it packed pretty good. We got the car cranked up all right, and I got in up front, beside Uncle Rudolph. We backed out and started down the road. I stuck my head out the window and looked back. Mama and everybody was standing on the front porch. I waved to them, and they all waved back. They were still waving when we disappeared around the curve.

We got to the market and helped the warehouse folks unload our tobacco. We placed it in the long rows where the buyers and auctioneer would come by. Then me and Uncle Rudolph laid down on our piles of tobacco and went to sleep. When morning came, we got up early. I asked Uncle Rudolph, Can we get us a hamburger and a Pepsi now?

No. We ain't got no money. But as soon as the tobacco gets sold, I'm going to make sure that we get us a hamburger and a drink.

How long do you think that's going to be?

Well, son, I think it's going to be before dinnertime.

Our tobacco got sold by dinnertime all right, and we took our sales tickets up to the teller window where the lady takes your tickets and gives you the money. Uncle Rudolph gave the lady our tickets and she counted the money out real fast. I'd never seen that much money and I didn't know money could be counted so fast. Now Uncle Rudolph, he just stood right there at that teller window and counted the money all over again.

It seemed like it took a good little while 'cause when he got done counting, the teller lady acted like she was real upset. I guess it was because there was a bunch of people in line behind us. She asked Uncle Rudolph, Well, is it all there? Uncle Rudolph took his pipe out of his mouth, leaned over, hit it on his heel, looked straight at the teller lady and said, Well, it just is. I didn't think that teller lady liked that at all because she told Uncle Rudolph, Now you take that little country hick and git.

We didn't say anything, we just turned around and left. I asked Uncle Rudolph, What we going to do now? He said, Well now, son, we're just going to get us one of them big, juicy hamburgers and a Pepsi.

꩜

After we got our tobacco sold, we paid all our bills to the store folks who ran us through the year with our fertilizer, seed, plow points and things like that. The next thing we wanted to see was them electric lights in our house. The men that were stringing electric wire on the poles were getting closer to our house. I asked Mama, Can we get electric lights when they get to our house?

Not yet, son. We got to make sure we got everything for our crop next spring. Then if we've got anything left, we'll get electric lights.

What all you think we got to get done before we can get our house wired up for lights?

Well, R.C., you know we got to get all that wood cut for curing the tobacco next year. We got to get them tobacco beds planted, and that means new canvas. Then all them sweet potatoes got to be dug and banked, and we got to kill all them hogs and get the meat in the smokehouse. There's just a lot of things we got to do before we start splurging on electric lights.

Mama, you think if everything goes along all right, we can get electric lights by spring?

We'll see how it goes, son.

School had started and Christmas had come and gone. We got some fruit and nuts, but we were all thinking about next spring when we'd get electric lights. I told Doris, When we get them lights, we won't have to mess with carrying them kerosene lamps around. Besides, there'll be enough light for us to get our homework done real good, and we can read all them library books we want to. I tell you something else, Doris.

What?

You know how Daddy likes to listen to the news on the radio?

Uh-huh.

Well, when we get electricity, we can have an electric radio. That way we won't have to worry about no battery running down and all.

Daddy needs some enjoyment, what with him just laying there suffering. He hurts so bad he don't want nobody to touch him.

I know, Doris. Last night Mama had to turn him over with a sheet.

The R.E.A. folks had gone on way past our house. When they came by us they put a pole on the front corner of our yard. Mama said we were going to plant a rose bush right beside that pole. It would be a climbing one with pink roses. I asked Mama, What you gonna do that for?

Well, son, this will be a bush that will spread over the ground and along that road ditch. It will thrive and have them pretty, small pink roses, and it will twine around that pole that our government put there. We'll call it our *rose of memories*. You children don't think about it now with all your cousins around and us being so busy all the time. But these times will pass and me and your daddy will pass away too, and this little old house will settle to the ground. The well will cave in, and these fields where we've worked so hard will be overgrown. But the bush with the pink roses will still cling to this spot in the corner of our yard. Oh, you'll grow up, get married and have children of your own. But in time, you'll pass this way again and when you see this bush of climbing roses, memories will flood your mind and just maybe some tears will fall.

That sounds real good, Mama. It's like a poem.

Maybe, but what I want you children to remember is that you are the roses of my life.

❦

Next morning Mama woke me and said, R.C., them hogs are out again. I thought to myself, I bet it's that same old sow that's always breaking out and causing all them other hogs to follow her. I hated that old sow. Most times when she broke out it was when we were sitting down to eat. Seemed like she just knew when it was our eating time. I wasn't much on killing things, but I was about ready to kill her, hog-killing time or not. Only reason Daddy kept her around was because she had all them pigs every year. But I didn't care. I thought, I'd like to shoot that old razorback cuss right between the eyes and invite all our cousins to eat her skinny self right down to the bone. I hate that sow!

We got the hogs back in and ate breakfast. I started off to work. Doris followed me out on the back porch and asked me did I hurt any of them hogs? I told her, No, but one of these days, me and that old mean sow's going to have a big run-in. I'm just tired of her mess. I don't care how many pigs she has.

Mama came out on the back porch and said she wanted to talk to me about something.

What, Mama?

We got to do something about getting your daddy some medicine.

What we going to do?

Well, son, I want you and your Uncle Rudolph to cut down one of them big pine trees. Then me and you're going to take that crosscut saw and saw it up in stove wood lengths. You can split it up. Then we'll gather some of them sweet potatoes and a few dozen eggs and put them and the wood in the back of the old Ford. Your Uncle Rudolph can take it to town, sell it and buy your daddy something for his pain.

That sounds all right, Mama. But can you pull a crosscut saw?

I'll do what I have to, son. Now you go talk to your Uncle Rudolph about cutting down that tree.

I asked Uncle Rudolph if he'd help me saw down one of them big pine trees.

Yeah, R.C., I'll help you. And I sure am sorry about your daddy being bad off sick like he is.

I know, Uncle Rudolph, but if you'll just help me cut down the tree, Mama will help me saw it up in stove wood. We're going to gather up some sweet potatoes and eggs and load it all in the back of our Ford. We was hoping you could take it to town and sell it for us.

Yeah, I'll do that. I'll just take it one day when I'm taking your Aunt Maybelle to work.

One more thing, Uncle Rudolph.

What's that?

We was hoping you'd sell it off for us and take the money and buy Daddy some pain medicine.

Well, I'll be glad to, son.

We got the pain medicine and it helped Daddy some, but he was still mighty sick. Everybody that came to visit said how he looked real bad and was losing a lot of weight and that it just looked like something could be done. I felt sorry for Daddy. I knew he thought it was about all over and that his dream of owning the inheritance land was gone.

&

We were back in the short, dreary days of winter. I still didn't like winter. I especially didn't like working by myself that time of year. I'd get real lonesome doing them winter jobs, like cutting wood for the next summer, cutting down them cornstalks, and getting the fields ready for planting in the spring.

One of my winter jobs was to take a grubbing hoe, chop up the manure in the mule lot, and stockpile it for use in the fields the next spring. Sometimes the manure would be nearly a foot thick, and if it was a wet time, my brogan shoes would fill up with brown water. And that cold stinging winter wind didn't help none.

Sometimes when I was working in the mule lot like that, I'd just prop my chin on the top of that grubbing hoe handle and look out across the fields. There was nothing there to see except dead grass and weeds and them long-dead cornstalks. And once in a while a crow flying low, looking for a passed-over grain of corn. I thought, these are the kind of days that make me want spring to hurry up and get here. Of course, I knew that meant we'd all be out in them hot fields again, but at least there wouldn't be that dreary, lonesome feeling that winter brings.

Besides that, it wouldn't be long after we started plowing that we'd have plenty of green crops growing all over. All we had out in the fields during the winter months was a real big crop of loneliness. I thought, if we could just figure out some way to sell loneliness, we could probably get electric lights before spring.

I knew it was kind of silly, me daydreaming and all, but I liked to do it anyway. I remembered when I used to lay on that old wooden davenport in

Grandpa Fowler's yard and look up at the clouds in the sky and just imagine they was shaped like all kinds of things. Sometimes I'd think, when I get more education, I just might like to try and write some stories and maybe some poetry or things like that. I bet Mama could help me 'cause she's pretty good at it. She wrote a poem about her Grandma Larkins, and I thought that thing about the memory rose was real good.

One evening just before spring, after I'd finished my jobs, I was sitting on our front porch watching the bull bats fly around and dive like they do. While I was sitting there, I heard something that sure enough wasn't no bull bat. It sounded like a man hollerin', and it seemed like it was coming from a long ways off. I went in the house and told Mama to come out on the front porch and listen. Mama came out and me and her stood there real quiet. It wasn't long before I heard it again. I asked Mama, Did you hear that?

I heard it all right.

What you think it is, Mama?

It's just a man hollerin' way off.

What's he hollerin' like that for?

Well, son, that's what they call a country holler. The man's just letting folks know where he is.

It wasn't long before the man hollered again.

Mama, what's he keep on hollerin' for?

He does that so we'll know that everything's all right and we can tell he's getting closer.

It sounds like he's coming down that narrow road by that old schoolhouse where you used to go.

Yeah, I think that's the road he's on all right. It sounds like he's right along where the old schoolhouse is.

It sure does, Mama. Who you think it is?

Well, I heard that Rufus Lee was going to be coming to visit your daddy. I just bet that's who it is.

I think I saw him one time, Mama. He's a kind of small man and he seemed real quiet.

That's him all right. Folks around here say he's a good man.

Mama went in the house and told Daddy that Rufus Lee was coming to see him and she thought he'd be here in about fifteen minutes. Mama said she was going to make a pot of coffee so's it'd be ready when Mr. Lee got here.

I walked through the living room and looked over at Daddy. He was just laying there on his bed still and quiet-like. It seemed like every time I walked by, his eyes would follow me across the room, like he was studying me or something. I wondered what he was thinking about.

I went in the kitchen where Mama was making the coffee. I asked, Why is Mr. Rufus coming to see Daddy so late in the evening?

Well, R.C., it's about the only time he can come. Like most of us, he has to work during the day. He just wants to visit with your daddy and sit a spell. He's just doing the neighborly thing. That's the way people are up here in the country. They know there's not much they can do except try to cheer him up a little. It's their way of showing that they care.

If he goes back home down that narrow dirt road, it's going to be so dark he won't be able to see nothing. I hope he can run as good as he can holler 'cause if one of them sinikin bears gets after him, he's really going to have to pick 'em up and put 'em down.

Well now, I don't think Rufus Lee's going to be too worried about that. Besides, I'm sure he's got his dog and a lantern with him.

Mama, if them sinikin bears is as bad as Lester says they are, that dog and lantern just ain't going to make no difference. If one of them bears gets ahold of Mr. Rufus, that old bear'll just use that lantern so's he can see how to eat him. And then he'll eat that old dog for dessert.

For goodness' sake, R.C., you know you're just trying to be funny.

Yeah, I am some, but we'll see.

It wasn't too long before I saw Mr. Rufus turn off the road and head towards our porch. He took his hat off before he started up our steps. I thought to myself that he must be a nice man like Mama said, him taking his hat off before he even started up the steps and all. Most of the time I just walk right through our house with my straw hat on.

Mama came out on the front porch and said, Hey, Rufus Lee. It's sure nice to see you.

Same here, Miss Carrie. I just thought I'd come by and see how Mr. Alton's doing.

Well, that's mighty neighborly. Come on in. We got a fresh pot of coffee.

Mama poured Mr. Rufus a cup of coffee and they went in the living room to talk to Daddy. Daddy was glad to see Mr. Rufus all right, but he didn't feel like talking too much. Mr. Rufus said he just bet it wouldn't be long before Daddy was back at work and just as good as ever. Mama said she thought so, too. I didn't know, though, it looked to me like he was getting worse off.

When Mr. Rufus got ready to leave, it was big dark. He lit his lantern, called his dog, and told us all good-bye and headed off down the road. I noticed he didn't put his hat on until he was almost out of our yard. I thought, well now, that sure enough is a nice man and he's got good manners, too. I just hoped them bears didn't get him on the way home. I knew he had at least a three-mile walk through them dark woods. I was just going to sit out there on our front porch and see if he started hollering when he got to going down that narrow dark road that went by the old schoolhouse.

It wasn't much more than half an hour before I heard him holler. I guessed he was just letting everybody on our side know where he was and that everything was all right. I told Mama, I heard Mr. Rufus giving that old country holler.

Yeah, R.C., he probably won't holler no more until he gets almost to where he's going.

It looks like he's going to make it home.

Yeah, he's going to make it all right.

I think so too, Mama, 'cause when he hollered, it was just a regular old holler, not like a scream or nothing.

Oh, for goodness' sake.

&

School was out and we'd all made our grades. I'd be in the seventh grade next year. I was always glad when school was out. 'Course, I was always glad when it started, too. Mama said she was happy that we made our grades all right, but that it was time for us to get real busy getting our fields ready for planting.

Somehow we'd gotten us a used fertilizer distributor. It looked something like a plow, except it had a hopper that you dumped fertilizer in. It was pulled by a mule, just like a plow. It was a lot easier than holding a bucket and putting the fertilizer out by hand. We got the fertilizer out and all the crops planted. Then we had to keep everything plowed enough to keep the grass down and the ground around the crops soft so they could grow. Me and Sam still traded off work now and then, but mostly we had to work on our own farms.

&

Daddy was still sick. Sometimes I'd see tears in his eyes. We all tried to keep him cheered up by saying things like everything was going along real good and it wouldn't be long before they'd be wiring our house up for electricity. Then he could listen to the radio all he wanted to and he wouldn't have to worry about no battery going dead anymore. Sometimes Mama'd tell Daddy that we were still making them payments on the inheritance land and that she was keeping account of everything in her little book. Most times he'd just look at us, then turn his head and look out the glass window beside his bed.

Eleven

One morning after breakfast I was going out the back door to do my regular jobs and start the plowing for the day when Mama said, Wait a minute son, I got something I want you to do.

What's that, Mama?

I want you to go with your Uncle Jessie to Burgaw. They got a place out there where they give out clothes and some food, like raisins, dried fruit and graham flour.

What's graham flour?

It's not like real flour, but it's not bad. It's just not refined like regular flour. The biscuits are kind of brown-looking when you bake them, but it's good for you.

Mama, we don't need none of them people's handouts.

Son, let me tell you something. There's times when you have to do things that you don't want to do. That's just the way life is.

I still don't like it. What's that place you're talking about in Burgaw called?

It's called relief, son. But don't get your pride up, just remember that it's something that President Roosevelt started.

Well, I guess if President Roosevelt started it, it's all right. I'll go, but can't I just take our mule and go by myself?

Now, son, you ain't been to Burgaw enough to know where the relief place is.

Mama, I'll go if that's what you want, but I'm scared to go with Uncle Jessie.

Why's that, son?

Because sometimes he'll just stand straight up in the cart and get the mule to going real fast. When he does that, I think, Now, what if this old cart swings around and turns over, you know, like Mr. Worley's did?

For goodness' sake. I wouldn't worry about that.

Everybody says that Mr. Worley was almost killed.

Son, that was our mule that was pulling the cart that turned over with Mr. Worley. Your Uncle Jessie's mule's not wild like ours.

I still don't want to go.

It's been decided.

Next morning I got me a sack and walked down to Uncle Jessie's house. He already had his mule hooked up to the cart for the trip to Burgaw. I climbed in the cart and sat down. I put the sack that I was gonna put the relief stuff in on the seat between us. We started down the dirt road towards Burgaw. Uncle Jessie said, We'll probably get there in two hours, maybe less. Far as I was concerned, the less the better. I wanted to see Burgaw, all right, but I wanted to get the trip over with. I just kept right on thinking, what if this cart gets turned over.

It seemed like everything was going along all right. We were riding along talking about plowing and things like that, and the mule was walking along real calm-like. I guess we'd been riding along about an hour when Uncle Jessie looked over at me and said, R.C., who you like the best, me or your Uncle Rudolph? I didn't know what to say. I thought about what Mama, Aunt Maybelle and Aunt Lanie had always told me, and that was to tell the truth. People might not like to hear it, but they'd just have to live with it. Most of all, you don't have to explain it. I told Uncle Jessie, I like you both the same.

I could see Uncle Jessie didn't like what I'd said because he stood straight up out of that cart seat and put that mule in a dead run. I was scared all right but I decided I was going to sit there on that seat like a knot on a log. I wasn't going to stand up or nothing. Besides that, I wasn't taking back anything I said, and that was that. After a while the mule settled back down to a walk and Uncle Jessie sat back down.

There wasn't much talking the rest of the way to Burgaw. When we got to the relief place, Uncle Jessie tied his mule to a telephone pole and got out of the cart. I asked him, Is this the place? I just didn't want to say *relief*. He said, Yeah, this is it, and he went on inside. I sat there on that old cart seat and just thought to myself, now what's he want to act like that for? I wasn't going to worry about it. Right then I was wondering why I was there anyway. It didn't make no sense, me hitching a ride to some old relief place in a one-horse town with my hand out, not as hard as our family worked. I didn't like nothing about it.

I got my sack and went inside. A lady asked me, What's your name, son?

I told her, I'm R.C. Fowler, oldest child of Alton Lee and Amelia Caroline Fowler. The lady was real nice. She looked through some papers and said we were on her list. Then she put some dried apples, peaches and raisins in some paper bags and set them on the counter. She set out a sack of graham flour and some overalls and shirts that was all the same size and color. They had real wide pockets that was cut straight across. It looked like they did all they could so everybody could tell you'd done got it from the relief.

I wanted to leave everything right there on the counter and just walk out. But being the lady was so nice and it was a program that President Roosevelt got going, I guessed it was all right. Besides, I kept thinking about one of Mama's sayings about the rabbit that got caught in the hailstorm. Sometimes there wasn't nothing to do but just hunker down and take it. Well, we might have to hunker down and take it for a while, but it was for sure we didn't have to like it.

I put the relief stuff in my sack and told the nice lady thank you and that we all appreciated what President Roosevelt was doing for us and all our family thought he was a real good man. The lady said, Now thank you, Curly. That's a nice thing to say. I didn't know why she done had to call me Curly. I guessed she'd forgot what my name was.

I threw the sack across my shoulder and walked outside. Uncle Jessie already had the cart turned around and was sitting on the seat, ready to go. I walked up to the back of the cart and throwed the sack in. I climbed up and sat on the back of the cart. Uncle Jessie said, You going to sit back there? I said, Yeah, I like to sit on the back and let my feet swing off. He said, Suit yourself.

It was a quiet trip, them seven miles from Burgaw back home. I just sat on the back of that cart thinking about all that relief business. I didn't think we needed none of it no how.

We'd been riding along for about an hour when the mule had to stop. While he was stopped, I thought, I'd just like to jump out of this old cart and fling that old sack of relief stuff in that ditch 'side the road. 'Course, I knew I wasn't going to do that.

Uncle Jessie turned the mule and cart off the road and up in his yard. I reached over, got my sack and jumped off. Uncle Jessie looked back and said, You okay, R.C.? I said, Yeah, I'm okay. I'm going to head on home now. I'll see you later. I slung the sack of relief mess over my shoulder and headed down the road towards home. It seemed like the sack was easier to carry if I leaned forward and down a little. I knew I had to hurry 'cause it was starting to get dark and I still had the feeding and milking to do.

When I got home I walked in the house and throwed the sack on our kitchen table. I didn't say anything. I just started walking out our back door. Mama said, R.C., that ain't no way to act. I still didn't say anything. I just left the back door wide open and went on out to do the feeding and milking.

That night after I got the milk strained and put down in the well, I just went straight to bed. I figured I'd just teach Mama a lesson, I'd just go straight on off to bed and not eat anything. I thought to myself, I just bet she'll be coming in here any minute and beg me to come on and eat. I laid there in bed listening to everybody talking while they was eating. I could hear the radio playing. It sounded like I wasn't being missed a whole lot. I raised up on my elbow and tried to hear what they were saying. I didn't hear my name mentioned. It seemed like nobody cared if I starved to death.

They all finished eating, turned the radio off, and went to bed, and still nobody hadn't come and begged me to go and eat. Well, I didn't care. I sure as heck wasn't going to starve to death before morning. I could see right then, though, that pouting wasn't going to get me anywhere. But one thing was for sure, I wasn't going to that Burgaw relief place no more.

After I finished feeding and milking next morning, I ate me a big breakfast. Mama didn't say anything about me acting up and pouting. I didn't either. When I started out the door to hook up the mule, Mama said, R.C., you might as well get on back to plowing the tobacco field today.

I know, Mama. That's what I was planning on doing. I think I'll have all the crops laid by in about two weeks.

That's right, R.C. I can tell you're learning a lot about farm talk, like laying by and all.

Yeah, Mama, I know. When you plow a crop for the last time, you call it laying by. And when you finish plowing all your crops the last time for the year, you just say, I've got everything laid by.

That's right, son. Now you better hurry on and get started with that plowing.

I walked out in our back yard and there was them sorry hogs out again, heading right for our garden. I called Mama.

What, son?

Them doggone hogs is out again.

We better get them back in real quick before they get in our garden or the corn crop.

Me, Mama, Doris, Bobby and Sister ran them hateful hogs until our tongues was hanging out before we finally got them back in the hog pen. Mama told me to get some hog pen nails and nail them boards around the hog pen up real good. I knew what she meant when she said hog pen nails. She meant for me to look through the ashes around the washpot. There were always a few nails there. They were rusty and bent, but they were good enough to nail up the hog pen with.

I found some nails and nailed up the pen as best I could. Then I hooked Old Bill up and headed towards the fields. Mama hollered out, R.C., take the bush axe with you. Them sassafras saplings needs to be trimmed around. You know wc got to keep them tended to. There's no telling when we're going to need some more of that sassafras tea.

I got the bush axe and took it with me to the tobacco field. Me and that old mule plowed real hard that morning. Seemed like he just knew it was the last time we'd be plowing the crops that year. The weather was still hot and me and Old Bill were washed down in sweat. I knew all the crops had to be laid by, but I didn't want me and Old Bill to be laid by too, so I just told Old Bill to whoa. I figured it was time me and him took us a break.

While he was resting, I went over to the edge of the woods, got me some sweet gum leaves and put them under my straw hat. It seemed like they kept my head a little cooler. When I got back to where Old Bill was, there were a lot of them old blood-sucking horseflies on him. I killed every one I could. I must have killed fifty anyhow. It wasn't right, us working hard as we could and them doggone horseflies just sucking the blood out of us.

Well, they didn't get much of my blood because I could hit them with my hands, but all our mule could do was just swish his tail, stomp his feet, and swing his head around. Them horseflies knew just where to get on him so he couldn't reach them. Sometimes I'd catch the flies, pull their heads off and let them go. I never could figure out how they did it, but they'd just fly off straight and level. One thing was for sure, they weren't going to bite me or Old Bill again.

I decided to let the mule rest some more because he was still washed down in sweat, and his head was hanging real low to the ground. It seemed like a good time for me to cut down some of that undergrowth around the sassafras saplings.

I cut the undergrowth and went back to check on Old Bill. I could tell he needed more rest, so I took the bush axe and walked over to the old walnut tree. I sat down and leaned up against it, pushed my straw hat back, and looked out over the fields. I could see the heat waves dancing.

There wasn't much shade under the tree, but it was better than nothing. I stretched out my legs and dug my bare feet into the ground where it was cooler, closed my eyes, and dozed off.

After a few minutes, I woke up to a strange noise. It was a kind of a huffing and puffing sound. The first thing I thought was maybe one of them sinikin bears was creeping up on me. It sounded just like what I thought a bear would. I'd never heard a bear, but I'd done made up my mind how I thought one would sound.

I jumped straight up and looked over towards where the sound was coming from. There was something there all right. It was our old razorback sow and she was acting real strange. While I was wondering what was wrong with the hussy, she lowered her head and started running towards me. I wasn't sure what to do. At first I thought, when that old hog gets close enough, I'll just give her a kick in the nose. I drew my foot back. She didn't even slow down. She just kept coming towards me, foaming at the mouth. I thought, what if she's done been bit by one of them mad foxes?

I turned real quick and started climbing the walnut tree. It didn't take me long to get to the first limbs. I sat there in the fork of the tree and looked down at that old sow. She was sitting there under the tree looking up at me and she was still making that huffing and puffing sound. I'd never seen a hog act like that before.

I sat there in the fork of the tree and tried to figure things out. I thought, now who's been taking care of that old sow, and who's been building all them pens she's been living in, and who's been putting all that nice warm straw in her shelter so she can have all them little pigs that Daddy's always bragging about, and who's the human being, and who's the regular old animal? It didn't take me long to figure that out. I guess some of Daddy and Grandpa Fowler's temper done flew in me. I started sliding down that tree trunk. I was thinking, hog-killing time or not, I'm just going to kill that razorback hog as soon as I hit the ground.

I slid down the tree real fast. Soon as I hit the ground, I grabbed the bush axe that I'd left leaning up against the tree and took a big swipe at that old sow. She just jumped back and acted like she couldn't figure out what was going on. She backed off a little more but kept her head lowered down and kept snorting-like. When she backed off like that, I thought, maybe I won't kill her, I'll just teach her one good lesson.

I took the bush axe and cut me a real good size sapling off that ditch bank that was beside that walnut tree. I trimmed it up real quick where I could swing it around like I wanted. Then I started after that old sow. She looked real surprised and turned and started running back towards her pen as hard as she could go. I caught up with her and warped her behind real good. She started running faster and I began falling behind. I'd done made up my mind though—that old hog was gonna get one good ass-beating.

When we got up close by our house, she turned and lit out straight for her pen. I was still behind her. I called the dogs. Old Dizz and Toby saw something was going on and came at a dead run. When they got close up, I hollered, Sic 'im, boys, get her, sic 'im. Well now, that just set Old Dizz and Toby on fire. There was that old sow heading for her pen, Old Dizz and Toby nipping at her heels, and me coming up behind her with that sapling. That old sow wasn't even looking back. Looked like she knew she'd done messed up bad. She got to her pen and tried to get under the wire where she'd broke out. But she was in such a hurry, she got hung up, and them dogs was nipping at her butt real good. When I got there, I called off the dogs and I warped her behind real good with that sapling. It didn't take but two or three warps before she got under that wire and run over to the back corner of that hog pen. I told Old Dizz and Toby, just stay there and don't let her out.

I went to our washpot, got some nails, went back and nailed up the pen real good. I told old Dizz and Toby, Good job, boys. Before we left I looked over in the hog pen and told that old sow, Well, guess what, you got the honor of being the first in line come hog-killin' time.

When I got back to the field, Old Bill had drug the plow up in the shade of the walnut tree. I didn't blame him for trying to get out of the hot sun. Besides, he hadn't hurt anything. I told him, Come on, me and you still got a lot of plowing to do before quittin' time.

That night at supper I told Mama what happened about that old sow and all.

Son, you done the right thing all the way. The first thing you got to do when something like that happens is take care of yourself. The next thing is, you don't let no animal treat you like you was just another animal.

I know. I ain't going to let no hog tree me like I was a possum or some other varmint.

That's right, son. That old sow's a troublemaker.

I know, Mama. I done told her today she was going to have the honor of being first in line come hog-killin' time.

Now, I don't know whether she's going to be first in line or not, but I think she's sure enough going to be in the line.

Mama, you know when I was real mad with that old sow today, I was ready to kill her right then and there. But I'll tell you, Mama, I just don't like to kill anything.

I know, son. You're tender-hearted all right, even though you get upset and say bad words every now and then.

Maybe so, but I don't get upset unless somebody messes with me, or sometimes when them animals think they're going to rule the roost.

Well, everybody gets upset sometimes.

Mama, you know sometimes when them little chicks are born deformed and I have to kill them? I don't let on it bothers me, but when I take them out in the woods to kill them, I just close my eyes and do it quick as I can. I know it has to be done. I just don't like to be the one that does it.

That night after I went to bed, I heard Mama, Aunt Lanie, and Sister talking. Mostly they were talking about how we came about our land. They said they understood it was given to the Larkins by King George III. I heard Mama say how she loved her grandma, Amelia Larkins, and how she was so proud that she was named Amelia Caroline after her. Then they talked about how many of their ancestors had been named Amelia, Ann, and Caroline. Mama told Aunt Lanie and Sister that it just seemed like we ought to keep them names going, especially since her grandma, Amelia Ann, was such a saint. I guess that's why Mama named my baby sister Ann Carolyn.

Mama read a poem that she had written about her grandma. Then they sang a song,

You can picture happy gath'rings
Round the fireside long ago
And you think of tearful partings
When they left you here below.

Will the circle be unbroken
By and by, Lord, by and by
In a better home awaiting
In the sky, Lord, in the sky.

I believe Mama wanted to see her grandma again as bad as I wanted to see mine. I didn't know why, but it seemed like a grandma's love could squeeze right inside you and just snuggle right up to your heart.

A few days later we got a letter about Grandma Fowler. Seems the sores on her leg had spread and got so bad that the doctors had to take her leg off, and the only way she could get around was in a wheelchair. We was all real sorry to hear about it. I knew how Grandma liked to sit and rock on her front porch. I just knew she was going to miss her rocking. It was sad news.

Twelve

Summer was slipping on by. We already had about half our tobacco crop cured and packed down in us children's bedroom, and our other crops were looking good, especially our sugar cane. Mama said the sugar cane was looking so good she was thinking about having it all made into syrup. I'd heard how much fun it was making syrup, how all the sweet juices got squeezed out of the stalks and then got heated all steamy in a big vat. I just knew all us cousins were going to get together and have a good ol' time come syrup-making day.

One night while I was sitting up curing our third barn of tobacco, I got to thinking how I only had about four more barns of tobacco to go and I'd be finished curing for the year, and I thought about how I wasn't near as scared as I was the first time I sat up with the barn at night. One reason was because I was older. I'd be thirteen in December. I'd heard Aunt Maybelle say that when you got past twelve, you were at the age of accountability. I believed what she meant was I had to get right with the Lord or I'd be doomed for sure.

I was still puzzled some about religion. I just couldn't understand why something that was so good for you was so scary. I hoped I hadn't already done something that had doomed me to hell. I just didn't believe that the Lord my Aunt Lanie loved so much was going to reach down and fling a boy that was just twelve years old into no burning pit. I knew I still cussed a little bit, but I said my prayers at night and asked the Lord to help me quit. I didn't think that God was going to turn his back on no little boy that was doing the best he could.

It was beginning to rain real hard. The lightning was flashing all around, like it did during the summertime. It was raining harder than usual and that old oak tree had done got struck by lightning again. I rolled up in the bench quilt and laid real still.

While I was laying there, I got to wondering why that oak tree got struck so much and the old log cabin didn't get struck none. I figured maybe the Lord was looking out for that old cabin because He was sorry for all them generations of hard-working folks that had been born and raised inside them cabin walls. I stuck my head out from under the quilt. It was still raining hard.

When daylight came, I went out to our tobacco patch to take a look. There was a lot of water on the ground. I knew that was bad and I'd have to tell Mama about it.

After breakfast, I told Mama, We might have a problem with the tobacco that was left in the field.

She said, Are you talking about all that rain last night?

Uh-huh.

Well, son, if the next day or two is real hot and we don't get some clouds, them leaves are going to wilt, and that'll be the end of our tobacco crop for this year. We'll just have to wait and see.

I'm going back out to the barn. I think I'll be finished curing that barn of tobacco today.

If that barn comes out all right, we'll be saved half our cash crop at least.

Mama, I ain't saying it 'cause I done the curing, but right now it looks real good.

That's good, son. Go on back to the barn and we'll check on the tobacco field later.

I went back to the barn and checked inside. It looked like by evening I could pull the fire, open the doors and let the barn cool down. That night at supper I told Mama that I'd pulled the fire and the tobacco looked good. She said, That's good, son. Tomorrow we'll check the tobacco in the field.

After we'd finished supper, cleaned the kitchen and washed the dishes, we went straight to our bedroom. Me and my brothers slept on pallets on the floor. Doris and Ann slept on a pile of tobacco. I lay there on my pallet with my hands under my head and thought, I sure wish we had a packhouse for all the tobacco. It's stacked so high around our pallets, we can't see out the windows. Before I went to sleep I heard Mama singing real low:

> *When at last I near the shore,*
> *And the fearful breakers roar*
> *'Twixt me and the peaceful rest.*
> *Then while leaning on Thy breast,*
> *May I hear Thee say to me,*
> *"Fear not, I will pilot thee."*

Next morning I checked the tobacco in the barn. It was ready to take out and pack down. Me, Mama, Doris, and Sister started getting the tobacco out. By mid-afternoon we had it all packed down. Mama looked at me and Doris and said, We might as well go out to the tobacco field and see how it looks. I told Mama, You know, the sun's been out bright all day and it's mighty hot. She said, There's no need putting it off any longer. If it looks good, I want to know, and if it's bad, I need to know.

Me, Mama and Doris started walking towards the tobacco field. When we went past the tool shelter we each got us a hoe. There was nothing we could do with the hoes, but it made us feel better walking out there like we were going to do something.

When we got to the tobacco patch and looked down them long rows, there was still a lot of water on the ground. We could see the heat waves coming up and the tobacco leaves were all wilted down and laying flat against the stalks. We knew it was the end of our tobacco crop for that year.

Nobody said anything. Me and Doris turned away from the tobacco and just kind of chopped at some hills of grass. Mama stood there looking down the rows. Then she turned and started back towards the house. Me and Doris walked along behind. I looked down the path and saw Bobby coming toward us. He didn't know what was going on, but he must have felt that something wasn't right. Mama was still holding her hoe. I could tell by the way she was holding her head to the side and down that she was trying to figure out what to do next.

Bobby had stopped and was looking in the brush beside the path. I knew he was looking at that partridge nest that I'd seen earlier. The hen was just beginning to hatch off her chicks. Bobby took a few steps towards her and she started flapping along the ground. They always did that. It made it seem like they were easy to catch, like they had a broke wing or something. Sure enough, Bobby ran after her. When the hen thought she was far enough from her nest, she just up and flew away. I'd been told that was her way of protecting her brood. She'd done fooled Bobby, all right.

❧

One morning early, Uncle Rudolph and Aunt Maybelle came over to our house. It seemed like they wanted to talk with Mama about something special. I could tell it was serious-like, but it was none of my business, so I went on and did my regular jobs. When I got back, Mama and Doris were washing the dishes. Aunt Lanie and Sister were already on the front porch grading tobacco.

Later on that day, I asked Mama, What was Aunt Maybelle and Uncle Rudolph doing over so early this morning?

Well, son, they're thinking about giving up on farming and moving back to the Mill Hill. Just seems like losing the rest of their tobacco crop was the last straw.

I guess so, Mama. I wish we could go back, too.

That's out of the question, son.

A few days later I told Mama, I think I'll walk across the branch to Aunt Maybelle's. I won't be gone long.

You run along over there. We need to check on one another right now, seeing as how we're all kind of down about losing most of our tobacco crop. Now don't you get over there and start playing and keep them Cottle boys from their work. And I want you to be sure and see how your Uncle Rudolph's doing. He's been mighty quiet lately.

He ain't never talked much, Mama, but he don't hardly say nothing now.

I know. He's feeling low. Rudolph's a good man, but he's got a lot on him. 'Course, we ain't none too well off right now.

Aunt Maybelle don't seem all that worried.

Well now, your Aunt Maybelle's concerned, but she puts her faith in God and believes that things are going to work out. Now you just run on across the branch and check on your Uncle Rudolph.

When I got to the branch that divided our land from Aunt Maybelle's, I stopped and watched the little stream of water that ran there most of the time. I didn't know why, but I always liked to watch running water. There were four or five little branch streams that ran through the old Larkins plantation. They just kept running along until they got to Long Creek. I'd been told that sooner or later it all ran into the Cape Fear River.

I'd heard Grandma Harrell and Aunt Lanie talk about how our ancestors took tar and turpentine from the pine trees. Then they'd take it down the Cape Fear River on barges to Wilmington and sell it off to the British. I just knew it had to be a lot of fun riding down the river on a barge.

When I got out of the woods and cut across the first small field leading up to Aunt Maybelle's, I saw Uncle Rudolph right off. He'd been plowing in the vegetable garden that was up close by their house. But it seemed like his mule, Old Blue, had stopped about halfway down the row and wouldn't move. I could tell Uncle Rudolph was upset. He looked up and called me over. When I got to where him and Old Blue was, he told me to hold on to the plow handles. He said it looked like Old Blue had made up his mind he wasn't going to pull that plow anymore.

After I got behind the plow and held on to the handles, Uncle Rudolph went over to the woods and cut a good-size sapling. When he got back he stood alongside the mule like he was trying to make up his mind whether to hit Old Blue with it or not. I was still holding on to the plow handles wondering what was going to happen. All of a sudden Old Blue's legs just crumpled and he fell straight down. Then he rolled over on his side and closed his eyes. A noise came out of his throat like a low rumble.

I looked over at Uncle Rudolph. His eyes were open real wide. He dropped the sapling, looked over at me and said, Son, you can let go of them plow handles now. I just stood there. Seemed like I couldn't turn the handles loose. Uncle Rudolph turned and started walking towards his house. It was kind of a stumbling walk. His head and shoulders were pitched forward like he was staring at the ground, and his arms were hanging straight down, like they just couldn't swing anymore.

I held on to the plow handles until Uncle Rudolph got to his porch steps, which were just two old pine boards laid across some wood blocks. He sat down on the steps, leaned over, and held his head in both hands.

I let go of the plow handles and walked off a little ways. Then I walked around in front of Old Blue's head, kind of slow-like. He wasn't breathing, and there was a yellow liquid coming from his mouth and nostrils. I started walking towards Uncle Rudolph. After I took a few steps, I heard something behind me. I looked back and saw that the old plow had done fell over, too. It was a strange feeling, seeing Old Blue and that plow laying there on the ground together.

I walked over to where Uncle Rudolph was sitting on the steps. He was rubbing his head with both hands. I stood there for a little while, wondering what to do. I drew a bucket of water from the well and asked Uncle Rudolph if he'd like a dipperful.

I don't want anything right now, son.

You didn't know Old Blue was sick.

Don't make no difference. I should have known something was wrong when he stopped like that and wouldn't move. I had no business trying to make him keep on pulling that plow. I just wish somebody would come along right now and give me a good horse-whipping. I wouldn't care if they killed me.

It was just Old Blue's time to go, Uncle Rudolph.

I guess so, son, but I sure feel bad about it.

I got to go now, Uncle Rudolph. You know, take care of my regular jobs and all. I'll be back over in the morning with our mule and we'll drag Old Blue off in the woods.

I cut across Aunt Maybelle's vegetable garden and headed for home. When I got to where Old Blue was laying, I walked by him real slow. It seemed like somebody ought to do something, but I didn't know what.

When I got to where the narrow dirt road entered the woods, I looked back where Old Blue and the plow were laying. It was a sad-looking sight, and I felt real bad about what happened. But it was like I'd heard Mama say—bad things are going to happen in life, and when they do, you just do the best you can and go on living.

I took a few steps down the cart path where it entered the woods, then looked back over my shoulder again. Uncle Rudolph was still on the steps, resting his head in his hands. I turned towards home and set off through the woods.

Next morning, I took our mule and went over to Uncle Rudolph's.

When I got there, he'd already hooked up Uncle Jessie's mule to a sled and pulled it up alongside the dead mule. I said, Hey, Uncle Rudolph.

Hey, son. I see you brought Old Bill all right.

Yeah, I got here soon as I could.

You're here in time enough. I just got back from your Uncle Jessie's. He let me borrow his mule long enough to help pull Old Blue off. It's just too much for one mule to pull.

That's for sure. How far down in them woods are we going to pull him?

We need to pull him somewhere's close to a mile.

I guess so. If we don't, we'll be smelling him.

That's right, son. Let's get him loaded on the sled.

We got Old Blue loaded and headed for the woods. Uncle Rudolph was right. It was about all them two mules could do, pulling the load. When we thought we was far enough back in the woods, we took the mules and pulled Old Blue off the sled. Then we started back the way we came. After we got off a little ways, we stopped and looked back. Uncle Rudolph said, I just hate to leave him laying there on top of the ground like that. But he'd be rotted away before we could dig a hole big enough to bury him in.

I know, Uncle Rudolph. It took me and Sam ten days to dig our well. Digging in this clay around here is something else.

Let's go on home. We've done all we can do.

When we got back to Aunt Maybelle's house, she came out on the porch and told Uncle Rudolph they had to hurry and get started towards town or she'd be late for her job at the cotton mill. Then she looked over at me and said, R.C., come here and sit with me on the steps a bit, hon. I want to talk with you and I've got something to show you.

I went over and sat beside Aunt Maybelle on the steps. I asked her what she had on her mind.

You see this book, son?

Yes ma'am, I see it.

The name of it is *Little Azar*, and it's by an author who imagined what Jesus' little friends were like, what they did, and how they got along. The story is about children that are about the same age as all you cousins.

It sounds like a nice book, Aunt Maybelle.

I think so. Me and your mama decided we're going to read some of this book every night over at your house after Aunt Lanie gets through reading the Bible.

Do all the cousins have to be there?

Yes. But my Billy and your little brother Jimmy will most likely be asleep.

When y'all going to start reading it?

Well now, son, we just thought we'd start tonight.

Aunt Maybelle, sometimes it's after dark when you get home from work.

No matter. Your mama's the one going to be doing the reading. She's a real good reader. Now, I know you're just going to like hearing about little Azar.

I guess so, but don't you think it might be better if we waited until it turns a little cooler? It's going to be mighty hot, all us sitting around huddled up like that this time of year.

Now, me and my family, we'll be gone when cold weather comes. Besides, it's done been decided, sugar.

It must've took a month getting that *Little Azar* book read. It was a nice book all right. Mama was a good reader, but she'd always stop reading for the night right in the middle of an interesting part. She'd just turn down the page and say, We'll find out what happened tomorrow night. I liked books all right, but I liked it better when I went off by myself and read. Another thing, it just took too long to read a book like that, what with all them cousins sitting around and asking questions about this and that. And every time one of them boys had to pee, the reading stopped until he ran out, peed off the end of the porch and got back. It just took too long.

Thirteen

One Sunday us cousins were out in the front yard shooting marbles. The grown-ups were sitting in the rocking chairs on the front porch, resting and watching us play. Everything was going along pretty good until Aunt Maybelle hollered out, R.C. shug, come here. I want to talk to you. I thought, Oh Lord, I bet she wants to talk about reading another book.

I walked up to the porch where Aunt Maybelle was sitting in her rocking chair.

What, Aunt Maybelle?

Son, I've just had you on my mind.

You have?

Yes, I have, sweetie.

What you had me on your mind for?

R.C., you know I told you some time back that you had reached the age of accountability.

Yes, ma'am, you told me.

You know what *accountability* means, don't you?

I think so.

What do you think it means?

I guess it means I'm old enough to know right from wrong.

That's right, son, and it's time you got serious about it. Don't you want to go to heaven when you die?

I don't like to think about dying, Aunt Maybelle.

Shug, everybody's going to die, and the thing we all need to do is to make sure that when we do, we're ready to go.

I don't want to get ready to die.

Now, son, what I mean is you need to confess your sins and accept Jesus Christ as your personal Savior so that when you do die, you can go to heaven. You understand that, don't you?

I think so, Aunt Maybelle. I've heard the preacher talk about it at them cottage prayer meetings.

They're going to start having prayer meetings at the Mosey Road house.

They are?

Yes, and I'd like for you to attend them meetings.

Maybe I will, Aunt Maybelle. How come they call it the Mosey Road house anyhow?

Well, it was the only house on the Mosey Road for a long time. I guess that's why.

There still ain't but two or three houses along that road.

You going to the meeting or not?

I guess I am.

You promise?

I promise. Now can I go back to playing marbles?

Yes, shug. Just remember your promise.

I went back to the marble game, but I knew I was going to have to go to them prayer meetings and do something about my sinful ways. It didn't look like none of us cousins was gonna die and go to no hell, not with Mama, Aunt Maybelle, and Aunt Lanie after us all the time like they was.

❧

One morning after breakfast, Mama said, Seems like things is getting a little too quiet around here. Just because we got all that tobacco ready for market don't mean there's nothing else to do. I asked Mama, What we going to do to keep it from getting too quiet?

Well now, son, I think it's about time we had us a real good rat killin'.

That's the best thing I've heard in a long time. When we going to have it?

Ain't no reason we can't have it today, just as soon as you get your regular jobs done.

I told Doris to run across the branch and tell the Cottle boys, and I told Bobby to go tell the Wells. It didn't take me long to get my regular jobs done, and when I got back to the house, all them cousins were there with their dogs, ready to start the rat killin'. I told Mama, We're ready to start.

Go ahead and get started. Just y'all be careful.

We will. Where you want us to start?

Don't make no difference, son. There's rats in all them outbuildings and them haystacks, too. Might as well make a day of it.

Okay, Mama.

Us cousins got together and planned out how we were going to kill the rats. It was decided we'd try about everything we could think of. First, we'd build us a fire around the washpot and heat a pot of boiling water. Then we'd pour the water down the rat holes, and there'd be at least two of us waiting there with tobacco sticks in our hands all drawed back, ready to start flailing the daylights out of them rats. If they got by the ones of us standing at the end of the tunnel, we'd have the dogs right ready to chase them down. If they got by the dogs, some more of us would be right ready to chop them up with the hoes. 'Course, we'd have to be careful not to hit the dogs with our hoes.

We thought we had a good plan, so it was decided that the Cottle boys would start finding the rat holes and that some of us would fill the washpot with water and pile the wood around it to get a good fire going. The rest of us would get the dogs all excited, like getting them to smell down the rat holes and saying things like, Sic 'em, and, Let's get 'em, boys, and, Yeah, let's get them dirty rats.

Pretty soon we had the washpot boiling and the dogs were all excited. They were sticking their noses down the rat holes and trying to dig them out. The Cottle boys had already found about fifty rat tunnels. We brought some buckets of the hot water to where the rat holes were and got ready. Me and Lewis took turns pouring the hot water down the holes.

It wasn't long before a rat came running out one of the tunnels. Everybody got real excited and started hitting at it with the tobacco sticks as hard as they could. The dogs started chasing the rat and caught him right quick. It wasn't long before that was one dead rat. Everybody ran over to where the dead rat was. While we were all standing there looking at it, somebody hollered, Look out! Here comes another one!

Everybody lit out after that rat. We was swinging them hoes and sticks, and the dogs was trying their best to get to the rat without getting killed themselves. Well, that rat done got killed in record time.

The rat killin' was going along real good. We was killing a lot of rats and everybody was having a good time. By dinner we'd done killed a peck bucket full. We were all getting tired and hungry, so we decided to take us a break.

A bunch of us boys went out to our watermelon patch and got four big ripe watermelons and laid them up on our barn bench. We sliced them up and helped ourselves. Everybody was laughing and talking and spitting out seeds. We was all saying we was the ones that killed the most rats and things like that. We danced all around like we was trying to keep rats off our feet.

Pretty soon we had watermelon juice all over us. We hadn't had that much fun in a long time. I went up to the house to tell Mama how things was going.

Mama, we done killed about a peck bucket full of rats.

That's good, son. Y'all going to be wanting me to fix some dinner?

Naw, we just decided to eat us some watermelon. Then we're going to get right back to the rat killin'.

Mama looked out the kitchen window towards the barn and said, Is that Lester out there?

Yeah. He just got here a little while ago.

What's he want?

You know Lester. He mostly wants to talk.

What's he talking about today?

He's telling us how he'd go about killing them rats.

I thought so. When you go back to the barn, you tell Lester that we know how to kill rats.

I'll tell him, Mama, but he don't mean nothing by it. He just likes to talk.

I know, but just remember this. Everybody's business is nobody's business, and this is our rat killin'.

All right, I'll tell him.

When I got back to the barn, all them cousins was still laughing and talking about them rats we'd killed. By then they'd done been in our vegetable garden and helped themselves to our tomatoes. It looked like everybody was full of watermelon and tomatoes and was ready to get back to the rat killin'. I told Lester, Mama said thank you for your help, but we know how to kill rats.

Lester said, What exactly did Miss Carrie say?

Well, Lester, she said this was our rat killin' and everybody's business is nobody's business.

Sounds like Miss Carrie. She's got a saying for just about everything.

Lester, I'll have to agree with you on that.

R.C., is Miss Carrie cooking dinner?

No, we ain't taking no time to sit around at the dinner table today. We're too busy with this rat killin' business.

I declare, that Miss Carrie's a good cook.

Yeah, I noticed you can put a lot of it away.

I can do that all right.

Lester, if you want to help with the rat killin', you can start bringing them buckets of hot water.

I wish I could, R.C., but I better be getting on home. Grandpa Worley just might have something he wants me to do.

I always knew how to get rid of Lester. All I had to do was mention work and he was gone.

By suppertime we were all lined up at our kitchen table waiting for Mama to bring on that big pot of food. After the blessings was said, we all started telling Mama about the rat killin', like how many we killed, who killed the most and all. Mama said, Did you younguns wash your hands real good? We all said we did. Then Mama started telling about all them diseases that rats carry around. We all got up and washed our hands again with lye soap.

We ate a good supper, washed the dishes, cleaned up the kitchen, and went to bed. We were just too tired to sit around the radio table and listen to the battery radio. We were tired all right, but one thing was for sure, we'd taught them rats a lesson that day.

It was Sunday morning, and us cousins got together and decided we was going to play baseball. Only thing was, we didn't have anything to play with. The balls and bats that we played with last year was done used up or lost. 'Course it didn't take us long to make a ball and bat. We just peeled the hull off a hickory nut, took some used tobacco twine, and wrapped it around the nut real tight until it was big as a baseball. Then we took a needle and thread and sewed it up all around. To make a bat, we used a dried-out hickory limb.

After we finished making the ball and bat, we chose up sides. There were nine of us, so it didn't work out to be the same number on each side. After we chose up four on each side, we still had Bobby left over. It seemed like neither side wanted Bobby, him being little like he was, so we drew straws. The loser got Bobby.

After we was all chose up, we put down the bases and home plate and started playing. My side was up first. We were doing pretty good. We made some runs, but their side started hollering *out* every time we hit the ball and ran for first base. Then there was just a lot of hollerin' and arguing. I told Sam, We need time out so we can talk things over.

R.C., what we going to talk about?

I'll tell you later, Sam. Right now I'm gonna call time out.

I hollered at the other side, Time out!

Lewis said, R.C., y'all don't need no time out. Besides, our side wants to keep on playing.

I can't help what your side wants, Lewis. Our side wants time out. It's legal and all, so we're gonna take it. Y'all can have a time out later.

We don't want no time out.

Suit yourself, we're taking a time out.

Me, Sam, and the other two that was on my side walked off a little ways. Sam said, R.C., what're we walking off like this for?

Well, Sam, we just don't want the other side to hear what we're gonna say.

What're we gonna say?

Not much, Sam. First, we're gonna lean over and put our arms around each other's shoulders.

What we going to do that for?

Now don't worry, Sam. I used to play ball on the Mill Hill and I know some tricks.

What kind of tricks?

I'll tell you when we get all huddled up closer here.

Our side got huddled up close-like and I told them, Now what we do is just talk real low and make plans. Then every once in a while we'll all raise up our heads and look over at the other side and just grin-like.

James Kenneth said, Now what're we gonna do that for?

James Kenneth, it don't mean nothing really, it just makes them think we've got some real good plan on our minds. But about all we can do when we hit the ball is run as fast as we can. If their side starts hollering foul ball or you're out, don't pay no never mind. Main thing is, just keep running. If you're going to do any arguing about whether you're safe or out, just wait until you get back to home plate. I learned that when I was playing ball on the Mill Hill.

We had a good time playing ball. When it got time to quit, we decided to call the game a tie because it was too hard to keep up with the score, what with all the arguing and fussing about who was out and who was safe. We were going to have to quit before long anyway. The string kept coming off the ball.

&

We got all the tobacco sold off, and me and Doris got the beds back up in our bedroom. It was a good feeling to get that tobacco out and sleep in our beds again. Another thing, it was good not to be out in them fields every day. 'Course, there was always something to do. Mama made sure of that.

October came and the days were beginning to get a little cooler. Aunt Maybelle and her family were getting ready to move back to the Mill Hill. Daddy seemed to be worse off. It looked like he was swelling more around the back of his neck and shoulders. Mama said we just had to take him to town. She said he could stay with Aunt Roxie and Uncle Red a while. That way he'd be close by the doctor.

Uncle Rudolph took Mama, Daddy and Aunt Maybelle to town and got Daddy settled in at Aunt Roxie's, and Mama got up with a doctor. He said he'd come by that evening. Uncle Rudolph picked us children up at the farm 'cause Mama didn't want us to spend the night at home by ourselves. It was late when Uncle Rudolph got there. We all squeezed in the old Ford and rode back to the Mill Hill.

When we got to Aunt Roxie's house, there were some more of our kinfolks there. Some were sitting around the living room and some were in the bedroom where Daddy was. It wasn't long before the doctor came and went right in to see Daddy. Somebody closed the bedroom door. I was sitting in the living room.

While the doctor was checking Daddy, Aunt Roxie and Aunt Maybelle came out and got a lot of towels and took them back in the bedroom. Pretty soon, I heard some of the women cry out, Oh my God!

After a few minutes the doctor came out carrying his little bag. He told the ones of us in the living room he just didn't see how Daddy had lived with all that corruption in him. He talked a little while about what ought to be done and left. I went into the bedroom. Some of the women were washing Daddy's back and shoulders, and some were cleaning off the wall and bed sheets. It seemed that when the doctor lanced Daddy's shoulder, the corruption had flown all over. When the women finished cleaning up all the mess, the towels were soaked with what came out of Daddy's neck and shoulders. Daddy was just laying there, quiet-like. Everybody seemed to think he'd get better for sure, now.

Uncle Rudolph took us children and Aunt Maybelle back home to Pender County. Mama was going to stay with Daddy a few more days. I asked Aunt Maybelle if somebody was going to stay with us while Mama was gone.

Yes, son. Rudolph's going back to town this evening and get Aunt Lanie. She'll stay with you until your mama and daddy get home.

I like it when Aunt Lanie stays with us.

I know, R.C., your Aunt Lanie's a good woman. She's always ready to help.

Aunt Maybelle, when are y'all moving back to the Mill Hill?

We're going to wait until your mama and daddy are back.

In a few days, Mama and Daddy came home. Daddy acted like he was feeling better. He said it didn't hurt to touch him anymore and he could turn over in the bed by himself. It seemed good to see him moving around more.

After Daddy'd been home a few days, Aunt Maybelle came over to our house and said, R.C., I want to talk with you, hon. I just knew what she wanted to talk with me about was my soul and how if I didn't do something about my sinful ways, I was sure enough bound for hell.

What you want to talk with me about?

Son, you know I've been telling you about how they were gonna be having them cottage prayer meetings at the Mosey Road house.

Yeah, I remember.

Well, shug, they're gonna start having them tomorrow night. I sure would like to see you go.

Aunt Maybelle, looks like I'm gonna be mighty tied up around here.

Now, hon, I know you stay pretty well busy, but this is important.

I'd sure like to go, but you know how Daddy's all stove up and he don't feel like taking me nowheres.

I've done thought about that. Your Uncle Jesse's gonna be taking his family and you can ride with them.

But Aunt Maybelle, there's five in their family and that old cart's gonna be mighty crowded.

It ain't gonna be that crowded. Besides, I already talked to your Aunt Ruth, and she said they'd love to have you ride with them.

Well, it looked like there was just no way I was gonna get out of going to that prayer meeting, but I wasn't ready to give up.

You know to get to the Mosey Road house you have to ride the mule and cart down that old dark Mosey Road for about two miles.

That's the way you have to go all right.

Well, I've heard there's a lot of bears that live along that road. Lester said that's where a lot of them sinikin bears live.

Now, hon, I don't care what Lester says about them sinikin bears. Do you realize that you're the only cousin around here that's reached the age of accountability that hasn't confessed their sins and accepted Jesus Christ as their Savior?

I am?

That's right.

Well, sometimes it takes me a while to make up my mind on them kind of things.

Are you going to the prayer meeting or not?

I'm going, Aunt Maybelle, I'm going.

Next evening, just before dark, I put on my clean overalls and walked up to Aunt Ruth's house. They were all sitting in the cart. Aunt Ruth said, Hurry up, R.C., we're all ready to go. I hopped up in the back of the cart and sat beside Sam. Uncle Jesse tapped their mule, Little Bill, with the lines and we started down the dirt road headed for the Mosey Road house. We had a mile to go down the road that ran by our house before we got to where we turned off on the old Mosey Road. I asked Sam how everything was going.

All right, R.C., how about you?

I guess all right, but Aunt Maybelle just won't let me alone. She says I'm the only cousin here in the country that ain't done confessed his sins and got right with the Lord.

I don't know about that, R.C., but everybody in our house has.

I guess it's time I did something. You know how I cuss sometimes.

Yeah, I know.

Another thing, Sam. I guess I stretched the truth a little when I told Aunt Maybelle that Lester said that most of them sinikin bears hung out along the Mosey Road.

Well, I don't know where them sinikin bears hang out. Maybe they do live along the Mosey Road. Maybe you didn't stretch the truth.

Thing is, though, I just made it up right off. I was trying to get Aunt Maybelle off my back.

We turned down the old Mosey Road. We still had about another two miles to go. There was only one house along the way, and that was just before we got to where we was going to have the prayer meeting. After we'd gone down the Mosey Road about a mile, Uncle Jesse lit the lantern and hung it on a short post that was beside the cart seat. I guess I must have dozed off, but that old cart jolting around in them mud holes woke me up. I figured it was a good thing, though, because them mosquitoes were eating on me something fierce.

I looked over at Sam. He was sitting on the back of the cart, holding on and looking down. Every now and then he'd slap at one of them mosquitoes. I thought, if I was good as Sam, I wouldn't have to be going to no prayer meeting. Uncle Jesse pulled Little Bill up into the Mosey House yard. Sam got out and tied the mule to a pecan tree. The rest of us got out of the cart and went inside.

Some folks were moving the furniture around in the living room and a lady named Laura Belle was warming up on the pump organ. Me and Sam sat in the living room listening to some of the men talking about what all they was going to preach about. After a while we decided to go to the kitchen, which was the next room back. There were some women there that looked like they'd just finished eating and were feeding two babies. The women were dipping their fingers in a bowl of cornmeal mush, then putting it in the babies' mouths. I told Sam I sure would hate to have to eat off somebody's fingers like that.

Yeah, me too, R.C., but it don't seem to bother them none.

I know, Sam. They've got mush all over their faces and in their hair and they're dropping it on the benches and all over the place.

Me and Sam sat on the bench at the kitchen table across from the babies and watched them eat. Pretty soon somebody hollered out, Everybody get in the living room, we're about to start. The women cleaned the mush off the babies and went in the living room. Me and Sam followed them in.

It was a big room, but it was pretty crowded. There must have been twenty people there. Miss Laura Belle cranked the organ up pretty loud and everybody started singing. When the song was over, the one that was going to start the preaching off told us to bow our heads because he was going to pray. When the prayer was over, some more songs was sung and then a bunch of people testified. When the ones that was testifying finished up, the preacher started preaching.

Everybody was seated around the edges of the room. Miss Laura Belle had done got off the organ stool and was sitting with the rest of us. After the preacher had been preaching a while, he started walking up and down the living room, swinging the Bible over his head and around in front of him. Every once in a while he'd thump it like he was trying to make a point. He kept saying over and over how we was all sinners and the ones of us that hadn't confessed our sins and accepted Christ as our Savior were sure enough bound for hell, where we'd burn forever.

It seemed like the preacher was looking at me most of the time. I wondered if Aunt Maybelle had told him about me and my cussing and all. The preacher looked right at me and said, I know there's somebody here tonight that's under conviction, and you know who you are. Don't let this night go by without confessing your sins.

I was feeling real guilty about my sins and I wanted to confess, but I just hated to do it in front of all them people. The preacher asked some of the men to go in the kitchen and bring out one of the benches from alongside the table and put it on the floor at the end of the living room. The preacher said, Now, brothers and sisters, this is our altar. If anybody feels led to accept the Lord Jesus Christ tonight, just come down and kneel at the altar and me and some of the other brothers and sisters will pray for you.

The preacher turned to Miss Laura Belle and said, Will you please play real softly on the organ *Just As I Am*. Miss Laura Belle sat down at the organ and started playing. Then everybody started singing real low.

I sat there knowing I needed to go up to that altar, but it seemed like I just couldn't. After they finished singing the song, the preacher said, I just feel like there's somebody here that needs to come forward tonight. Then he said, Let's just sing one more verse, and they started singing again. Next thing I knew I was walking down that long living room towards the altar. I couldn't believe what I was doing. When I got to the altar, the preacher took my hand and said, Bless you, son. Just kneel here at the altar. I knelt down by that old wooden kitchen bench, put both my arms on it, laid my head in my arms and cried. Seemed like I was going to cry my heart out.

The preacher and some more folks came over and put their hands on my head and prayed. Miss Laura Belle was still playing the organ real soft and some folks was still singing.

After they was through praying over me, I stood up and looked around. Everybody was still standing and singing real low. The preacher raised and lowered his hand, and the singing stopped. He looked me straight in the eye and said, Son, are you confessing your sins here tonight?

Yes, sir. I've sinned all right, and I'm confessing 'em.

Well, now do you accept Jesus Christ as your Savior?

Yes, sir. I do.

Well, we're all happy for you tonight. I want you to stand here by the mourners' bench and I'm gonna ask everybody to come by and welcome you to the fold.

Everybody came by, shook my hand, and said things like, You did the right thing, child, Bless you, son, and Welcome to the fold. When they'd all come by, I walked out on the porch. Sam was untying the mule and Uncle Jesse was lighting the lantern. We all climbed up in the cart and Uncle Jesse headed Little Bill back down the Mosey Road towards home.

It was a quiet trip. I guessed everybody was thinking about what all had happened at the prayer meeting. About the only noise was the frogs croaking in the little ditch alongside the road and the sound of the cart wheel jolting back and forth in the mud holes. Once in a while the mule would snort like he smelled something. I hoped it wasn't one of them sinikin bears.

Uncle Jesse pulled the cart up in their yard and I hopped off the back and told them all I'd see them tomorrow. They all told me bye, and Aunt Ruth asked if I wanted to take the lantern. I told her, no, I'd be all right. I started walking down that lonely country road towards home. As I walked along I was thinking how I was usually scared some when I walked alone at night, but it seemed like I wasn't scared then, and I felt like I wanted to be friends with everybody and everything. Even the frogs and crickets making them sounds along the road seemed friendly.

It wasn't long before I saw the light of the kerosene lamp in our living room window. I thought, I just bet Mama's still up waiting on me. I turned up in our yard, walked up on the porch, and put my hand on the doorknob. Mama said, R.C., is that you?

It's me, Mama.

I opened the door and went inside.

Well, son, how'd everything go at the prayer meeting?

Mama, everything went just fine. I confessed my sins and accepted Jesus as my Savior.

Well now, son, that's wonderful.

Mama gave me a big hug and said, I just know your Aunt Lanie and Aunt Maybelle are gonna be mighty happy.

I guess so, Mama.

Son, what have you got on your shirtsleeves?

I raised my arms and looked at my sleeves. It looks like mush, Mama.

How in the world did you get mush on your shirtsleeves?

Mama, it's a long story. I'll tell you sometime.

O.K., son. You might as well get to bed.

I slept good that night.

&

Aunt Maybelle and Uncle Rudolph moved back to the Mill Hill. Their boys were going to a new school there. It was a lot quieter around our place. We'd started back to school, too. I was glad because we could see all our classmates again. One good thing about school, besides learning, was being with all our friends. Another thing, the days just seemed to pass easier and didn't seem so lonely.

We'd finally got electricity. We had a light bulb in every room and one on the front porch. It was a lot easier to do our homework and our radio played better. It looked like Daddy might be going back to work regular before long. He was getting out and walking around in the yard some.

One night while we were eating supper, Mama said that we were going to start making syrup the next day. We were all glad to hear that because it was going to be some excitement. Making syrup was probably as exciting as hog-killin' time and nearly as exciting as rat killin'. Mama said Uncle Jessie was going to bring the equipment to our house early the next morning.

It was hard for me to sleep that night thinking about cooking the syrup. Me and my little brothers lay in bed talking about what all was going to be going on the next day. Bobby was just eight and Jimmy was only three, but they knew that syrup-making day was going to be special.

Uncle Jessie got there with the equipment early the next morning, and pretty soon we had everything ready and the mule hooked up to a long pole. When he pulled the pole, it made some wooden rollers turn. The rollers mashed the juice out of the sugar cane stalks. Then the juice ran down into a vat that we'd built a fire under.

It wasn't long before steam started coming off the juice and smelling real good. When the vat was full, we unhooked the mule and the grown-ups stirred the juice. When the juice was cooked down enough, it turned into syrup and we poured it into fifty-pound cans called lard stands. It was a lot of fun for us children, watching the mule pull that long pole around, getting those cans cleaned and keeping the fire burning.

By late evening we had all the syrup cooked and poured into the cans. Everybody thought that we had enough syrup to last us two, maybe three years. We children knew that having all that syrup meant we were going to have a lot of molasses cookies and we'd be able to sop syrup anytime we wanted. Besides that, when most of that sugar got settled down in the bottom of the cans, we could pour off the syrup and get to all that sugar and molasses mix that always settled on the bottom. It was as good as candy. That night at supper, I told Mama we'd got all the syrup made and put away.

Did you put the cans in the smokehouse?

Yes, ma'am. We lined them up along the wall so they'll be easy to get to.

That's good. That way they won't be in our way when we go to the smokehouse for meat.

Mama, you know, we sure got a lot of food right here at our back door.

That's right, son, we got all them sweet potatoes in the potato bank, and all that hickory-smoked meat and molasses in the smokehouse, and we got plenty of corn to make cornmeal and grits. We're not going to go hungry, that's for sure.

That's right, Mama, but when I looked in them cans where we keep our grits and cornmeal, they were both getting low.

I was going to talk with you about that.

What you thinking about, Mama?

You know where the Sutton mill is, don't you?

It's out on the paved road, about eight miles from here. I used to go there with Daddy before he got sick.

That's right, son. One day before long me and you are going to take us a cartload of corn to the Sutton mill and have it ground into meal, grits, and maybe some animal feed.

I'm ready to go anytime, Mama. I like to go to the mill and see the corn ground, and Old Bill, he sure likes to pull a cart.

We'll be going in a few days. We'll just go on a Saturday, so you won't have to miss school.

I'll miss school if you want me to.

We'll see.

&

Christmas came and went. We all got a few toys. Me and Bobby each got a BB gun and a box of BB shots. We were excited about the guns. Only problem was, we shot all the BBs up the first day. It seemed like we ought to be able to do something besides just carry around empty air rifles. I told Bobby, I just bet them dry okra seeds would shoot about as good as them store-bought BBs, them being about the same size and all. We took some of the okra pods, shelled out the seeds and loaded them in our air rifles. They worked real good. Looked like we done figured out how to get all the rifle shots we wanted.

Fourteen

It was a new year, 1941, and I was thirteen years old. Things seemed to be going along all right. 'Course, the nights in our house were mighty cold. We still got a skim of ice in our water bucket some nights. One night when I was laying in bed with my brothers, Mama called out from her bedroom, R.C., are you awake?

Yes, Mama.

I think it's snowing.

What makes you think that?

I don't know. It's just the way the wind sounds outside. Sounds like there's snow swirling around out there.

I got up, turned on the front porch light and looked through our front room window. Sure enough, it was snowing. My mama was something else. She just didn't miss anything.

It's snowing all right.

I thought so. You'd best get back in bed and cover up real good, son.

I got back in bed and snuggled up to Bobby and Jimmy. It felt good all huddled up together under the quilts. The snow started coming in the hole over our bed. I tilted my head back and just let the snow fall right in my face.

Mama, guess what?

What, son?

You know that hole that's in the wall here beside us boys' bed? The one where we put the stovepipe in during tobacco season?

What about it?

Well, the snow's coming in through it pretty good.

It won't hurt you.

I know. It kinda feels good.

You just keep your brothers covered up.

Mama, they're all covered up and fast asleep.

I know you're excited about the snow, but you need to go to sleep, too. Me and you got to take some corn to the Sutton mill tomorrow.

Next morning when I got up, the ground was covered with snow. It wasn't very deep, but it was pretty. I hooked Old Bill to the cart and loaded it down with ears of corn that we'd shucked. I pulled the mule and cart up to our back porch and told Mama everything was ready to go. Mama told Doris to clean up the kitchen and make sure she watched after the children and Daddy. Then she came out and crawled up on the seat beside me and asked if I had sacks to put the grits, cornmeal and cracked corn in.

Yeah, Mama, I got plenty of extra sacks. I think we better get going.

I tapped Old Bill with the line and we started off. Pretty soon we were going down the road headed for the mill. I thought, here I am driving this old mule and cart all the way to the mill. Looks like I'm in charge. 'Course, I knew Mama was really in charge. If I got to making too many suggestions, I knew she'd tell me right quick that it was her rat killin'.

It was a good ride, our old mule pulling the cart through that little blanket of snow and the cart's wheels making that sloshing sound. The paved road was about five miles from our house and by the time we got there, the snow was beginning to melt.

We got to the mill around dinnertime. Mr. Sutton saw us drive up and came over to the cart. Mama said, Mr. Sutton, it's me, Mrs. Fowler. How are you today?

Oh, yeah, Mrs. Fowler, I'm fine. How're you?

I'm fine, too.

What can we do for you?

We'd like to get this corn ground.

How do you want it ground, Mrs. Fowler?

I was thinking one bushel of cornmeal, one bushel of grits, and one bushel of cracked corn. You can grind what's left, cob and all, for animal feed.

We can handle that all right.

Now, Mr. Sutton, I was hoping you'd take out your pay in toll.

I can do that, Mrs. Fowler.

Mr. Sutton told Mama how much of our corn he'd keep for the grinding and Mama said that would be all right.

While the grinding was being done, me and Mama ate some biscuit sandwiches she'd brought along. I watched while Mr. Sutton ground the corn. It didn't take much more than an hour to get the corn ground. Mr. Sutton took out his toll and helped me load the rest in our cart. Mama thanked him and we started towards home.

I'd fed Old Bill some corn and gave him some water while we were at the mill. He felt good and was walking pretty fast. Mama said it was a good thing because we needed to get home as soon as we could, being Doris was the only one at home to look after Daddy and the small children.

The ride home was kind of quiet. After we turned off the paved road and got a little ways down the dirt road, Mama started talking about what we were going to do to make up for losing half our tobacco crop. I asked Mama, What you thinking about doing?

I was thinking that we might plant us some produce.

You mean like lettuce, squash, cucumbers and things like that?

That's right.

Mama, we always plant some of them vegetables in our garden.

I know, but I'm thinking about planting about an acre of each. We can pack the vegetables in bushel baskets and take them to Burgaw to sell.

Do we get our money right then like we do at the tobacco market?

No, son. They ship it up North. Then when it's sold, they'll send us the money.

That's kind of risky, ain't it?

Yes, but we need to do something to make up for the tobacco we lost last summer. Them folks that's been supplying us all year have been mighty good and we've got to make sure they get paid.

Everybody knows we're doing all we can.

I know they do, son. Now make that mule step it up. We need to get on home.

I tapped Old Bill with the lines. He stepped it up a little.

About an hour later we pulled up in our yard. I let Mama out, put away the corn we'd had ground, put the mule in the stable, and went back to the house. When I opened the back door, Mama and Doris were cooking some of that country ham, sweet potatoes, biscuits and grits. I ate a good supper, then went into the living room and listened to the radio with Daddy.

Since we got electricity, we didn't have to worry about a battery going dead anymore. Another thing, with electric lights, you could read and get your homework done in any room in the house. Most times, though, me and Doris got our homework done in the kitchen after everybody had finished eating and the kitchen was all clean. It worked out good because Daddy was feeling a lot better and he wanted to listen to the radio in the living room. He was real interested in what was going on over in Europe. Seemed like the war over there had really heated up.

Daddy was feeling better, but not good enough to do some of the things he used to, like repairing shoes. I needed my shoes repaired 'cause the soles were flapping all around. I got the shoe last out but I couldn't get the hang of it, so I punched some holes through the soles and tops of my shoes and wired them together. Only thing was, the twisted wire was sticking out where it showed. It looked a little strange, but it didn't bother me all that much.

♣

Things were going along pretty good in school. I liked being in the seventh grade, and I liked my teacher, Mrs. Brown. She seemed real interested in what she was teaching. She especially liked literature. Sometimes when she read things like *Abou Ben Adhem* or *The Ancient Mariner*, she'd stop reading, lean back in her chair, look up at the ceiling and just roll her eyes back. I wouldn't have hurt her feelings by saying it, but she sure couldn't read like my mama, no way.

One day, Mrs. Brown said she was going to call on everybody in the class to read, and she wanted them to read their parts with feeling. Then she said it looked like somebody in the class could use a clean handkerchief. I knew she was talking about me because my handkerchief was real wet where I'd been blowing my nose a lot. She didn't call my name, but some in the class turned and looked at me. It made me feel bad, because I was sitting there with them wired up shoes and relief clothes on. I thought to myself, when it comes my time to read, I'm just going to show Mrs. Brown a thing or two. And another thing, I bet if she had to sleep where I slept at night, she'd just be blowing her ugly nose in a feed sack! I thought, to heck with her, she don't make me no never mind, no how.

Mrs. Brown started calling on the class to read. She had each one go up and stand in front of the class. When they got through reading, they'd look over at her. She'd just smile and they'd go back to their seats. After a while she called on me.

Mrs. Brown, if it's all the same to you, I'd just as soon stand here and read.

I understand, son. You just go ahead right where you are.

Thank you, Mrs. Brown.

Mrs. Brown leaned back in her chair, crossed her arms and looked straight at me. I stood up, looked real slow-like all around the room and said,

I'll be reading from *The Ancient Mariner.* Then I took the book in both hands and read like I'd heard Mama read that book, Little Azar, to all us cousins.

Every once in a while when I got to a part that had a special feeling, I'd just stop and stare off like I was looking at somebody that wasn't there. When I got through looking, I'd start reading again. I noticed Mrs. Brown had leaned forward and was resting her chin on her hands.

When I finished reading, I gave Mrs. Brown a slight bow and sat down. She just sat there quiet a little while. Then she took her hands out from under her chin, stretched one arm out towards me and said, Now, class, that's what you call reading.

Daddy was beginning to use his left arm pretty good and was driving our old Ford again. It seemed good to see him getting out and walking around the farm. Some nights I'd hear him and Mama making plans about what all we were going to plant come spring. Daddy was back sleeping with Mama in their bedroom. Me and Doris were able to get our homework done in the living room again, and we could listen to the radio if we kept it turned down low.

Next morning, Daddy said he was going to town to see if he could trade our old Ford in on some kind of truck. That sounded good to me. I was getting tired of us having to take the back seat out of that old car every time we needed to haul something. I sure wished I could go with him. I said, Daddy, I was just wondering, seeing as things are pretty well caught up and it's Saturday and all, could I ride into town with you? I sure would like to see Grandma Fowler and Aunt Til. Daddy said he didn't see why not.

I didn't know why Daddy agreed to let me go, but I sure wasn't going to ask any questions. I was just going to get myself ready to go real quick. I told Mama that Daddy said I could go to town with him.

Well, you run and wash up real good, and don't you worry Grandma and Aunt Til.

I ran out to our well, drew a bucket of water and stuck my head right down in it. I washed up real good and combed my hair the best I could. I was still having some trouble with my curly hair, but I wasn't going to worry about it.

Daddy told me to get in the car and sit behind the wheel. There were two little levers on the side of the steering wheel. He said one was for the gas and the other was for the spark. I asked him what he wanted me to do.

Well, R.C., I'm going to try and crank her up. Now just look at me. I'm going to turn the crank. When I turn it down and start back up, I want you to push up on them spark and gas levers a little. If it starts, just push the gas lever a little more.

Daddy, I'm not sure which lever's which.

Just do like I showed you. Now get ready.

I kinda half stood up and looked over the steering wheel. Daddy looked at me, spit on his hands, rubbed them together and put the crank in the slot. When he got it fitted good, he turned it hard, down and up. When the crank started up, I pushed both the levers up a little. Nothing happened. Daddy just shook his head, spit on his hands, and stuck the crank back in again.

I crouched up over the wheel and leaned a little closer to the windshield. The crank went down, and when it started back up, I pushed both levers up just a little more. Nothing happened. I could tell Daddy was getting upset. I thought, I hope he don't get mad enough to throw the crank in the woods. He spit on his hands, stuck the crank in, and tried it again. The old Ford started up. Daddy ran around to the driver's side and threw the crank in the back seat. I scooted over, and he crawled in, got behind the wheel, and moved them levers around a little. The motor started running better.

It wasn't long before we'd done backed out of our yard and was headed down the road towards town. We passed Lester and some other folks we knew. I waved and they waved back. I thought, I just bet they think we are going to the store to get a horse collar or a plow point or something like that, but if they knew how special this trip was, they'd watch us 'til we was clean out of sight.

When we got to town, Daddy put me off in front of Grandma Fowler's house and said, Now R.C., don't you worry your grandma.

I won't, Daddy.

I'm going to look around and see if I can trade this car, but I'll be back to pick you up about four o'clock. You make sure you're ready to go.

I'll be ready.

I looked towards the house and sure enough, Grandma was sitting on the front porch. She was looking towards me all right, but I could tell she didn't know who she was looking at. I stood there a few seconds and started down the walk. When I got pretty close up to the porch, she eased her wheel-chair up a little and put her hand up over the top of her eyes, like she was trying to get a better look. I took a few more steps. She put her hand down and said, R.C., is that you?

Yes, it's me, Grandma.

You just come here right now and give me a big hug.

I walked up on the porch, and she hugged me, patted me on my back, rubbed me across my shoulders, and hugged me some more.

R.C., I sure am glad to see you, son.

I'm real glad to see you too. I've really missed you. I've thought about you a lot.

I've missed you a lot, too, son. I've thought about you just about every day since you've been gone. Now, drag up that rocking chair and we'll just sit here and talk like we used to.

I drug the chair over beside Grandma and sat down.

Grandma, this looks like the same rocking chair I used to sit in.

It is. Now I just wasn't about to get rid of that rocking chair.

I'm glad you kept it. It seems good to be back here rocking on the porch and looking across the street at the company store. I wonder if Mr. Mooney's still got that big candy counter?

I think so, son, but I believe you've been eating something besides candy because you sure have grown.

I've grown some, Grandma. We get plenty to eat and you know Mama's a real good cook.

I know. It seems like she's just a natural-born cook. Son, do you want a mayonnaise sandwich?

Yeah, but I'll fix it. Do you want anything?

No, but you go on and fix whatever you want. Then come on back and we'll talk.

On my way to the kitchen, I passed through the dining room where I used to sit on my blue stool at the long table. I thought, now, last night was Friday night. I just wonder if Jeanette was here and if she'd got any money. I fixed a sandwich, got a glass of milk, and went back out on the porch. It seemed sort of like old times. But there were some changes, like Grandma sitting there in a wheelchair with just one leg. And it seemed quieter. I asked Grandma, Do them young men still gather over at the company store late in the evening like they used to?

Not as much. A lot of them have gone into the service. You know, like the Army, Navy, and Marines. Lots of folks around here think we're going to be in the war before long.

I know. Daddy listens to the news every night, especially since he started getting better and we got an electric radio.

I bet. I heard about y'all getting electricity. I just know you were all happy about that.

We sure were. It beats kerosene lamps. Grandma, I noticed you still got that blue high-stool sitting at the end of the dining room table.

Yes, it's still there, right where you used to sit.

I was just wondering, uh, does Jeanette come over on Friday evenings and sit there and collect money?

She comes over some, but not regular like you did. You just never missed a Friday.

I always got my money on Friday evenings. Sometimes I'd get as much as a dollar and seventy-five cents.

Well, son, she don't get that much because I only got three children left here now, Ralph, Otto and Helen. Robert, he's in the Merchant Marines, and all the rest are married and gone. There's been right many changes since you left.

Things seem different all right. You know, I was just nine when we left here and moved to Pender County. I'll be fourteen in December.

I know. It seems like things are changing real fast here lately. Your grandpa is talking about retiring from the mill and moving back to our farm in Columbus County.

Grandma, I hate to see you leave this house. I've got a lot of good memories here.

I hate it too, son, but Luke hasn't been feeling too good lately and he's just tired of the cotton mill.

I done found out farming is real hard work. You think Grandpa's going to be able to farm?

Oh, no, he won't be able to work on the farm. We'll have to get somebody to sharecrop it for us.

I think I'm going to see Aunt Til a little while.

Now, you make sure you come back and let's talk some more before your daddy gets here.

I will, Grandma.

I walked down the street to Aunt Til's. I wondered what she was going to think when she opened the door and saw me standing there. I just knew she had a big stack of funny papers and books piled up in her attic ready for me to start reading.

I knocked on the door, and pretty soon Aunt Til opened it. She said, Well, bless my soul! R.C., is that you?

Yes, it's me, Aunt Til.

Well now, you just come right on in. I'm so glad to see you.

I'm glad to see you too, Aunt Til.

You know, honey, you sure have grown and you're a good-looking thing. I bet you've heard that before.

You're just teasing, Aunt Til.

No, I'm not. Come on in, honey, and get you a Coca-Cola out of the refrigerator and we'll talk some. Then you can go up in the attic and read if you want. I've saved up a lot of funny papers.

Now, Aunt Til, I just figured you was doing that.

I got me a drink and me and Aunt Til talked a while. She said she'd heard about all them good grades I'd been making and how hard I'd been working. I told her that we'd all been working hard and that so far my grades had been pretty good.

After I talked with Aunt Til a while, I went up to the attic and read some. I knew I couldn't stay too long because I had to be back at Grandma's to meet Daddy by four o'clock, and I wanted to go by the company store before we started back home. When I got ready to leave, Aunt Til gave me a package of funnies all tied up and said, Now take these home and enjoy reading them. I know how you like to read.

Thank you, Aunt Til. I'll take them, but you know Daddy don't like to have funny papers around.

Now, son, you take them home and don't worry. I just might have to have a talk with your daddy.

Okay, Aunt Til. I've got to go now.

Bye, sugar. Now, you just come back to see me soon as you can.

I will.

When I got back to Grandma's, she was still on the front porch. I told her that I went to Aunt Til's all right, and that we talked and I read some funnies up in the attic like I used to.

I just know she was glad to see you.

Yeah, she was. Grandma, I think I'll go across the street to the company store. I want to see Mr. Mooney before Daddy gets back.

Go ahead, son, but don't stay too long. Your daddy'll probably be back shortly.

I went across the street to Mr. Mooney's store. When I walked in, he was busy with a customer. I walked around in the store some and went over to the candy counter. Pretty soon he finished with the customer, came over to where I was, and said, What can I do for you, young man? I turned around and looked at him.

Hey, Mr. Mooney.

Hey, son. You interested in some of that candy?

No, I'm just looking. I came into town with Daddy today and I just thought I'd come by to see you.

Mr. Mooney looked at me real close and said, Is that you, R.C.?

It's me all right.

Well, Lord have mercy, son. It's good to see you. How've you been?

I been doing all right.

Us folks around here sure have missed you. How's your dog doing?

He's doing all right, I guess. But I don't think he likes the country as good as he did the Mill Hill.

I guess dogs get homesick, just like people do.

I guess so. You been getting along all right?

Yeah, pretty good, son. This war business in Europe worries me.

Maybe we won't get in the war.

I don't know, son. It don't look good. How long you going to be in town?

I'll be leaving in just a little while. Daddy's going to pick me up at four o'clock.

Well, you be sure and come by and see me next time you're here.

I told Mr. Mooney I would. Then I went back over to Grandma's and sat with her on the front porch. I told her I'd be leaving in a few minutes and I didn't know when I could come back.

Well now, you come to see me as often as you can.

I will. That looks like Daddy pulling up out front in that truck, or whatever it is.

Daddy got out of the truck and came up to the porch and said, Hey, Ma. How you doing?

I'm okay, Alton. You doing all right?

Yeah, Ma. I just traded my car for this truck.

So I see. I thought maybe you'd get a pickup.

Yeah, I was wanting me a pickup, but I got a better trade on this. It's called a panel truck.

I was wondering what it was called.

R.C., what do you think about the panel truck?

I don't know, Daddy. I was just expecting you'd come back with a pickup, too.

Well, maybe we'll make one out of it later on. Now tell your grandma bye. We got to get on our way.

I hugged Grandma and told her bye. She said, Now, R.C., you come back real soon, you hear?

Me and Daddy got in the panel truck and headed towards home. We got there in time to feed up and do the milking before dark. Mama and Doris had a good supper cooked. While we were eating, I told Mama and my brothers and sisters all about my trip and what a good time I'd had.

After supper I listened to the radio with Daddy. It sounded like the war was going real bad for Britain, with them Germans bombing them everyday like they was. Daddy said he thought we were going to be in the war before long.

I was tired when I went to bed that night. It just seemed like I had to do some thinking about my trip. I'd had a good time all right, but it seemed like things was different from what I remembered.

Next morning at breakfast Mama was saying that her brother Buddy was wanting to come up and stay a while. He wanted to live in that old log cabin that was on his part of the inheritance land. 'Course, now we were buying it. He knew that all right, but he was twenty-one and just felt like getting out on his own. I told Mama, I like Uncle Buddy. I hope he comes real soon.

He's talking about coming in the spring.

Mama, when Uncle Buddy starts living in the log cabin, maybe I can spend some nights with him.

I think that would be a good thing because he might be scared there at night by himself.

Well, I can stay with him nights until I have to start setting up with the tobacco barn.

I just know he'd like that, son.

The next morning I got up early and walked through the kitchen on my way out to do the feeding and milking. Mama was cooking breakfast. I said, Mama, you've sure got some good-smellin' cooking going on in here.

R.C., all cooking smells good to you.

I guess you're right about that, Mama.

Son, you'd better put your coat on before you go outside. It's rainy and cold out there.

I opened the back door. Mama was right. It was a cold, gray, overcast day, and there was a slow rain falling. I put my coat on and went outside. Our back yard was wet and muddy and it seemed like chicken manure was everywhere. I thought, I just believe them chickens do their business in our yard on purpose when it rains.

I could picture in my mind what went on in the chicken coop at night when it started raining. I could just see that old head rooster hopping off the roost, standing in front of all them other chickens and saying, All right, all you chickens, I've got something to say. And the head hen would say, What you got to say, head rooster?

Shut up, head hen. Now, here's the plan, nobody messes in the chicken coop tonight.

Why not, head rooster?

Head hen, I told you to shut up. But being you asked, here's what we do. We all just hold everything until morning. Then we get up early, go up to the human house and drop everything in the back yard. That way R.C. will have to walk through it all to do the feeding and milking. Do y'all understand?

We understand, head rooster.

I did the feeding and milking and then went back inside and ate a good breakfast. I told Mama, Don't look like we're going to do much of anything outside today.

Yeah, I know it's pretty bad outside, but you'll think of something.

Well, I was kind of thinking about climbing up in that old potato bank and doing me some thinking.

R.C., you do some strange things.

I just like to get off by myself sometimes.

Suit yourself, son.

I crawled inside the potato bank, lit the lantern, leaned back against the pile of potatoes, and pulled some of the straw up around me. The lantern didn't give off much light, but it seemed a comfort to have it close by, kind of like a friend. Besides, when my fingers got cold and stiff, I could wrap them around the globe and warm them up. I pulled my knees up and wrapped my arms around them. I had some serious thinking to do.

It'd been almost five years since we'd left the Mill Hill. All that time I'd been wanting to get back to the things I'd left behind, but things weren't the same back there. I'd done found that out. Things were changing all right, but it seemed like I was changing too. My voice was even beginning to sound different. Another thing, I was starting to notice girls more, and I was getting strange urges when I looked at the pretty ones. There was just too many changes to try and figure them all out at one time. I decided I just wasn't going to worry about it for a while. I was just going to lay up in that old potato bank and think about girls.

I laid down on my stomach with my head close to the opening in the potato bank and looked outside. The rain started to sound different, coming down slow and easy-like, making a clinking sound when it hit the straw that was laying outside. I could see the ice beginning to build up already. It seemed almost peaceful.

After a while I crawled out of the potato bank and went into the house. Mama and Daddy were sitting at the kitchen table, talking. Seemed like a Mr. Wiggins, somebody that Daddy and Mama knew, had died. He lived about three miles away on another road. Daddy said that he'd ride over the next morning and see if there was anything we could do.

The next morning Daddy rode over to the Wiggins' place. When he came back he said it looked like they had the arrangements pretty well made, but they was all tore up over Mr. Wiggins' death. It was decided that me and Daddy would represent our family at the funeral the next day. That evening we got the panel truck all cleaned up.

The next day me and Daddy rode over to the Wiggins' place. When we got there, the hearse was pulled up in the yard. Everybody was pretty much gathered in the house and it sounded like they was getting ready to start the funeral. Daddy sat on the running board of the truck but I wanted to see if I could hear anything, so I set on the front porch steps. Pretty soon the preacher started preaching and you could hear people crying. Every once in a while somebody would just scream out. The preacher preached on a while. Then some folks testified about what a good man Mr. Wiggins was.

I looked over to where Daddy was sitting on the running board. He'd done lit another cigarette. He blew some smoke out and looked down at the ground. Then he glanced over at the door where they'd be bringing the coffin out. I thought, I just bet Daddy'd like to get a look behind that door. I wanted to look in there, too.

There was a creaking noise behind me, and I swung around real quick. It was some lady coming out on the porch. I figured she must be coming out to spit. Seemed like most people around where we lived just couldn't do without their snuff. She walked over to the end of the porch, spit real big, wiped her mouth, and turned around and looked at me. I felt like I needed to say something.

Ma'am, we're sure sorry about what happened.

I know, son.

When the lady went back inside, she left the door open a little. I wanted to look in, but I didn't want to be disrespectful. It wasn't long after the lady got back inside before somebody started singing. Then pretty soon somebody else joined in and before long it sounded like they was all singing.

The door was still open. I thought I'd just go up on the porch and look inside. I knew it wouldn't be right to just go prancing up to the door, stand straight up and just look right in, but I wanted to see in there. I walked up on the porch real easy-like. When I got up close, I put my arms behind me, stuck one foot out a little, bent over real respectful-like and looked in.

I saw the coffin over against the side wall under a window. I couldn't see the dead man. I was glad I couldn't. I just didn't like to see or think about no dead people.

Pretty soon they sang another song. It was one I'd heard sung at them cottage prayer meetings. I stood there and listened.

Swing low, sweet chariot
Coming for to carry me home.
I looked over Jordan, and what did I see—
A band of angels coming after me.
Coming for to carry me home.

When the singing was over, some of the men walked over to the coffin and it looked like they were getting ready to bring it out the front door. I jumped off the porch, ran over to where Daddy was sitting on the running board and said, Daddy, I think they're getting ready to bring the coffin out.

Okay, son. Now get over here off to the side, stand still and act real respectful-like.

Daddy, I know how to be respectful.

Yeah, I guess you do.

They brought the coffin out, carried it down the steps, walked over and slid it real slow-like in the back of the hearse. It wasn't long before we got to the clay hill where the cemetery was. It was a small cemetery. It didn't look like there was more than two or three graves. I thought, I'd just hate to be buried in a place where there ain't hardly nobody else buried. The hearse pulled up close to the grave and stopped. The same men that had put the coffin in came around to the back of the hearse, opened the doors, slid the coffin out and sat it down by the open hole. I walked up close to the hole and looked down. My heart felt like it jumped up in my throat.

The preacher came over, talked some, and said a prayer. Then he shook hands with all the family. When he got to the dead man's wife, he took her by the hand, put one arm around her shoulder, leaned over and said something only she could hear. Pretty soon people started drifting back down the road away from the cemetery. Me and Daddy got in the panel truck and drove off towards home.

That night after supper I felt like I just had to do something to keep me from thinking about the funeral. I just couldn't get the thought of that deep, dark hole out of my mind. After me and Doris washed the dishes and put them away, I told Mama, I think I'm going to take a bath tonight. She said, That's good, you could use a good bath.

I got the big washtub, put it on the back porch and heated a pot of water on the wood stove. I drew enough water from the well to fill the tub about half-full. I knew by the time I added the pot of hot water and got in, the water would be almost to the top.

I got a washrag, a towel, and a piece of our homemade soap, eased down into the water and just leaned back in the tub and relaxed. I wet the washrag and put it over my eyes and let it stay a while. When I took it off I saw the moon coming up over the trees in the back of our field and I began to feel better.

I could tell by the sounds coming from the kitchen that Mama and Doris were fixing supper and I could hear the radio playing kind of low. I knew Daddy was sitting there beside the radio table waiting for the news to come on.

Sitting there in the tub and listening to the frogs and crickets made me sleepy. I thought maybe I'd better get out of the tub before I fell asleep. When I stood up, Mama hollered out, R.C., make sure you wash up as far as possible and then wash down as far as possible. And while you're at it, you might as well wash possible.

Oh, Mama.

I'm just teasing.

Well, don't nobody come out here.

Oh, for goodness' sake. Ain't nobody going out there on that back porch.

Mama opened the door and threw me a clean pair of overalls. I put both hands over my private parts. She closed the door real quick.

When I got back inside, I told Mama, I might as well be the one that churns the butter tonight.

You go ahead, son.

I'm just trying to stay busy, Mama.

I know, son. You know, tomorrow's Sunday, and I think what we need is a good chicken dinner.

That sounds real good.

Well, after you get your feeding and milking done in the morning, pick us out two of them fat chickens. You kill them and get them ready, and me and Doris will cook us some good chicken and rice.

Next morning I caught one of our big fat roosters. I was getting ready to wring his neck when Doris came out on the back porch. She said, R.C., let me see if I can do it.

Doris, are you sure?

Yeah, R.C. I've seen you and Daddy wring them chickens' necks a lot of times.

I don't know, Doris. You ain't never killed nothing.

Well, let me try. It don't look like there's anything to it.

All right.

I handed the rooster to Doris. She took him by the neck and swung him around over her head. She was swinging that rooster around and around like a windmill. Now, I thought to myself, poor old rooster. That ain't going to kill him, but he sure is going to be one dizzy bird when she lets him go. Doris flung that poor thing around four or five more times and dropped him on the ground. He got up, shook his head, staggered around some, and started running as hard as he could. Doris watched the rooster run off. Then she looked at me like she just couldn't believe it.

R.C., why didn't he start flopping around and die?

Well now, Doris, it's because you didn't break his neck. You can't kill a chicken flinging him around like no windmill.

I saw you and Daddy do it.

We didn't do it like that. What you do is you take him by the neck and just flip him around with your wrist. That breaks his neck real quick.

Oh.

Doris went back inside. I killed two roosters and put them in a pot of scalding water so I could pluck them easy. Then I lit some paper and singed off the pin feathers and took them in to Mama.

Now, R.C., them's two nice, fat roosters.

Mama, you ought to have seen Doris trying to kill one of them. It was real funny. She flung him around and dropped him on the ground, and he just got up and run.

I bet that was some sight. Doris ain't never killed a chicken.

I know, Mama. I think she just better stick to cooking them.

We had us a good chicken and rice Sunday dinner. Then me and Bobby went to Aunt Ruth's house and played marbles with Sam and James Kenneth. Every once in a while we'd lose one of our marbles in a patch of grass, but we had a special way of finding them. What we'd do was stand where we shot the marble and spit in our left hand. Then we'd take two fingers of our right hand and hit down on the spit real hard. Whichever way the spit went, that's where we'd look.

Sometimes we'd find the marble, sometimes we wouldn't. When everybody that was playing had spit in his hand and hit it and we still couldn't find the marble, we'd call Aunt Ruth and she'd walk around real slow with her head down and her hands behind her back. She hardly ever said anything, but she most always found our marbles. We'd heard about secret weapons when the newsman talked on the radio. Looked like Aunt Ruth was our secret weapon.

Fifteen

School was out and we'd all made our grade. Me and Old Bill were back out in the fields plowing up the land and getting ready for spring planting. 'Course, we'd been plowing in the evenings before school was out and already had a pretty good start on getting the land ready. It looked like we were gonna be ready when it came time to plant all them squash, cucumbers, and beans that we were planning on selling come spring. It was a good thing, because we were going to be tending Aunt Maybelle's farm that year, too.

Daddy was getting along a lot better. He'd even been making trips into Wilmington, looking for a job. One evening, when he got home, he had somebody riding up front with him. Us children all ran to the truck to see who it was. It was Uncle Buddy, Mama's brother. His real name was William, but he liked to be called Buddy.

Hey, Buddy.

Hey, R.C.

Buddy, you going to be staying for a while?

Uncle Buddy had a big chew of tobacco in his jaw. He took a few steps off to the side and spit real big. Then he wiped the back of his hand across his mouth and said, Yeah, I'm planning on staying in the log cabin for a while.

Buddy, there ain't no furniture in the cabin.

I know. I brought some things with me. They're in the back of the truck.

What all you got?

Well, not much. I brought a mattress, a table and two chairs, and some pots and pans.

Buddy, there ain't no lights in the log cabin, but we got some kerosene lamps.

I figured I could use one of y'all's lamps.

Yeah, we don't use them anymore. We got electric lights now.

I heard.

That night we were all sitting around the kitchen table talking while Mama and Doris were cooking. I told Buddy that Mama said I could spend some nights with him in the cabin if he wanted me to. He said he was hoping I would. Mama said the blessings and we all helped ourselves. It seemed like food just tasted better when you had good company.

After supper Daddy went in the living room and turned the radio down low. I told Buddy, When Daddy turns the radio down low like that, you can just bet he's going to start playing on that old guitar. Buddy laughed and said, I heard he can't play all that good.

You heard right, Buddy.

R.C., can you help me get set up in the log cabin tomorrow?

Yeah, I sure can. You going to cook in the fireplace?

Yeah. That's what I was thinking.

Well, I got plenty of firewood cut. We'll just throw some in the cart and take it to the log cabin in the morning.

That sounds good.

Buddy, you want to go out to the well with me?

Yeah, I'll go with you. What you going for?

I got to pull up the milk jar.

Me and Buddy walked outside. The moon was full and the stars were out.

It sure is a pretty night, ain't it, Buddy?

It sure is.

We walked over and looked down in the well.

Hey, Buddy, look at that full moon down in the bottom of the well.

Boy. That sure is pretty, ain't it?

Yeah, it is, Buddy. But wonder who them two faces is down there looking up at us?

Me and Buddy looked at each other and grinned.

I pulled the milk jug up, untied the rope, and told Buddy, This jug's all cream.

It is?

Yeah. You see, every evening we put the day's milking in jugs and let them down in the well on a rope or in a bucket so the milk will stay cool overnight. Next morning, we pull the milk up, dip the cream off the top, and put it in another jar. Then we put the jars back down in the well so they'll stay cool. After about four days, there's enough cream so we can churn it and make butter.

Yeah, I know about that.

Well, Buddy, tonight's churn night.

It is, huh?

Yeah. We can sit out here on the back porch steps and talk while I churn if you want to.

I started churning the butter jar back and forth across my knees. We talked about getting the log cabin ready to bach in. Around where we lived, if a man was old enough to be married but wasn't and he was living by himself, people would say he was baching it. I asked Buddy if he liked being a bachelor.

Well, I like it all right for now, but I've been kind of looking around for a wife.

Have you found anybody?

I got my eyes on this girl.

I just bet you have, Buddy.

Mama stuck her head out the kitchen door and said, R.C., everybody's gone to bed except me and your daddy, and we're getting ready to turn in, too. Buddy, I put a quilt down on the living room floor for you.

Me and Buddy went inside and he got him another cup of coffee. I sat in the chair by our icebox and started back churning. Buddy sat down at the kitchen table with his coffee. When the butter was ready, we got us some leftover biscuits from the warmer over the wood stove and put some of the fresh-made butter in them.

Now, that's good eating, ain't it, Buddy?

You're right about that, R.C. I'm gonna turn in now.

Me too, Buddy.

Next morning, after breakfast, I hauled a load of firewood down to the log cabin. Then I hooked the mule to the plow and stopped by the well. While Old Bill was drinking water from the trough, I filled my half-gallon jar with water and screwed the lid on. Buddy came out on the back porch with a cup of coffee and said, R.C., you getting out kind of early, ain't you?

No, Buddy, I'm out early most every morning. I done took some wood to the log cabin and this evening after work I'll gather us up something to cook tonight.

That sounds good, R.C. I think I'm going back inside and have me another cup of coffee.

Okay, Buddy.

When I got to the field, I stopped long enough to bury my jar of water in the ground. It stayed cooler that way. I tapped Old Bill with the lines and said, Come on boy, we might as well get started, it's going to be a long, hot day.

Me and Old Bill did a good day's work, and that evening when I put him in his stable, I gave him a few extra ears of corn. Then I got a sack and went into our smokehouse. I got some lard, molasses, and cured ham. Then I got some cornmeal and some jars of vegetables and pickles we had canned up. When I went in the house, Mama asked if I was going to spend the night with Buddy in the log cabin.

Yeah, Mama. I got us something to eat in this sack. I'm getting ready to head for the cabin now.

Well now, don't y'all burn that old log cabin down.

Aw, we ain't.

When I got to the cabin, Buddy had the mattress on the floor. The table and chairs were all set up and he was sweeping.

I got a good fire going, and pretty soon we was frying us some cornbread and country ham and boiling up some rice. We set the table, said our blessing, and just dived right into that good supper.

What you think, Buddy?

Man, now this is good eating.

I tell you, Buddy, it's hard to beat cornbread, molasses, country ham and them tomatoes poured over rice.

Ain't no way you can beat it.

After supper we'll just snack on them sweet pickles.

Yeah, man, I like pickles.

After we'd finished eating, we went out and sat on the front steps. I wasn't much of a coffee drinker, but that night seemed kind of special, so I thought I'd just have a cup with Buddy. He took a big swallow of his coffee, looked over at me and said, R.C., do you ever see any bears around here?

Nah, Buddy. I believe I might have heard one a time or two when we was hunting. 'Course, Goldie and Doris said they saw one, one day when they was walking along the road. Then there's this boy named Lester that's always talking about them sinikin bears that lives around here, but I ain't never seen no sign of a bear.

Well, I just don't know what I'd do if I run up with a bear.

Aw, there ain't nothing to be afraid of. I sleep outside at least two months out of the year when I'm setting up at the barn curing all of that old tobacco. There ain't nothing got me yet, and I been sleeping outside every summer for five years now.

You ain't never seen nothing at night?

Oh yeah, I've seen plenty of raccoons and possums, and sometimes a fox, but they ain't never bothered me.

R.C., I've got to take me a leak.

Yeah, me too, Buddy. We don't have to go to that outhouse way out back, we can just go right here in the front yard. Just don't pee over by the well.

Oh, I won't.

Buddy, you know us children's got us a slop jar in our bedroom, but I haven't used it in about three years now. I'm just getting too old to use a slop jar inside like that. Whenever I have to go at night, I just go out in the back yard. When the ground's too cold or muddy, I just pee off the back porch. 'Course, Daddy does the same thing. I hear him get up at night and go out on the front porch.

The dogs came up and I fed them some of our leftovers from supper. Then me and Buddy sat back down on the front porch steps.

It sure is a pretty night, Buddy, with all them stars out and that old moon as full as it can be.

It sure is, R.C.

Buddy, I got to turn in 'cause I got to get going early in the morning.

Well, I'm just going to finish my coffee and then I'll be turning in too.

When I got up to go in the cabin, I heard one of them hoot owls start hooting. Buddy jumped up.

R.C., what was that?

Buddy, that ain't nothing but a hoot owl. Look over there in that old pear tree. You can see him sitting there on that bottom limb. The way that moon's shining behind him, it kinda looks like he's sitting right in front of it. I got to turn in sure enough now, Buddy.

Yeah, I'm going on in now, too.

I called the dogs in and got them settled by the fireplace. Then I laid down on the mattress. Buddy came in and after he closed the door, he kept fiddling with it. I said, Buddy, what you keep messing with the door for?

Well, it don't look like there's no way to lock it.

There ain't no way, Buddy. That old door ain't never had no lock.

Buddy took one of the chairs and propped it up against the door. Then he turned up the kerosene lamp, came over and laid down on the mattress.

Next morning, I got up and fed the dogs the rest of our leftovers, blew out the lamp, and me and the dogs left the cabin. When I got home Mama was putting breakfast on the table.

Well, son, how'd it go last night?

It went all right, Mama. But I don't think Buddy's going to stay in that old log cabin for long.

I don't think so either, son.

Buddy didn't stay the whole week. He said he just thought he'd get on back to town and see if he couldn't get in the horse-trading business. We told Buddy that we was real glad he'd come and stayed with us for a while and that he was always welcome. He said he just might come back again and bach some more. I didn't think he would.

🐾

Sister came to live with us again so she could help out in the fields. We needed all the help we could get because it was time to start gathering all them squash, cucumbers and beans that we'd planted to ship up North. One morning Mama told Doris to stay in the house and cook a good dinner because the rest of us were going out in the fields.

After breakfast, me, Mama, Sister, Bobby and Ann went out to our vegetable patch and started gathering and packing. By nightfall we had our cart loaded down and ready to take to the railroad depot in Burgaw the next morning. That night at supper, we were talking about how pretty all them vegetables were and how we thought we'd get a real good price for 'em.

Next morning after feeding and milking, I ate breakfast, hooked Old Bill up to the cart and started for Burgaw. I'd be there in plenty of time for the agents to check out everything and give me the papers before the train pulled out. Me and Old Bill were making pretty good time. I knew he was glad to get a day off from plowing. Pulling the cart was a lot easier. I could tell he was feeling good because he was walking kinda fast. He had his head stuck out and down, and his ears was just flopping around. He didn't know it, but I had six ears of corn in a bushel tub in the back of the cart. I thought while we was waiting around in Burgaw, I'd just give him a little treat.

When we got to the depot, I pulled the cart up to where the buyers and agents were. They came over, opened our baskets and looked at the vegetables. They took everything off the cart, gave me some papers, and one of them said, Son, you got some mighty pretty vegetables here.

Yeah, I know. When you think we're going to get our money?

It's hard to say. You'll probably be getting a check in the mail in about a week.

Well, I sure hope so. We've worked mighty hard getting all these vegetables growed.

I can imagine, son.

I tied Old Bill to a telephone pole by the railroad track. I'd saved me up a little money from picking strawberries, so I just thought I'd go around the corner to the barbershop and get me a real haircut like I used to get when I lived on the Mill Hill. I liked the way the barber put that cloth around my neck, and the way he talked to me the whole time he was cutting my hair. But I guess the best thing I liked was when he sprayed that good-smelling tonic water on my hair after he was through cutting and all.

I put the tub and corn where Old Bill could help himself and walked around the corner to the barbershop. When I walked in, the man said, Hey, son, what can I do for you?

Well, I just thought I'd get me a haircut.

It looks like you could use one.

That's why I'm here.

Okay, young man, just crawl right up here in the chair.

I got in the barber chair and the man put the cloth around my neck.

Son, how you want it cut?

I don't know. I just want a haircut.

Your hair's going to be kind of hard to cut with all them curls.

My mama don't seem to have no problem with it.

Oh, I can cut it all right. What's your name, son?

My name's R.C. Fowler. I'm the oldest child of Alton and Carrie Fowler. We got a farm about seven miles from here.

Oh yeah? You work on that farm?

You could say that. How much this haircut going to cost me?

Aw, it ain't much. Just fifty cents.

That seems kinda high. Last time I got a haircut in a barbershop, it was just twenty-five cents.

How long ago was that?

It's been a little more than five years.

You want the haircut or not?

Yeah, I want the haircut and I got the money. What's your name, Mr. Barber?

Well now, son, my name's Mr. Porter, and I been cutting hair a long time. Where was it you got that barbershop haircut five years ago?

It was in the cotton mill village in Wilmington, and the barber man was real friendly.

I see.

He started cutting my hair. It seemed real relaxing and I liked looking out the big front window. Maybe somebody that knew me would walk by and see me getting a barbershop haircut. I settled back in the chair and crossed my legs. Mr. Porter said, Now, son, I wish you wouldn't cross your legs. It throws off my haircutting.

Well, sir, like I said, I ain't had me a barbershop haircut in a long time and I just want to sit here and relax, and I relax better with my legs crossed.

It throws me off with my haircutting.

Just do the best you can. I'm keeping my legs crossed.

Boy, you're something else.

You ain't cutting the hair on my legs. I just want a good haircut.

I don't think he liked what I said, because he swung the barber chair around where I couldn't look out the big window anymore.

I heard the train coming. It reminded me of when I used to live on the Mill Hill and heard the train every day. The thought of the circus train came to my mind. I started to feel sleepy. I hoped I wouldn't fall asleep. The barber said, All right, son, keep your head still, looks like you're going to fall asleep on me. You tired or something?

You could say that. You about finished?

Yeah, I'm just about done.

He finished cutting my hair, took the cloth from around my neck and said, Okay, son, that's it. That'll be fifty cents.

Mr. Porter, I thought I was going to get some of that tonic water on my head.

You did?

Yeah. The Mill Hill barber always put some good-smelling tonic water on my hair.

Boy, you want a lot for fifty cents.

Well, fifty cents is a lot of money.

He put the tonic on my hair. I paid him and started for the door. When I opened the door, Mr. Porter said, Hey, son, I kind of like you. Come back to see me, you hear? I said, Well, Mr. Barber Man, I just might. I put my straw hat on and went outside.

I went around to where I'd left Old Bill tied. My heart jumped up in my throat and started pounding real hard. Old Bill and the cart was gone. There was nothing left but the bushel tub on the ground and his bridle and lines hanging on the telephone pole. Now, there I was, standing all alone on Fremont Street in Burgaw, with nothing but a tub and an empty bridle. I just knew Daddy was going to kill me. I was in deep trouble, but I guessed I deserved it, going in that barbershop and smarting off at the barber man like I did. I untied the bridle, picked up the tub and started walking towards home. I figured that train that came by must've scared Old Bill real bad and he just tore loose from the pole and headed for home. I just hoped nobody would see me walking down the street with that tub and bridle, my neck shining from a new haircut and smelling to high heaven from that tonic water. I felt like a fool.

After I'd walked about three blocks, I saw Old Bill and the cart. He was standing still in front of the funeral home. I walked up to him slow-like and talked to him real easy and soft, like Uncle Rudolph had taught me. It looked like he was glad to see me. I knew I was glad to see him. I walked up, patted him on the shoulder, and slipped the bridle on him. Then I put the tub in the cart and crawled up on the seat. I told Old Bill, Let's go home, boy. We done had enough of Burgaw town today.

Old Bill set off at a good walk. I knew he just wanted to get back to his stable and some of that good hay and corn, and I wanted to get home and get my feet under our kitchen table and help myself to some of Mama's good cooking. I tapped Old Bill real lightly with the lines. He stepped it up a little. We got home before dark.

That night at suppertime I told Mama about my trip, about shipping off them squash, cucumbers and beans. I gave her the papers them folks gave me. I told her I didn't know if we'd done right or not, letting all them vegetables get loaded on that train headed up North and not getting any money.

Now, son, just don't you worry about it, we've done all we can do right now. I see you got you a haircut.

Yeah, Mama. I took the fifty cents I'd saved up from picking strawberries and got me a barbershop haircut.

Well, it looks good.

I don't think it looks no better than when you cut my hair.

I don't know, son. It looks mighty good.

Mama, I just felt like I wanted to sit in a barber chair again.

I didn't tell Mama about Old Bill breaking away like he'd done.

&

We were gathering tobacco again. I was having to watch two barns, ours and the one across the branch where Aunt Maybelle used to live. I didn't get much sleep because by the time I got one barn fired up and checked the heat, it was time to walk across the branch and check the other one. I wore my high-top shoes at night so I wouldn't step on one of them rattlesnakes barefooted. Besides the kerosene lantern, I took along a flashlight so I could see better going through the woods. Some nights I'd carry along our twenty-two rifle. I'd learned to shoot it pretty good. It came in handy for snake killin'.

&

It had been about ten days since our vegetables had been shipped up North. I'd walked the mile and a half to our mailbox most every day, hoping we'd got a letter with a check from New York, but every time I pulled the mailbox door open, it was empty. I told Mama, Looks like them Northerners done beat us out of our money.

It's beginning to look that way, son. But we'll check the mail one more day. If we don't hear anything, I'll just write to the address we got on our receipt.

Okay, Mama. Can Jimmy go with me to the mailbox tomorrow? He keeps asking me if he can.

I guess so, son. Just you take real good care of him.

Now, Mama, you know I will. I know he's just four years old, but he wants to walk down the road with me. He'll be all right.

That night, when I was laying out on the barn bench, I got to thinking about my little brother Jimmy. He'd never known anything but the country and our farm. He'd never been able to sit on the porch with Grandma Fowler or go to the company store and check on the candy counter. He'd never even heard the humming of the cotton mill. About all he'd ever heard was them old crickets and frogs. I decided for sure I was going to take Jimmy with me to check the mail.

Next morning, while we were eating breakfast, I told Mama, I'm going to take Jimmy with me to check the mail today.

Just be careful when you go by that house that's got all them bad dogs. You know how mean they are.

Mama, now just you quit worrying. I know all about them dogs. I've done fought them off lots of times. I'm going to look out for Jimmy John. Jimmy didn't have no John in his name, it was just a nickname we'd gave him. He didn't seem to mind.

After breakfast, I told Jimmy, Come on, me and you's going to see if we got any mail. He looked back at Mama. She said, It's all right son, you can go with R.C. Me and Jimmy walked out in the yard and started down the dirt road, both of us barefooted. I had my straw hat on and Jimmy had him a soft cloth hat.

I walked a little ahead, and every once in a while I'd look back to see how he was doing. He didn't seem to be in any hurry—he just kept stopping to stomp his feet in that thick dust that covered the road. It looked like he just wanted to see the dust fly.

Every once in a while I'd holler back and say, Come on Jimmy John, I'll carry you on my back for a while. Then I'd squat down in the road and wait for him. Before long, little Jimmy would catch up to where I was, crawl up on my back, and put his arms around my neck. Then I'd stand up, take his legs up under my arms and we'd set off down the road again.

It wasn't long before we got up close to the bad dogs' house. I told Jimmy, Now, you just hold on tight. We're getting ready to go by the bad dogs.

Can they get me up here, R.C.?

No, ain't no way they can get you up here on my back. Besides, they ain't nothing but mouth anyway. You just watch, Jimmy John. When they come running out here snapping at me, I'll just kick at them a few times. Pretty soon they'll go on back to the house.

Sure enough, just before we got in front of the bad dogs' house, three of them shaggy dogs come running out and started barking and snapping at us. I stood there and kicked at them a few times, then started walking on again. They followed me a little ways. Then they turned around and left us alone. I said, You see, Jimmy, I told you they wasn't nothing but mouth.

I hate them dogs, R.C.

Well, I ain't exactly in love with them.

How much further to the mailbox?

It ain't far.

Pretty soon we got there. I put Jimmy down and opened the box.

Guess what, Jimmy? We done got us a letter in here.

What does it say?

I don't know yet. It's addressed to Mr. and Mrs. Fowler. That means that Mama or Daddy's got to be the one that opens it. But I can tell you one thing, it's from New York, New York.

How comes it says New York two times?

Jimmy, you'll learn all about that in school. You'll be starting school in about two more years, but right now we've got to get on back home. Mama's going to be glad to get this letter.

R.C., can I carry the New York, New York letter?

Yeah, Jimmy, you can carry it.

Jimmy was real proud to be carrying that letter. He walked along beside me and every once in a while he'd raise his arm up to look at the letter, then look at me and grin. I told Jimmy, Now you just hold on to that letter real tight. You're going to be in charge of that letter until we get home. I think Jimmy liked that, because he kept looking at his hand that was holding the letter.

Before we got to the bad dogs' house, I let Jimmy crawl up on my back again. We got by the dogs all right, and after we got past them a little ways, I put Jimmy down and we walked on down the road towards home. When we got there, I told Mama, Well, we got us a letter from New York all right and Jimmy John's got it. He's carried it all the way from the mailbox. Mama said, Well now, ain't that something, we finally heard! Jimmy gave Mama the letter and we all sat down around the kitchen table.

Mama opened it and started reading. All us children were watching, our elbows propped on the table and our heads resting in our hands. When Mama finished reading the letter, she said, Well, children, it's kind of like we thought. They done took all our vegetables, baskets and all, and now they say they couldn't sell them and that we owe them for the freight.

I asked Mama, Are you sure?

Yeah, I'm sure, son.

You know what I think, Mama? I think them New York, New York Yankees can just kiss my skinny Southern ass.

Now, R.C., you just watch how you talk around these children.

I got up and walked out the back door. I thought to myself, To hell with them Yankees from New York, New York.

Summer was over and we had all our tobacco cured and packed down. Us children were sleeping on pallets on the floor again. I was hoping we could pack all our tobacco in Aunt Maybelle's old house, but it took both of them rooms to pack the tobacco that we'd raised on her farm.

It was grading time again and Aunt Lanie had come to help us. We were always glad to see her. It seemed like everything went along real smooth and easy when she was around.

Most everything was the same as the last few years. We'd sit on our front porch grading and tying tobacco all day. It'd get mighty hot there on that old porch, especially in the evenings with the sun shining smack dab on us.

We'd sit there with the sweat running down, and when a log truck, pickup or car came down the road, the dust would come across the yard so thick you could hardly see the sun. Sometimes we'd laugh at how funny we looked, sitting on our front porch covered with dust, especially when the sweat ran down and got mixed with it. It'd look like we hadn't had a bath in a month.

One good thing, though, the Rawleigh Man, the Watkins Man, and the candy man still came by once a week. We were always glad to see them. I couldn't figure out why they kept stopping by because we hardly ever bought anything. Mama said that maybe they just wanted to stop and talk a bit. Anyway, it gave us a little break.

We got the tobacco all sold off and were back in school. I was in the eighth grade. My homeroom teacher was real nice. I especially liked the way she taught algebra. It seemed like she just knew what to say and how to say it to get us to understand them complicated formulas.

When we got home from school in the evenings, Mama always had something for us to do. We didn't mind, though. Mama always said idleness was the devil's workshop. There was just no way Mama was going to let the devil set up his workshop around our place.

Every evening we'd get off the school bus and walk that mile and a half to our house. Just before we'd get home, I'd start sniffing the air to see if I could tell what Mama had cooking. I didn't know how, but I could almost always tell. Most times Mama would be standing on the front porch. When we children turned off the dirt road, I'd wave at Mama and call out, I know exactly what you got cooking.

What you think, son?

Well now, Mama, my nose tells me you done cooked up some of them molasses cookies and, besides that, you got some chicken and rice.

R.C., I declare, you got a nose like a hound dog.

Aw, Mama, it's just your good cooking.

Sounds like you're just looking for a second helping, son.

Well now, that could be. But I just want to ask you one thing.

What's that?

Did that chicken you're cooking get run over by a log truck or did it get killed by the electric fence?

R.C., it sounds like you just might not get one helping tonight, smarting off like that.

You know I'm just teasing, but I just can't see you killing no good laying hen so we can have chicken on a school day. Maybe on a Sunday, but not on a school day.

Now that's enough of that. You younguns get on in here, change your clothes and get on out to work. I got y'all a ham biscuit and a sweet potato ready. That'll last you 'til suppertime.

 Sixteen

It was spring and the year was 1942. We were at war with Japan, Germany, and Italy. Daddy was talking about quitting his job and going to work at Camp Davis in Holly Ridge, a little town about twenty miles from where we lived. They were building a camp there where our service men could get trained to fight.

Everybody in our school that was old enough had already joined some branch of service. The ones that weren't quite old enough were talking about how they were going to join up soon as they could. They all wanted to go overseas and kick some butt. Sam and me had been talking about what we could do. I was fourteen in December and Sam was fifteen in January. We'd figured out it'd be three or four more years before we could join up. 'Course Sam could go before me, him being nearly eleven months older.

Our government had started rationing a lot of things. It didn't make much difference to us 'cause we didn't buy much of what they was rationing anyhow. We grew just about everything we needed. Biggest thing that concerned us was gasoline and tire rationing. Daddy got us a regular pickup truck and built a wooden cover over it so he could haul workers back and forth to defense jobs. That way we were able to get enough stamps for gas and tires. If we got a little low on sugar, we'd dig down in them molasses stands and get some of that molasses sugar.

Uncle Ralph joined the Army, but before he left, he bought me and Bobby each a used bicycle. Bobby's was smaller than mine. We had a lot of fun riding the bicycles all over the farm and up to Aunt Ruth's house. Besides the bicycles, we'd all gotten a little something the past Christmas. I got me a dollar Ingersol pocket watch, like the one Grandpa Fowler had.

I really liked my watch. There was a pocket in my overalls made special for a watch and I kept it there. I took a leather shoestring and tied the watch to my overalls. It fitted just right in my watch pocket. I liked my bicycle a whole lot, but I liked my pocket watch more. I must have pulled that watch out a hundred times a day to see what time it was getting to be.

When the sawmill whistle blew at twelve o'clock, I'd always tell Old Bill to whoa up there. Then I'd pull out my Ingersol watch to see how close the whistle was to being on time. Seemed like it was about always right. If it was off a little, I'd just tell Old Bill that it looked like the sawmill whistle was a little bit off that day. Sometimes in the bed at night, I could hear that old watch ticking away in my overalls that was hanging over the foot of the bed.

❧

It was September and we were grading the last of our tobacco. All we had left to grade was across the branch in Aunt Maybelle's old house. One night after we finished cleaning up the kitchen, me and Doris went in the living room to get our homework. Mama came over to the radio table and told Doris, tomorrow's Saturday, the day the fish man comes by. I'm going to leave a dollar on the kitchen table after breakfast. When that fish man comes, I want you to buy a dollar's worth.

Mama, I ain't never bought no fish before.

There's nothing to it. When the fish man comes by, he always pulls up in our yard and tries to sell us some. All you got to do is just say we want a dollar's worth of fish.

Well, Mama, I guess I can do that.

I know you can, honey.

Mama, I ain't never cooked no fish.

Now, Doris, I know you can do it. You've done got real good at cooking.

Me and Doris finished our homework. There wasn't no big hurry, being the next day was Saturday. We just wanted to get it done and off our minds. That night after we went to bed, I noticed Doris kept tossing and turning, so I asked her, Doris, what's the matter?

I just can't seem to go to sleep.

What you got on your mind?

I just keep thinking about talking to that fish man tomorrow.

Aw, Doris, there ain't nothing to that. You just show him that dollar and tell him that Mama said she wants a dollar's worth of his best fish.

I guess I can do that.

I know you can. Another thing, when that fish man sees that dollar, he's going to be so happy he'll just wrap them fish up real quick. He might even throw in a little ice to boot.

I guess I can do it.

Now, Doris, there ain't no guess to it. What you do is, you walk right up to the fish man like you know what you're doing. Just remember to hold that dollar kind of out in front of you so's he can see it right off.

Okay, R.C., if you think so.

Now, Doris, you just go on to sleep.

Next morning after breakfast, me, Mama, Bobby and Aunt Lanie walked across the branch to start grading and tying what was left of the tobacco. When we got to the old house, Miss Perlie and Miss Flossie Mae were there. We were all thinking that, with that many of us working, we just might get finished with all that grading and tying by the end of the day. We were just tired of messing with that old tobacco.

Me, Mama and Aunt Lanie were grading and Miss Perlie and Miss Flossie Mae were tying. Bobby would bring us the tobacco that was packed down. Then he'd take the tobacco that we'd graded over to Miss Perlie and Miss Flossie Mae so they could tie it.

Everything was going along pretty good. It seemed like Mama and the other women talked more when we were working at Aunt Maybelle's old house. I guess one reason was there was no electricity and we couldn't listen to the radio. I knew Mama missed them silly old radio programs that said about the same thing every day. I didn't care anything about them, but I missed the country music. Every once in a while we'd just get up off that little front porch and walk around in the yard to stretch our legs and shake the sand off of us. Sometimes, whether we were thirsty or not, we'd walk over to the well and draw up a bucket of water. I got up, shook the sand off me, walked out to the well and drew up a bucket of water, then leaned the bucket towards me and started drinking some of the cool water. When I looked over the top of the bucket, I saw Ann coming across the field, headed towards us. I said, Mama, I see Ann coming.

Are you sure, R.C.?

Yeah, she just came out of the little woods road and now she's cutting across the field, headed this way. It looks like she's carrying something in her arms.

What's it look like?

I can't tell yet, but she's holding her arms out front like she's carrying an armful of stove wood.

Mama got up and walked to the end of the porch. She saw Ann coming across the field. Mama hollered out, Come on, *Ann-Darling*. That's what Mama called Ann sometimes. Mama had nicknames for most all us children. She called Jimmy *Jimmy-John* and Bobby *Bob-Tooser*, and she called Doris *Dar-Linda*. Everybody just called me by my initials.

Ann cut across the field and came up to the porch where we was working. Mama said, Ann, aren't you supposed to be helping Doris cook dinner? She said, Yes, ma'am, but Doris told me to bring you this.

She handed Mama what she was carrying in her arms. It was a bundle all wrapped up in newspaper with a piece of writing paper and a pencil tied around it. At the top of the writing paper was a note. Mama read the note and started laughing real hard. It kind of reminded me of how Grandma Fowler used to laugh. I asked Mama, What's so funny?

Mama kept on laughing. I looked at Ann and said, What is it? Ann just shrugged her shoulders and looked away. I asked Mama, For goodness' sake, what is it?

Well, it's them fish that Doris bought from the fish man this morning. She's done sent them to me by Ann with a note.

What does the note say, Mama?

Just a minute and I'll read it.

Mama told Aunt Lanie, Miss Perlie and Miss Flossie Mae to listen to Doris' note. By then we were all looking at Mama. Ann was just standing there waiting for Mama to tell her something. I asked Mama, Are you going to read the note from Doris or not? Mama told me, Keep your shirt on, boy. She put down the package and started to read.

> Dear Mama,
> Please write on this piece of paper how to cook these fish.
> > Signed,
> > Doris

I asked Mama, Was that all the note said? Mama was still laughing. Her stomach had gotten pretty big and was just a-jiggling. It looked like we might have us another brother or sister before long. She had laughed so much there were tears in her eyes. The other women were still laughing, too. I asked Mama, What's so funny? Mama said, Well, son, I just think it's funny Doris sending little Ann over here with a note like that. But what tops it all off is, she's done sent the fish, too.

Mama took the pencil and wrote on the piece of paper, telling Doris how to cook the fish. She tied the note and pencil back around the fish and told Ann, You best be getting along, honey, and don't waste any time. Them fish has got to be cooked right away. You just can't carry fish back and forth over these hot fields. They'll spoil for sure. Now, honey, you get on back to the house as soon as you can.

That little Ann took the package of fish, held it out in front of her like she was carrying a turn of wood, and lit out for home. I watched as she headed back across the field. She was just a-hopping over them old rows where we'd already gathered our corn. Pretty soon she disappeared into the woods down the cart path. I told Mama, That Ann's done took what you said to heart. She's out of sight already.

Mama and the other women were still laughing. I told Mama, Ann was running so fast that her hair and the bottom of her dress was just flouncing up and down. Mama just shook her head and rubbed her stomach.

&

One evening when Daddy got home from work, he said that Grandma and Grandpa Fowler had moved back to their farm in Tabor City and that he had something in the back of the truck. I asked Daddy what it was and he told me to just go see for myself.

I went out to the truck and there in the back was that old davenport that I used to lay on and in a box beside it was the set of encyclopedias. I crawled up in the back of the truck and looked around for the picture of the Titanic. It wasn't there. I asked Daddy, Did Grandma or Grandpa say anything about the picture of the Titanic? He said that Grandpa wanted to take the picture to the farm with him. Seemed like he just couldn't part with it yet.

We put the davenport in our side yard under the black gum tree, and us children took the encyclopedias in the house. That night we stayed up late looking through the books. I hated we didn't get the picture, but I was glad we got what we did.

&

We got all our tobacco sold off and us children were back sleeping in our beds again. School had started back, and things were going along pretty good. Of course, when we got home in the evenings, Mama still had plenty for us to do. One evening when we got home, Mama was gone. Aunt Lanie said that Daddy had to take her to the hospital, but she'd be home in a few days.

When Daddy brought Mama home, she had a little baby boy with her. She said his name was Dennis Alton, but that we were going to call him Denny. All us children thought that our new baby brother was as cute as he could be.

ꙮ

We got a different school bus driver. His name was Henry K. and he lived down the road past our house. We didn't have to walk a mile and a half to catch the bus anymore. It seemed good, that old bus pulling up and stopping right in front of our house. It looked like things were going along all right. We had glass windows, electric lights, and the school bus was stopping right in front of our house.

It looked like I was wrong about things going along all right, though, because a few days later our teacher, Mrs. Brewster, told our class, Now, everybody pay attention. Then she said, I'm going to call out some names, and if I call yours, I want you to come to the front of the room. Mrs. Brewster called out some names, and I was one of them.

After we got to the front of the room, Mrs. Brewster said, Now, children, you all know about that cafeteria they've been working on here at school. Well, it's going to start serving lunch tomorrow, and all you children I've called up here are eligible for free lunch tickets.

I asked Mrs. Brewster, How come it's just us that's eligible for free lunch?

Well, I've been given a list by the county for the ones that are eligible, and you're the ones that's on it.

Mrs. Brewster, I'll tell you what the county can do with that list.

Now, R.C., I know how you feel, but you just better watch what you say.

I'm telling you, I'm not taking any handouts. I don't have to, and I'm not.

Go to your seat, young man.

Mrs. Brewster, I've got to be excused.

Well, go on, but hurry back.

I left the classroom and went downstairs to the new cafeteria, opened the door, walked in and looked around. There were some ladies working. It seemed like they were in a big hurry. One of them asked if she could help me.

I don't know. I just want to ask you something.

What is it, son?

Our teacher says y'all are going to be serving lunch here tomorrow.

That's right.

I was just wondering, are y'all going to be cooking and serving sweet potatoes?

We sure are, son. They're going to be on our menu nearly every day. How come you ask that?

I was wondering if I brought you a bushel of sweet potatoes, how many lunch tickets I could get for it.

I don't know, but I'll ask our supervisor.

Well, ma'am, I'd appreciate it if you would.

I can let you know tomorrow.

I'll bring you a bushel of sweet potatoes in the morning, and maybe you can get me the tickets then.

I don't see why we can't.

I'll bring the potatoes in the morning. Thank you, ma'am.

You're welcome, son.

When I got back to the classroom, Mrs. Brewster asked why I was gone so long.

Well, ma'am, there was complications.

Looked like Mrs. Brewster didn't know what to say. She just told me to hurry up and sit down. I sat down and looked straight ahead. I was thinking about one of Mama's sayings—hold your head up if your tail drags the ground. Well, I held my head up and pretty soon everybody went on about their studying.

Next morning when the school bus came by, I had a bushel of potatoes all bagged up. After my brothers and sisters got on, I put the sack inside the bus. Henry K., our bus driver, asked, What you got there, R.C.?

Well, Henry K., I got a bushel of sweet potatoes. I'm going to take them to the new cafeteria.

Be sure you put them under the seat so nobody'll trip over them.

I will.

I drug the sack down the aisle and pushed it under one of the seats. When we got to the schoolhouse, I put the sack of potatoes over my shoulder and walked around to the cafeteria. The lady I'd talked with the day before was there. She said, I see you brought the sweet potatoes.

Yes, ma'am, I got them.

Well, son, I talked with the supervisor. She told me how many tickets you could get for the bushel of sweet potatoes and I got them right here.

Well, here's the potatoes.

Okay, son. Here's your lunch tickets.

I sure thank you.

You're welcome.

I took the tickets. It looked like there were enough to last me at least a month.

A few days later, we were on the school bus headed for home when our bus driver saw a log truck coming down the road ahead. The dirt road we were on was kind of narrow, so Henry K. pulled over real close to the edge of the road. It looked like that log truck driver was in a real big hurry. He didn't slow down at all.

Our driver got a little too close to the road ditch and the bus slid right over in it. What children were still on the bus were flung up front and over towards the side that was laying in the ditch. Henry K. was real upset. He checked all us children out. Seemed like everybody was okay but me. My ear was bleeding and it felt real funny. Henry K. asked me if I was going to be all right.

I guess so. My ear feels funny, though, and it's bleeding some.

I can see that, but I believe you're going to be all right.

I reckon.

What'd you hit your head on, R.C.?

Henry K., you see that broke window there? My head's what broke it.

Aw yeah, I see it now. How's your ear feel?

Well, it's ringing and it feels like it's beginning to swell up, and when I touch it with my hand, it feels like it's folded over.

It's folded over, all right. I think that's the first time I've ever seen a broke ear. Fact is, I ain't never heard tell of a broke ear.

Well, I ain't never heard of one, either, but it sure feels like I got one.

Henry K. tried to start the bus, but it just wouldn't start. He asked me if I'd go outside and blow in the gas tank.

Yeah, I'll do it.

Now, R.C., just take the gas cap off and blow in the tank hard as you can.

Okay.

I took the gas cap off and blew in the tank. When I took my mouth away from the tank, gas come flying out and went all over me. I had gas on my clothes, up my nose, and all over my face and hair. It scared me real bad. I ran back a little ways and tried to wipe the gas off me. I heard the bus start up, but right then I didn't care if that old bus ever ran again or not.

There I was standing beside that ditch soaked in gasoline and my ear throbbing to high heaven. I could hardly breathe. Henry K. stuck his head out the bus door and said, Okay, R.C., she's running good now. Get in and I'll see if I can get her out.

You go on. I'll get back in after you get the bus out of the ditch.

What's the matter, R.C.?

I'm just going to stand out here a while. My ear's throbbing real bad, and I'm soaked in gasoline.

Henry K. tried to get the bus out. He tried going frontwards, and then he tried going backwards, but that old bus wasn't about to get out of that ditch by itself.

After a little while, another log truck came by and stopped. When the driver heard that it was a log truck that run us in the ditch, he said he'd pull us out. He backed his truck up to our bus. Then he took some of his log chains, tied them around the front bumper of the bus, hooked them on to his truck, and pulled us out.

When we got home I took me a good tub bath on our back porch and got most of the gas smell off me. Then I went inside and Mama doctored my ear up. She shaved the side of my head just over my hurt ear and bandaged it up straight. In a few days it was good as ever.

Daddy was getting along good working on his job at Camp Davis. There had been some talk about a shipyard opening up in Wilmington. Daddy said if it did, he was going to quit his job at Camp Davis and get him a job at the shipyard. He said he thought he could help the war effort more by building ships than driving nails.

With two brothers in the Army and one in the Merchant Marines, I knew that Daddy wanted to do all he could to help win the war. They wouldn't take him in the service because he was getting too old. Besides, he had six children and was working on a defense job and trying to run a farm. I wished

I could do something besides plow them old fields.

&

One evening when Daddy got home from work he said, You know, son, we ain't been coon hunting in a good while.

That's right, Daddy.

Maybe we just ought to go tonight. It's real cold and the moon's shining bright. Why don't you go get Sam and we'll go.

I trotted down to Sam's house. They were just finishing supper.

Hey, Sam. How's everything?

Everything's okay, R.C. What you doing up here after dark?

Well, Sam, Daddy said it's a real good night to go coon hunting, and we were wondering if you'd like to go with us.

Yeah, I'd like to go. I'll ask Daddy.

Uncle Jessie said it was all right. Me and Sam trotted off back to my house. When we got there, Daddy had everything ready to go. I asked him, Where are we going to start hunting?

I just thought we'd start off in that branch in back of our field, work our way down it until it runs into that second branch, then hunt our way down it, pretty far back in them woods.

Me and Sam looked at one another. We'd heard there was sure enough bears down in them woods. We didn't say anything, though, 'cause we'd heard there was lots of coons down along that second branch and back in them deep woods, too.

We weren't all that anxious about hunting in that part of the woods at night, but me and Sam had us a plan. We were planning on saving up all the coonhides we could get. Then we was gonna catch us a ride into town and sell them right off. We'd done found out there was a place on Dock Street in Wilmington that would buy them.

We got the lantern, flashlight, axe, rifle, and a sack, just in case we caught something. Then we called the dogs and started for the woods. We hunted down along the first branch for about an hour and the dogs hadn't picked up a trail. After a while, we got to the second branch. There was a log laying across it, which was a good thing because it was too deep for wading. It wasn't long after we got across that the dogs started barking. It sounded like they had something treed for sure. When we got to where the dogs was, Daddy shined the flashlight up in the tree. Looked like all you could see was eyes. Daddy said, Well, boys, it looks like we're in luck tonight. We let the dogs bark a while. Then Daddy shot the coons out of the tree. There were three of them, full-grown.

Me and Sam put the coons in the sack. Daddy sicked the dogs off again, and while they were hunting we sat around the tree talking about what good luck we was having. All of a sudden the dogs started yelping like they was real scared. While we was wondering what was going on, the dogs run by us headed back the way we come in. It wasn't long before they'd done crossed the branch on that log. While we was wondering what was going on, we heard something crashing through the woods headed our way. Daddy hollered, Grab everything and run, boys! Sam grabbed the sack of dead coons, I grabbed the rifle and the flashlight, and Daddy got the axe and lantern. Right then, we just wanted to get out of them woods as quick as we could.

Me and Sam got across the log and kept on running. We heard a big splash. I turned and shined the flashlight back towards the branch. Daddy had slipped off the log and was in the water up to his waist. In a few seconds he climbed out with the axe, but the lantern was in the bottom of the branch water someplace. Daddy hollered out, Keep on runnin', boys! We all kept running until we got out of the woods and about halfway up in our field. Then we stopped and rested a while.

When we got to our house, we stood around our back yard talking. We was all wondering what it was that chased us out of them woods. We all figured it must have been a bear for sure. The more we talked about it the funnier it seemed, getting chased out of them woods like that and Daddy slipping off that log. Daddy was still soaking wet and he said he was gonna go on in the house and dry off, but first he was going to tell us about one of his hunting trips. I asked Daddy what it was.

Well, I was hunting one night and I slipped off a log that was laying across a deep branch and the lantern sunk to the bottom like it did tonight.

Sam asked, What happened, Uncle Alton?

Well, the next day I went back to get my lantern, and would you believe it was still burning?

Daddy turned and started for the house, but I saw him grinning before he turned around. Me and Sam looked at one another and shook our heads. Then we threw our sack of dead coons in the corncrib. We figured the next day we'd hang them hides on our smokehouse wall. Sam took the flashlight and started off towards home.

When I got in the house, Daddy was all dried off and listening to the news.

Daddy, how's the war going?

Well, it looks like our boys is running them Germans clean out of North Africa.

That sounds good. What they saying now?

Just sit down and listen.

I sat down with Daddy at the radio table and listened for a while. It sounded like a lot of soldiers had died on both sides and the newsman talked like there was a lot of killin' still going on. I was tired and sleepy. I told Daddy I was going to bed. Last thing I heard when I left the living room was the newsman saying, Huge fires were seen burning in the vicinity of El Alamein. I thought, well, at least tonight Daddy knows what vicinity them huge fires are burning in.

# Seventeen

It was spring and the year was 1943. School was out and I was promoted to the eleventh grade. I never did go to tenth grade because our whole class skipped it. In 1943, the Pender County school system decided we'd have twelve grades instead of eleven and go to school nine months out of the year instead of eight. To make things work out, they just had our class go from the ninth to the eleventh grade. I didn't understand why and it didn't make any difference to me. I was just glad I only had two more years to graduation.

Me and Sam were still trading work back and forth. We just liked to work together. It gave us a lot of chances to talk. Most times when we were out plowing, we'd plow real close together. Sometimes we'd be side by side and sometimes we'd plow one behind the other. When the mules got all washed down in sweat, we'd stop under one of the trees in the field and let the mules rest. Then we'd just sit down and lean against the tree and talk.

Most times we'd talk about all them soldiers that had started camping on our piece of land. They were scattered all over the woods. They never bothered us or anything in our fields. We were just glad we had a little piece of land they could do their training on.

One day me and Sam were plowing up some new ground at his place. New ground was ground that hadn't been plowed before. It already had all the trees, stumps and brush cleaned off. I didn't know what got into me and Sam that day, but it just seemed like everything was funny to us.

When we plowed new ground that time of year, every once in a while we'd plow up a snake. Sometimes we'd plow one up and it'd run up one of our britches legs. We'd just holler, Whoa up there, mule, let the plow fall over, kick out our leg and shake the snake out.

When dinnertime came we put the mules up, fed them and started walking towards the house. I asked Sam, What you think got into us this morning?

I don't know.

I just hope Aunt Ruth didn't see us out there acting like dunces.

I hope she didn't either.

Sam, I smell coffee.

Me too.

What you think Aunt Ruth's going to have for dinner?

I don't know.

I'm just about ready to eat anything.

Me too, R.C.

When we got to the house, Aunt Ruth and Goldie were cooking dinner. It was country ham, corn bread, and there was a jar of molasses on the table. The coffee that we'd smelled was coffee beans being cooked in a pan on top of the wood stove. Goldie was setting the table. Aunt Ruth took the roasted coffee beans and put them in a little wooden coffee grinder. Pretty soon they were ready to put in the coffee pot. Then, sure enough, everything got to smelling good.

Me and Sam went to the well and got a bucket of water. It wasn't long before we all sat down to a real good dinner. Goldie said, Sam, what was you and R.C. doing out there plowing that new ground? Looked like y'all were doing a lot of jumping around.

I told Goldie, Well, now, that's kinda hard to explain. It's like this— me and Sam don't know why, but we just thought everything that happened was funny.

You and Sam can do some crazy things sometimes.

246

Now, Goldie, we ain't the ones that's got a little soldier boy coming up to see us every chance he gets.

What you talking about?

Goldie, you know what I'm talking about.

Aw, he's just lonesome and looking for somebody to talk to.

Well, he could talk to me and Sam.

R.C., I don't know about you.

I was just teasing, Goldie. I don't blame your soldier boy. What's his name?

His name is Art, and he's real nice.

I know, Goldie. Like I said, I was just teasing.

It was summer and it seemed extra hot. We'd moved our hog pen down in the edge of the woods to give the hogs some shade. One evening, when I was feeding them, I heard somebody say, Halt, who goes there? I didn't see anybody right off. I thought it might be one of them soldier boys having fun with me, so I just kept on feeding the hogs. I heard it again, so I looked over in the woods where the voice was coming from and said, It's me, who do you think?

I know it's you, R.C., but you're not supposed to say *It's me.*

Well, what am I supposed to say?

You're supposed to give your name, rank and serial number.

Art, is that you?

You're not supposed to ask me that.

Why not?

Because I'm the sentry, and I'm the one who asks the questions.

Now, Art, that don't make no sense. You know it's me who goes here. I go here every day to feed these stinking hogs.

Okay, so your name is R.C. What's your rank?

Now, Art, you know I don't have no rank.

Everybody's got to have a rank.

Well, I guess my rank is plowboy.

What about serial number?

Let me think a minute.

Hurry up.

I can't think of anything.

You've got to have a serial number.

Just put me down as 1-0-F-6.

What's that stand for?

Well, I'm the first of six children. You reckon your Yankee brain can figure that out?

Come on back, R.C., and have a cup of coffee with us.

Me and Art walked on down in the woods to where their camp was set up. Art poured us a cup of coffee and we sat down on a log and started sipping. I told Art, Now this is all right, but it's not as good as Aunt Ruth's.

You're right about that, R.C.

You drank some of Aunt Ruth's coffee?

Yeah, she makes good coffee.

You know, Art, seems like you been hanging around Aunt Ruth's house a lot lately, and I don't think it's because she makes good coffee.

What do you think I've been hanging around there for?

Now, Art, don't play dumb with me. You know you been hanging around Aunt Ruth's house 'cause of Goldie.

I like Goldie a lot.

I think she likes you too, Art.

You do?

Yeah. I don't understand why, but I think she does.

You really think so?

I done told you, didn't I?

Yes, you did, but you can be tricky.

Well, I'm serious now.

You know, R.C., when I get back from the war, me and Goldie might get married.

Well, I hope you get back all right, but I just hate to see my cousin marry a Yankee. If she's going to marry one, though, I guess you'd be the one I'd pick. Art, I got to get on back to the house now.

The next time you come to feed the hogs, come on back and we'll talk some more.

I'll do that.

I got up and started towards home. When I got a little ways through the woods, I hollered back to Art, I sure hope one of them rattlesnakes don't crawl up in your sleeping bag tonight.

I hope not, too.

Well now, Art, you know what to do if one of 'em does, don't you?

What?

You just ask him for his name, rank and serial number.

You're something else.

See ya, Art.

See ya, R.C.

Fall came. We got all our tobacco sold off and started back to school. I was in the eleventh grade. I still liked school. My classmates seemed more like brothers and sisters, except maybe some of them prettiest girls. I didn't think about them like sisters, and they weren't looking at me like I was their brother either.

During recess and lunch, all us big boys would meet behind the gym. Most of the boys smoked and gambled, and there was always a pair of boxing gloves handy. I didn't smoke or gamble, but I boxed some. Sometimes we'd tell jokes and sometimes we'd have a contest to see who could tell the biggest lie. I tried my best, but somehow I couldn't think of lies like some of the boys.

Seemed like Marvin, one of the older boys, could always tell the biggest lie about anything. Most times we'd let him go first. That way, if he told his usual good lie, we'd declare him winner right off.

One day when we was out behind the gym, one of the boys said, Let's see who can tell the biggest lie about cold weather. Right away everybody turned and looked at Marvin. Now Marvin, he kinda grinned and stepped to where he was in the center of us. He put his foot out a little ways and drug his toe across the ground. All the time he was doing that, he was looking down.

That Marvin, he played everything to the hilt. He said, Well now, boys. When he said that, we all stepped towards him a little. Everybody just knew he was going to come up with a good one. Marvin drug his toe back and forth one more time. Then he looked up and said, Well, boys, it wasn't as cold at my house this morning as it usually is, but when I milked the cow, I just squirted the milk across my arm and carried it in like stove wood. Everybody just walked away. He'd done won again, hands down.

&

It looked like Daddy was liking his job at the shipyard because at night when we were sitting around in the living room, he'd draw a lot of diagrams about how the pipes were going to be fitted in the ships. Sometimes he'd get aggravated with the drawing, but when he was finished, he seemed satisfied.

He made pretty good money too. Some of the workers were making as much as a dollar and fifty cents an hour. He wasn't making that much, but he thought if he kept working on the drawings at night, he'd be making that before too long. He was still hauling workers like he did at Camp Davis.

&

It was January 1944. I was sixteen. Us big boys were still meeting behind the gym, and we were still having them lying contests. One day we had a contest about who had the skinniest cows. We all gathered around Marvin. One of the boys said, Marvin, you might as well start off. If it's as good as most of your lies, we'll just declare you winner right off.

Marvin did like he always did. He got right in the middle of us, looked down at the ground and started dragging his toe back and forth. Then he looked up at us and waited a little before he said anything. One of the boys said, Marvin, you going to tell us a good lie about your skinny cows or not?

He drug his toe across the ground one more time, then looked up and said, Well, boys, I hate to tell you, but our cows have done got so skinny, we just tore our cow stalls down. One of the boys, whose name was George, asked Marvin, How come you tore the cow stalls down? Where do they go now to get out of the rain? Marvin stopped dragging his toe, looked up at us boys and said, Well, they done got so skinny that when it rains, they just run and get under the clothesline. We all walked off and left Marvin standing there.

&

Our school had a scrap iron drive on. They told us it would be used to help fight the war. Everybody brought all the scrap iron they could find and put it in a pile in the schoolyard. I gathered up all our old plow points and broke tools I could find and took them to school.

One night when I was laying in bed, I thought about our old truck contraption out there in the woods. We hadn't used it to cut wood in a long time. I decided I'd just break some pieces off that old truck and take them to school.

Next evening, after I got home from school, I went down in the woods where the old truck contraption was, took a sledgehammer and beat off all the pieces I could. I put what I could carry in a sack and took it to where the school bus stopped by our front yard. The next morning when the bus stopped to pick us up, I loaded the scrap iron on.

When we got to school, I took the sack of scrap iron and dumped it on the pile. One of the big boys, George, came up and said, R.C., you might not need to bring any more scrap iron to school.

What you mean, George?

Marvin says he's got a plan to end the war.

How's that?

Well, he says he's got a plan to kill Hitler.

Now, you know that Marvin's the biggest liar in school, bar none.

He says he's serious this time.

I doubt that.

Get your sack and come on back behind the gym. Marvin's there now, waiting to tell us about his plan.

Me and George walked around to the back of the gym. Sure enough, Marvin was there, and there were a bunch of boys waiting to hear what he had to say. Me and George joined them. Somebody said, Okay, Marvin. Tell us about your plan to kill Hitler. Marvin did what he always did. He got in the center of all us boys, looked down and started dragging his toe back and forth.

One of the boys said, Now, Marvin, this is serious business. Quit dragging your foot back and forth like that. If you got a plan, tell us about it.

One of the other boys said, That's right, we ain't got long before the school bell rings.

It looked like Marvin knew us boys wasn't in no mood for his messing. He quit dragging his toe back and forth and said, Well now, boys, here's my plan. Everybody got real quiet. Marvin said, First, I'll get me a way over to Germany.

George asked, Now, how you going to do that? We all looked over at George. He shut up. Marvin started back telling about his plan.

Now, when I get over there, I'm going to find out where Hitler lives and then I'm going to catch me a ride pretty close up to his house.

George started to say something. We all looked at him. He didn't say anything. Somebody said, Okay, Marvin, so now you got you a ride up pretty close to Hitler's house. What's next?

I figure after I get up pretty close to Hitler's house, I'll just walk along that dirt road kinda leaned over-like until I get up real close to his house.

Now, Marvin, you know them Germans can follow your footprints down that road.

George, I've thought about that. What I'll do is walk along the edge of the road where the grass grows. That way I won't leave any footprints.

That sounds okay. What next, Marvin?

When I get right up to Hitler's house, I'll just hide right across the road.

Where you going to hide?

I'll just hide in the ditch 'side the road.

Then what you going to do?

I looked over at George and said, George, if you don't shut up, I'm going to strangle your ass. Now be quiet and let him finish.

R.C., you ought not to talk to me like that. We're distant cousins.

Well, we ain't distant enough. Now let Marvin finish. Hurry up, Marvin, we ain't got all day.

After I get all hid up in the ditch, I'll take out my squirrel rifle that I've kept hid in my overall legs and then I'll settle down for the night.

George started to say something. One of the boys kicked him in the shins.

Marvin went on, Then I'll just sit there real patient-like, and when daybreak comes, I'll prop my squirrel rifle on that ditch bank and wait.

George said, What you going to be waiting for? Nobody said anything to George because by that time we was all wondering what Marvin was going to be waiting for. Marvin went on with his plan.

I'll be waiting for Mr. Hitler to come out on the porch to take his morning piss. And when he does, I'll just shoot his ass.

George said, Is that it, Marvin? Is that the whole plan?

What's wrong with it?

All us boys walked off and left Marvin standing there. George came up beside me and said, R.C., looks like we better keep on bringing that scrap iron, huh?

It sure does, cuz.

&

Spring came and school was out. I'd made my grade. Soon I'd be a senior. It was hard to believe that would be my last year in school. I still liked spring better than any other time, mostly because them dreary winter days were over and everything was beginning to bloom and bud.

It was time to start plowing and planting again, but I didn't mind so much because I liked the smell of fertilizer and newly turned earth, and I liked to pick the wild huckleberries and briarberries. Mama knew just how to cook them with pastry and sweet juices. Another thing, I liked to look for hens' nests. All us children looked for nests in the spring. When we found one, we'd get excited and run tell Mama. Sometimes we'd find a nest with the baby chicks already hatched out. Then we'd really get excited.

Another good thing that happened in the spring was our Easter egg hunt. Mama started having the egg hunt the first Easter we lived in the country. Seemed like every year more people would show up. 'Course, it was only our kinfolk on Mama's side. There was Grandma Harrell, Aunt Lanie, all Mama's brothers and sisters, and all them that were married brought their wives and husbands. And there were nineteen of us first cousins. All the smaller children had a real good time hunting the eggs. We all had fun playing ball, shooting marbles and eating that big Easter dinner.

&

We got us another mule. Her name was Kate. She couldn't hear very good. You had to tap her with the lines when you wanted her to go and pull 'em back a little when you wanted her to stop. She wasn't all the way deaf—she could hear when you whistled.

Bobby had started to plow some. He always plowed Old Kate. Maybe she couldn't hear so good, but she was real gentle. Our Old Bill was still pretty ornery. It really helped out, having an extra mule and plowboy.

We got all our crops planted. It was like all the other years. We'd take off in the middle of the day to eat our dinner, sit out on the front porch, listen to the radio and let the mules rest.

One day when we were sitting on the front porch, I saw a man come riding down the road on a big white mule. When he got in front of our house, he stopped beside our memory rose bush. I went out to where he was and said, Hey, how you doing, mister?

I'm doing all right.

Where you headed?

Son, I ain't headed nowhere in particular, I'm just riding this old mule.

Is that all you do, mister?

It's all I've done for the last year.

You want something to eat?

I could use a good meal.

Well, you just come on in our house. We've got plenty left over from dinner.

The man tied his mule to the black gum tree in our yard and Mama fixed him a big plate. He ate it all, thanked Mama and told her how good it was. Then he said he'd better be getting on his way. I followed him out to where his mule was. He untied the mule, climbed up and started towards the road. When he got out of our yard I ran and caught up with him.

Hey, mister, are you the man that rode the mule around the world?

Not yet, son, but I hope to be.

I stood in the road and watched him and his mule disappear around the curve.

That evening when Daddy got home from the shipyard, he went in the kitchen where Mama and Doris was cooking supper, got a cup of coffee and sat down in his chair at the end of the table. I started telling him about the man on the mule. I asked him if he thought it was the man that he sang about when he sang that song, *I'm The Man That Rode The Mule Around The World.*

I don't think so, son.

Daddy, he said he ain't done nothing but ride that old mule for the last year.

Did he say that?

Yeah, and I asked him if he was the man that rode the mule around the world.

What did he say?

He said, not yet, but he hopes to be.

That can't be the one I sing about.

Why not, Daddy?

Well, the one I sing about already rode his mule around the world.

Oh.

I asked Mama, What you think?

I don't know, son, but we got to be real careful. That man on the mule could've been a German spy.

You think so, Mama?

You never know.

                        🐾

All the soldiers that were training on our land had left. I guess they were overseas fighting. I kinda missed them soldier boys. Goldie hadn't heard from Art in a while. We all hoped he was all right. I wished I could do something to help. I thought I'd just go out and see if I could beat some more scrap iron off our old truck contraption.

We heard on our radio that our boys had landed in Europe. It was called *D-Day.* Looked like before long we were going to get old Hitler hemmed up. I guess Marvin's plan wasn't good enough because he joined the army and was sent to Germany. Looked like he got him a way over there all right.

We weren't too worried about that man that rode the mule by our house. There wasn't much he could report to Germany from what he saw around our place, but there was an old German hermit named Mr. Ludwig that lived about a mile through the woods from our house. One day Mama said that maybe me and Daddy might just ought to pay him a visit and see if we could see anything suspicious.

One Sunday not long after that, me and Daddy walked through the woods until we came to a small patch of cleared land. We looked across the little clearing and saw the hermit's house. It was about the size of Aunt Maybelle's old place. We could see a well, a hog pen, a small garden and some beehives. It looked like the hives were all turned over. Bees were flying all around.

When we got closer to the house, we saw an old man sitting on his front steps with his head in his hands. When we got up real close, the old man looked up and Daddy asked him if he was Mr. Ludwig.

Yeah, I am.

My name's Alton Fowler. Me and my son were walking around today and we just decided to pay you a visit.

Now, that's mighty nice.

How's everything going, Mr. Ludwig?

Well, not too good right now, Mr. Fowler.

What's the matter?

You know I'm way out here in these woods in the middle of nowhere, and these wild varmints give me a hard time.

Yeah, I noticed your beehives were turned over.

That's what I'm talking about. Them bears came last night and turned over my beehives and got most of the honey.

That's a real shame.

It is. I got my garden, chickens and hogs, and I get along pretty good with them. But I usually sell a little honey to get some staples, like flour, salt, pepper, molasses and leather to fix my shoes.

I know what you mean. Can we help you set them beehives back up?

No. I'll just wait until them bees calm down a little. Then I'll set up some smoke around them, and that'll keep them calm enough for me to set the hives back up. I thank you anyway.

Okay. I guess we'll be on our way.

Mr. Fowler, I'm real glad you and your boy come by. It gets mighty lonesome out here. Come back anytime.

We'll be back to see you, Mr. Ludwig.

When we got back home that evening, we told Mama about our trip to Mr. Ludwig's place. She said it sounded like he wasn't no spy, just a good American. Like the rest of us, he was just trying to get by in hard times.

                🐝

Goldie got a letter about Art. He was killed in some battle. She was heartbroken. They had planned on getting married when the war was over. We just all wished that old war was over and done with. It was a sad time.

Eighteen

I got to be good friends with one of them Herring boys that lived about a mile and a half down the road. His name was Benny Frank. Benny had a brother named Bruce. It seemed like Bruce got to where he was hanging around our house a lot and rolling his big eyes towards my sister Doris. It looked like we'd have to keep our eyes on that boy. 'Course, I couldn't blame him because Doris was real pretty with her long blond hair and blue eyes.

I liked Benny Frank, though. He'd been helping me cut wood and work around our place. We'd talked about girls a lot and was talking about catching a ride to Burgaw on Saturday evenings to get a hamburger and a soft drink. Then we was planning on walking up and down the sidewalk and looking at the pretty girls. Maybe we'd even get us a barbershop haircut and go to the movie show. We'd even been talking about staying out late and seeing the owl show. That was the one that didn't let out until midnight.

Daddy must've been making pretty good money at the shipyard because Mama told me and Benny she'd give us two dollars a cord to cut tobacco wood. Now, me and Benny done figured out we could make about two dollars a week apiece. With that kind of money, we decided, for sure come Saturday, we were going to catch us a ride to Burgaw and paint the town.

One evening when me and Benny were cutting wood, I said, Benny, I think I know how we can make us some extra money.

How's that, R.C.?

You know, we still got all them coonhides that we caught last winter nailed up on our smokehouse wall.

What you got on your mind?

I know a place in Wilmington where we can sell them hides and just stick the money right in our pockets.

Yeah?

I done told you, me and Sam's done it before.

Well, let's do it.

I asked Mama if me and Benny could go to town next Saturday and sell our coonhides. She said that we'd been working pretty hard and she didn't see why we couldn't. Next Saturday morning, Benny was down at my house early.

Hey, Benny. Looks like you're ready to go.

Yeah, I'm ready.

I can tell. You done got your hair all slicked down.

It looks like you got something on your hair, too.

Yeah, it's supposed to keep your hair down. It's advertised on the radio.

I don't know what I got on, R.C., but it keeps my hair from flying all around.

It looks good. Come on back to the smokehouse and we'll take them coonhides off the wall.

How many you got?

Well, we got twelve, and the last time I sold coonhides, I got fifty cents apiece for them.

That comes to six dollars.

I know. Seeing as how we're real good friends, what we're going to do is just divide them coonhides up. You get six and I get six.

That sounds all right.

Me and Benny got two sacks and put six coonhides in each one. Then we started walking down our dirt road. We figured we'd be out to the highway in about two hours. We walked along talking and laughing. Mostly we talked about girls. I thought that Benny was girl crazy. 'Course, I liked them too.

It seemed good, me and Benny walking down that old road with nothing to worry about. We was just looking forward to getting into town, selling them coonhides, getting us a hamburger and a Pepsi and going to the movie show.

When we got out to the paved road, we started thumbing for a ride. It wasn't too long before a car came along and stopped. Me and Benny got in the back seat. We put both our sacks of coonhides on the floor in front of us.

There were two men in the car that picked us up. They looked like brothers. They both had red hair and freckles. The one that was driving had a big chew of tobacco. I was sitting behind him and Benny was sitting behind the other man. He wasn't chewing tobacco. The driver asked if we were going all the way into town. I told him we were. He asked what we had in the sacks.

We got coonhides in them.

What's your name, son?

My name's R.C., and my friend's name is Benny.

Well, my name's Rufus and my brother's name is Seth.

Nice to meet you.

Nice to meet you too, boys.

Just then that Mr. Rufus stuck his head out the window and spit real big. Now, the wind must have been blowing just right, because all that tobacco juice hit me square in the face. I looked over at Benny. He saw what happened and started grinning. I wiped the tobacco spit off the best I could. I reached over to roll the window up, but the handle was broke off. I wished I'd brought a handkerchief. I sure hoped Rufus didn't keep spitting out the window like that.

We hadn't been riding very long before Rufus drew his head back and spit again real big. It hit me in the face just like the last time. Benny looked over at me and grinned again. I gave him a hard look. He turned and looked out the window on his side. I asked Benny, How about let's trade places?

No way.

I tell you what, Benny Frank. I'll give you one of my coonhides if you'll trade places with me.

No.

You know, if I give you one of my coonhides, you'll have seven and I'll just have five.

I can add and subtract.

You going to be sorry, Benny.

Maybe.

Now that red-headed Rufus, he drawed back to spit again. I tried to duck, but he got me anyway.

Benny, I'll give you two of my coonhides if you trade with me.

Nothing doing.

We rode on a little ways. I never knew Wilmington was so far away. Now that red-headed, freckle-faced Rufus done spit out another big mouthful of that tobacco juice. Same thing, right in my face. This time Benny didn't even look at me. He was still staring out the window on his side. I said, Hey, Benny. He didn't answer.

I took my foot and slid my sack of coonhides, all six of them, across the floorboard until they touched Benny's foot. That Benny, he didn't even look my way. He just kept staring out that window. I gave my sack of hides a little nudge against Benny's foot. He still didn't look, he took his foot and pushed them right back to me and kept looking out the window on his side.

Benny, you can see the river from my side.

I seen the river before.

In just a little bit we got to the Smith Creek bridge. I thought to myself, Thank goodness, it's only about two more miles to downtown Wilmington.

That Rufus fellow that was driving asked where we wanted to get off. I told him, Right here will be just fine. Now that smart aleck Benny, he asked Rufus if he was going by Dock Street.

Yeah, we're going right by there.

Well, how about letting us off there.

I'll do that.

Benny looked over at me and grinned again. I wanted to kill him. I figured in about another five minutes we'd be out of that piece-of-junk car, and for sure that Rufus idiot couldn't have much spit left. I was wrong, though, because that redheaded, freckle-faced, no-count idiot done drawed his head back and spit again. I leaned away from the window quick as I could. This time it got me on the side of my face and in my ear. Thank goodness, I saw a sign that said Dock Street.

We got out of the car and walked about a half-block to the store that bought coonhides. We told the man that ran the store that we had some coonhides to sell. The man looked at me and asked, What you got all over your face, son?

It's a long story, mister. My friend, Benny, he'll be glad to tell you all about it. Can I use your bathroom?

Yeah, it's straight back.

I went to the back of the store. When I opened the bathroom door, I looked back and saw Benny leaning over the counter, talking to the man. I just knew he was telling him all about how I got that tobacco juice on me. I washed up real good, and when I came out of the bathroom they were both laughing and grinning. It looked like I was going to have to kill Benny for sure.

After we got the money for the coonhides, we went to a cafe and got a hamburger and Pepsi, then walked around the corner to the Bijou theatre.

We bought our tickets, some popcorn and a drink, and got us a seat. The show was just starting. It was a cowboy show. Me and Benny both liked it. I decided not to kill him.

&

We got all our tobacco sold off. School would be starting soon. I'd been picked to drive our school bus that year. I thought I'd like driving the bus. It paid thirteen dollars and fifty cents a month. All us drivers took the test and paid the examiner two dollars. He gave us our driver's licenses, shook our hands and told us we were officially school bus drivers. I asked him what my bus number was going to be.

He looked through some papers and said, Looks like your bus number is five, son.

Just five?

That's right, son. Just five.

I was hoping I'd get a bus with a number like ninety-seven or ninety-nine.

Son, like I said, the bus that's been assigned for your route is number five.

I'd settle for a number like forty-four.

It's number five.

All school bus drivers liked to say old in front of their bus number, like old number ninety-seven, or old number ninety-nine or something like that. It just wasn't going to sound right to say old number five. I guessed if somebody asked me what bus I was driving, I'd just say number five.

All us drivers got in our buses and drove them home. When I pulled up in our yard, my brothers and sisters came running out to see the bus. They looked it over inside and out. All five of us brothers and sisters that was going to school that year liked having the bus parked in our yard.

&

Things were going along good in school. Me and my classmates were looking forward to graduation. There weren't as many of us older boys gathering behind the gym as there used to be. A lot of them were already in the service. Bruce, the one that had been hanging around our house a lot, was in the Army.

It was January 1945. I was seventeen. Me, Sam and Benny had been working together a lot after school. We had a good time talking while we worked. Mostly we talked about girls and what we were going to do when we got off the farm. We talked a lot all right, but we kept on working because Mama kept a check on us.

Daddy was drawing plans for a new house. I didn't know much about house plans, but they looked pretty good. There was going to be an inside bathroom and a fireplace, and there were going to be two rooms upstairs. The new house was going to be across the road and down a ways from where we lived. We'd already cleaned off some land.

Daddy was having some of our timber cut and made into lumber to build the new house. On evenings and Saturdays I was helping him work on the foundation. Some Saturdays I'd quit work about four o'clock so me, Sam and Benny could go to Burgaw. We'd just quit everything, take us a tub bath, put on our best clothes, slick our hair down and start walking towards town.

Sometimes we'd catch a ride, but most times we walked. We were always there before the show started, though. When we got there, we'd get us a hamburger and a soft drink and walk up and down the sidewalks. We were always looking for girls. They were walking up and down the sidewalks too. Sometimes we'd have a whole hour to walk around before the show started.

When we'd see girls coming towards us, we'd start talking to each other like what we were saying was real important. When we'd get alongside the girls, we'd kind of glance over at them. Most times they'd look back at us. If we caught them looking, they'd just turn away, laugh, and put their hands over their mouths. One time I told Sam and Benny, That pretty blonde girl looked right at me.

Benny said, Did she really?

Yeah, I'm telling you, and I looked right into her big, blue eyes.

What'd she do?

She just kinda smiled. I started to wink at her.

Well, why didn't you?

I wish I had. I wonder what her name is?

Sam said, One of them girls looked at me too.

I told Sam that didn't surprise me none. We went to the show. It was a western movie and the cowboy star could sing, play the guitar, and yodel real good. We liked the show all right, but we was mostly looking around for girls.

After the first show was over, we got us another hamburger and a drink and walked down the sidewalks some more. Then we went back to see the late show. It was over about midnight and we started walking towards home. There were just a few people on the sidewalks, mostly country boys like us.

We were all getting pretty tired, but we still had to walk the seven miles home. It seemed like when us boys got together, we could just do some crazy things. When we got in front of the funeral home at the end of Fremont Street, we all started hollering and running. We ran for about three blocks. By then, we were at the town limits. We all stopped, rested a while, then started walking back down that dark dusty road towards home. We still had about another six miles to go. There wasn't much talking going on by then, but every once in a while one of us would let out a country holler. I just wished I was home. I knew Mama would have the porch light on. I knew when I walked up on our porch and grabbed ahold of that doorknob, she'd say, R.C., is that you? and I'd say, Yeah, Mama, it's me. Then I'd go in, get in my bed, and just be glad I was home.

It was spring and me and Bobby were breaking up the land for planting. It seemed good, me and Bobby plowing together. We got twice as much done in a day as I did when I was plowing by myself. It was a good thing, because we were tending nearly twenty acres of tobacco. We helped Uncle Jessie plow his farm that year because Sam was in the Army. He'd been sent overseas somewhere. We missed him a lot.

Daddy bought a horse named Nell. She was brown with white on her head and feet. Sometimes Daddy would plow with her. When we had both mules and the horse plowing, we really got a lot of work done.

Nell was big and pretty all right, but she was real nervous. She didn't like any strange or sudden noises. One evening after school me and Benny were going to rake some hay at our place. I hooked Nell up to the hay rake, and Benny asked if he could sit up on the hay rake seat.

Benny, have you ever rode on a hay rake before?

Oh yeah, I've raked hay before.

Are you sure?

Yeah, I'm sure.

Okay. I'll hold the bridle while you climb up on the seat.

Benny climbed up and took hold of the plow lines.

You all set, Benny?

I'm set.

Now, Benny, you know old Nell here, she's real nervous and sometimes when she hears a strange noise, she'll just jump and take off in a dead run.

I can handle her all right.

Think so, huh?

Yeah, let her go.

We were up kinda close to our back porch. The porch didn't have any roof, just a floor and a pair of steps. I told Benny, Be careful and don't run into the porch when you start off.

I ain't going to run into the porch. Now let her go.

I let go of the bridle. Benny tapped Nell with the lines and said, Giddy-up. She took a few steps and that old hay rake started moving and making a loud clanking noise. Old Nell got scared, snorted, jumped around real crazy-like and took off in a dead run.

Benny looked like he was scared to death. He was pulling back on the lines, but that crazy horse wasn't paying him no mind. She ran straight towards where I was standing. I jumped out of the way and one of the wheels on the hay rake ran across the corner of the porch. When it did, the wheel went way up off the ground. I saw Benny fly off the seat and go sailing through the air.

Nell turned away from the porch real quick, and Benny landed face-down in the mud right in front of the hay rake. The wheel that was in the air came down and hit Benny on his tailbone and slid all the way up to his head. That crazy old horse ran towards the stable, and the wheel that had slid up Benny's back got caught around our clothesline post. That flung her around and in a ditch that ran between our house and the stables.

I didn't know what to do. There was Benny laying face-down in the mud and our horse standing in the ditch with the hay rake wrapped around our clothesline post. I ran to Benny and turned him over. His face was covered with mud and he was groaning and rubbing his back with his hand. Just then Doris came out the kitchen door and hollered, What on earth's happened?

Doris, that crazy horse got scared when the hay rake started moving and just went wild.

What in the world you gonna do?

I don't know. Right now I've got to get Benny out of this mud.

I got Benny up and helped him over to the back porch steps.

Benny, you all right?

I don't know.

Well, just sit here. I'll get some water and you can wash off.

Okay.

I helped Benny clean up a little and told him to just sit there until I got the horse put up. I told Doris to stay with him until I got back. Then I unhooked Nell from the hay rake, got her out of the ditch and put her in the stable. When I got back, I told Doris, I'm going to use Daddy's truck and take Benny to the doctor in Burgaw.

R.C., I don't know what Daddy'll say about that. Him and Mama rode into town with one of the neighbors.

Doris, I'm taking Benny to the doctor. I'll just have to talk to Daddy about it later.

I helped Benny in the truck and we started out for Burgaw. When we got to the doctor's office, he examined Benny real good. The doctor said he wasn't hurt, only shook up and his back was skinned up some. He painted Benny's back with some red medicine and told him he was going to be all right. When we got out of the doctor's office, I asked Benny if he was feeling better.

Yeah, I think so.

Benny, you want to go to the picture show?

Yeah.

Well, after what you been through, I think you deserve a little fun.

Yeah.

Me and Benny went to the show. It looked like he was going to be all right because he really liked the show. When it was over, we went outside and the first thing I saw was my school bus going by. I told Benny, There's my bus. I wonder what in the world's going on.

I don't know, R.C., but it looks like your daddy's driving.

Yeah, it does, and it looks like your daddy's in there with him.

It sure does.

I got to find out what they're doing driving my bus around like that.

I could get in a lot of trouble.

Well, from the look on their faces, we just might be in trouble already.

I walked out to the street and waved Daddy down. He stopped the bus and opened the door. I got in and asked him what he was doing driving my bus. Daddy was real upset. He said, Now, what the hell do you think I'm doing here?

I don't know.

Well, when me and your mama got home we saw the hay rake tore all to hell and the younguns said that Benny had got hurt.

He did, Daddy, so I took our truck and brought him out here to see the doctor.

Well you been gone long enough to see ten doctors. What you been doing?

We ain't done nothing but go to the show after we got out of the doctor's office.

Now that was a stupid thing to do. Your mama is worried to death.

We was just getting ready to leave.

Well, you get on home and I mean now!

Daddy, I took Benny to the show because he was all shook up and nervous. We ain't hurt nothing, and Benny's feeling better. Here's the keys to your truck. I'm driving my bus back home.

You talking mighty big, ain't you, boy?

I'm just saying I'm in charge of the school bus and that's your truck parked over there.

Daddy gave me a hard look, took the keys and got out of the bus. Then him and Benny's daddy went over to the truck. Me and Benny got in the bus and I took him home. When I got home Daddy had calmed down. I told Mama what all happened. She said maybe I'd done wrong going to the picture show like that, but the main thing was that Benny was all right. I thought she was sure enough right about that, because Benny was a good friend. I was just glad it was all over.

❧

It was April thirteenth. We heard on our radio the night before that President Roosevelt had died. Everybody in our house that was old enough to understand had tears in their eyes. It seemed like a member of our family had died. I plowed our mule, Old Bill, in Uncle Jessie's tobacco patch that day. I couldn't get it out of my mind about our president dying. Tears eased down my face. I thought, well, I guess I can cry if I feel like it. Besides, nobody can see me way out here in the back of this old field.

❧

Aunt Ruth got a letter from Sam. He was in a town in Northern Italy called Trieste. I wondered if he knew I was helping with the plowing on his homeplace.

Nineteen

There was a real pretty girl that started going to our school. She'd come up from Wilmington to spend the school year with some of her relatives. She was two grades behind me. I'd never seen such a pretty girl. One of her relatives, Danny, was in my class at school and was one of my best friends. I talked to him about her a lot. She rode the school bus I drove. When she got on the bus we'd look at one another and smile. Her name was Cassie.

I'd been talking to Cassie some and found out she went to church and Sunday school at Long Creek Baptist Church. I told her I'd been thinking about going to Sunday school and church there myself. I thought she liked me, but she didn't hang around me at recess and lunch as much as some of the other girls did.

I bought a sport coat with some of the money I got from driving the school bus. Some of the girls would get my coat out of the cloakroom at lunch and recess and wear it around the schoolyard. Everybody knew when a girl wore your coat it was because she liked you. I liked all the girls that wore my coat, but I wished that Cassie would wear it.

One Sunday I rode Old Nell all the way to Long Creek Church. It was about a six-mile ride when I took the shortcuts through the woods. I had to be careful riding Old Nell, because if she saw or heard anything that looked or sounded strange, she'd rear up or stop dead in her tracks. When she did, I'd just go sailing through the air. When she threw me off like that, I'd usually land on my feet, crawl back up, and ride on.

When I got to the church, I tied Old Nell to a tree in the churchyard, went inside, and walked down the aisle looking for Cassie. When I found her, she was sitting beside her little brother Arnie. He looked like he might have been about seven years old. I was hoping she'd be by herself. I sat down between her and Arnie. She looked at me and smiled.

Pretty soon the preacher started preaching. I couldn't get my mind on what he was saying. I knew it was wrong, and I hoped I didn't go to hell over it, but I hadn't come to hear the preacher. I'd come to sit by Cassie and I hoped I could walk her home. She was acting like she was listening to what the preacher said, but every once in a while she'd give me a smile. I wanted to reach over and hold her hand, but I didn't.

Her brother, Arnie, got up as close to me as he could. I was hoping Cassie would slide over closer to me. It seemed like things was kinda mixed up. After church was over, I told her I'd like to walk her home. She said it'd be okay. She liked horses and thought Old Nell was real pretty. I left Nell tied to a tree. Then me, Cassie and Arnie started walking towards her house. It was about a mile and a half away. I walked along close to her. I was hoping we could hold hands, but that little Arnie kept running up and asking questions.

I thought to myself, now, here I've rode that old horse six miles down them dirt roads and through the woods hoping I could have some time alone with Cassie, but that Arnie is following us every step we take. I decided I'd just reach over, hold her hand, and see what happened. I took hold of her hand and she just looked over at me and smiled. I never knew it would feel so good to hold a girl's hand. I just wished that Arnie would run on ahead or something, but he didn't.

When we got to the house where Cassie was staying, my friend Danny came out to meet us and said, Hey, R.C.

Hey, Danny. How're you doing?

Okay. What you doing over this way?

Now, Danny, you know what I'm doing over here.

I know. I was just teasing.

Cassie thanked me for walking her home and went in the house. But Arnie, he kept hanging right around me. I didn't know what that boy saw in me. I wished his sister would hang around me like that. I told Danny I had to go because I had our horse tied up at the church and I'd better get back before she broke loose or something.

&

School would be out soon. We were going to have a father-and-son banquet. That was where your father came to school and you and him sat beside each other. All your classmates got to meet him, and he got to meet them and their fathers. The banquet was for all us members of Future Farmers of America, called FFA. Just about all us boys belonged to FFA. It was sponsored by our agriculture class.

The ones in charge of the banquet set up a long row of tables in the gym and set the tables up real nice-like. They had places set for all us boys, and places were set beside each of us for our fathers. I told Daddy, We're going to have our father-and-son banquet on Friday night.

What's that, R.C.?

It's a nice dinner for all the boys in the FFA and their fathers.

Why're they doing that?

They have it every year so all the fathers can meet each other and our classmates. I was hoping you'd come because this is my last year in school. I'll be graduating soon.

We had our banquet, but Daddy was busy and couldn't come. I had a good time, but I felt bad because the seat beside me was empty. The school folks were nice enough to set a place anyway, just in case he showed up.

&

I graduated in the upper third of my class and got a certificate for being a good bus driver. Grandma Harrell sent me a wrist bracelet with my name on it. I thought that was mighty nice of her. I knew I was going to miss my classmates. I told everybody good-bye. It was kind of a sad time. Some of the girls cried. I hated to leave that graduation day. I knew that I'd probably never see some of them again.

I thought that maybe after I graduated I'd get me a job in town and do something besides follow behind an old plow. It'd been eight years since we moved to Pender County. I was nine then. I was seventeen when I graduated. I hated to leave all my brothers and sisters and Mama and Daddy, but I felt like I just had to get off the farm and see what else was out there in the world.

I got letters from several different colleges that wanted me to enroll. I wished I could, but I didn't have the money. I'd already found out that if you were going to get anything in this world, it was going to take money. I didn't have any money, but I was sure going to try to change that. I told Mama now that I'd finished high school, I was planning on leaving home and going out on my own. She said, Son, come sit down at the kitchen table. I want to talk with you. We sat down on the long benches at the kitchen table, me on one side and Mama on the other. She had that serious look on her face that she got sometimes.

What you want to talk about, Mama?

Well now, son, I know you've finished high school, but me and your daddy was hoping you'd stay on until fall.

Mama, I had my heart set on going back to town and getting me a job.

I know, but your daddy's trying to get the new house built, and we've got twenty acres of tobacco this year. If you could stay until fall, it would really help out.

I don't know. I really wanted to leave the farm.

Well, here's what me and your daddy was thinking. If you stay on until fall, we'll let you have all the profit off an acre of tobacco.

Let me think about it, Mama.

That night I lay in bed trying to decide what to do. Something was pulling at me to get off the farm, and something told me to stay on and help Daddy with the new house and the crops. I knew when Daddy got the new house finished, it'd have an inside bathroom, a fireplace and a refrigerator. I thought my family deserved that. We'd all worked hard ever since we'd been big enough to work. 'Course, I knew they'd get it someday, whether I stayed or not. That night while I was laying in bed I thought about it and decided to stay on until fall. I looked at the moon through the hole in the wall and thought, well now, old moon, I guess me and you will just be staring at one another a while longer.

Next morning I told Mama I'd stay on until all the crops were in and the tobacco was sold off in the fall. She said, Son, I think that's the right thing to do. That way you'll have some money to help you get started.

I think it's the right thing too, but I'll be leaving in the fall. I just want to get out on my own.

It's been decided then, huh?

Yeah, Mama, it's been decided.

It felt kind of strange, me saying something had been decided. Up until then, it was always somebody else that told me when something was decided.

&

Me and Benny were still making about two dollars a week apiece with the wood cutting. I missed the thirteen dollars and fifty cents a month I was getting for driving the school bus. I got me an evening job with Mr. Ballard. He had a portable sawmill set up down in the woods about a half-mile from our house.

I just worked in the evenings after everybody knocked off. I got two dollars a week to shovel sawdust that had built up under the shed during the day. It wasn't hard work, and the extra money came in handy. Me and Benny had enough money to go to Burgaw on Saturday nights. We were still good friends.

&

The war in Europe was over. Everybody was real happy about that, but we still had to finish off them Japanese. It looked like it wouldn't be too long before we got them whipped too. We'd just be glad when it was all over. We'd done lost enough of our boys. Sam was still over in Trieste, Italy, and Bruce was still in Germany. We hoped they'd be coming home soon.

&

One Saturday evening me and Benny caught us a ride to Burgaw. When we got there we did like we always did. We got us something to eat and drink, walked the sidewalks and looked at the pretty girls. That night we stopped by the barbershop and looked in. I said, Hey, Mr. Porter, how's everything going?

Hey, boys. Everything's going all right. What can we do for you this evening?

Nothing, Mr. Porter. We just thought we'd stop by and say hello.

Well now, you boys stop by anytime.

We'll be back, Mr. Porter.

I told Benny, I like getting a barbershop haircut.

Me too.

You know, Benny, it seems like whoever's in that barber's chair just sits back like he ain't got a care in the world.

Yeah, and it seems like whoever's looking at him is thinking he ain't never done no hard work.

I know. It looks like he's being taken care of hand and foot.

It sure does.

Another thing, Benny, I just like the smell of the barbershop. You know, that tonic water and all.

Yeah, it does smell good.

Benny, you like Mr. Porter?

He's all right.

Well, I like him all right now. But the first time he cut my hair, we had a little misunderstanding.

What was that, R.C.?

It's a long story. I'll tell you sometime.

Me and Benny went to the show. We liked it all right, but mostly we were looking around for girls. When the show was over, we started walking the sidewalks again. We walked by the drugstore, but didn't go in because we didn't know what to order. We could see people sitting around tables laughing and talking like they was having a lot of fun.

I'd heard some boys say they'd order a shake or a malt when they went to the drugstore. Well, I didn't know what the difference was, and I just wasn't going to go in no drugstore and make a fool of myself. We'd been doing all right stopping by the cafe and ordering a hamburger and a Pepsi. We just walked by the drugstore like we didn't want to go in there anyway.

We went to the owl show and when it was over, we decided to take the long way home. There were some other boys that were going to be walking that way. Besides, the first five miles was a paved highway with houses along the way. Me and Benny walked along with the other boys. We didn't know them—they went to school in Burgaw. We got along all right, but we were glad when it was time for us to go our own way.

Me and Benny decided to take a shortcut off the highway. The shortcut was the old Mosey Road that ran through the woods. When we got to the turnoff, we told the other boys we'd see them later. Me and Benny started down that lonely, dark road. I said, Benny, you know there ain't hardly nobody lives on this road.

I know, R.C. After the first half-mile, don't nobody live on it. Then there's a mile and a half of nothing but woods until we come out on the road that goes by our houses.

I know, Benny. Are you scared?

No. Are you?

Naw.

Me and Benny talked some while we walked, but not as much as usual. The second house we got to was the old Mosey Road house. It was where I had accepted Jesus Christ as my Savior when I was twelve years old, during one of them cottage prayer meetings. I still felt like I was in the fold, as Aunt Maybelle would say. I sure hoped so. I didn't hardly see how, though, the way I still cussed every now and then. Aunt Maybelle always said that we'd all sinned and come short of the glory of God, but we just had to keep asking for forgiveness.

Benny, we got one more house to go by. Then there's nothing but woods until we get to the road that goes by our houses.

I know, R.C., but the moon is shining bright. I think if there's one of them big rattlesnakes across our path, we can see him all right.

Yeah, I think so, too. I think I can just about smell a rattlesnake.

I don't doubt it.

Benny, you know that job I got in the evenings at Mr. Ballard's sawmill?

Yeah.

Well, I always take an axe with me when I walk down that old tram road going towards his mill. I've done killed me a bunch of rattlers crossing that road.

That don't surprise me none. This is rattlesnake country.

Me and Benny talked about girls some, but not as much as usual. We kept looking off to the side of the road. It seemed like it was a lot more narrow than it used to be. Some of the tree limbs came clean across the road, but there was still some moonlight that hit the ground in front of us.

We had about another half-mile to go before we got to our road. It seemed like every once in a while we'd hear something by the edge of the road. We started walking a little faster.

Benny, do you hear anything?

I ain't sure, R.C., but it seems like I heard a rustling in them bushes back there.

Me too.

Me and Benny stepped it up a little and we weren't talking anymore. I was looking on my side of the road, and Benny was looking on his. We were walking real fast. If we'd went any faster, we'd have been running.

Just then, something came crashing through the bushes. It sounded like a tree was falling. Me and Benny took off running as fast as we could. We knew we still had a half- mile to go before we got out of them woods. I didn't know what Benny was thinking, but I thought for sure a bear must be after us. We kept running. The limbs and briars were tearing at us, but we weren't paying no mind. I was breathing real hard, and I could hear Benny panting too.

Everybody said I could run like a deer, but that Benny was staying right along beside me. After a while, we came out of the woods onto our road. Me and Benny stopped running and just leaned over and put our hands on our knees. Our chests were heaving real hard. It was a few minutes before we could say anything. After a while, I raised my head up and looked over at Benny.

What the hell you think that was?

Benny didn't even look up. He just shook his head and said, Damned if I know.

We stayed leaned over with our hands on our knees a little longer. After a while we straightened up some and were breathing easier.

Benny, I just wonder what that was come crashing through them woods like that?

I don't know, but I ain't going to be walking down that Mosey Road no more at night.

Me either. You know that might have been one of them sinikin bears that Lester keeps talking about.

I think it was some kinda bear for sure.

Well anyway, we threw something at him.

We did?

Yeah.

What'd we throw, R.C.?

We just threw ass in his face.

Me and Benny both got tickled and laughed about that. Then we each picked up a clod of dirt and threw it down that dark Mosey Road.

Benny, I guess I'd better be getting on home.

I'll walk with you a little ways.

Your house is a quarter-mile the other way.

I know, R.C., but you've got more than a mile to go. I'll keep you company a little ways.

You can if you want to, but I'm going to be all right. If one of them bears or anything else comes out on the dirt road, I can see him in this moonlight.

I'll walk a little ways with you anyway.

Benny walked along with me a little while. Then he said he was going to turn around and head on back to his house. I told him I'd see him later. I still had a mile to go. I thought to myself, I must be crazy walking along this country road at night, it must be two o'clock in the morning. I started singing some country songs that I'd been hearing on the radio. I liked listening to the Grand Ole Opry. I hoped someday I could go to Nashville.

There were two houses along that stretch of road. Aunt Ruth's was one of them and an old man and woman lived in the other one. I didn't want to disturb them that time of night, so I just didn't sing when I got close by their houses. After I got past Aunt Ruth's a little ways, I could see our house. Mama had the porch light on. Our house was small, but right then it looked real good. I knew my family was sound asleep, except maybe Mama. She never slept much until I got home. I walked up on the porch and turned the doorknob.

Is that you, R.C.?

Yeah, it's me.

Well, come on in, son, and cut the porch light off.

Okay, Mama.

Author at 16-17 years of age

Twenty

It was the end of August and the Japanese had surrendered. It looked like the war was over for sure. Bruce had come home, but Sam was still over in Trieste. We'd gotten all our crops in and the tobacco sold. We made pretty good that year. I made a three hundred fifty dollar profit on my acre. Mama was right, I had some money to help me get started on my own. I thought I'd put most of it in a bank. I told Mama I was ready to go to town and get me a job.

I know, son. I'd like for you to get a job inside. I think you'd do good working in some office.

I don't know. I've never worked inside.

Well, see if you can get on with the Atlantic Coast Line Railroad.

All right, Mama, I'll try there first.

Your daddy's going to town in the morning. You can ride with him.

That night I lay in bed with my hands behind my head thinking about the next day. I didn't know how I was going to make out in town. I was just going to do the best I could. I knew I was going to miss our little bedroom. There were six of us children that slept there. It was a little crowded with two beds and two small dressers, one for us boys and one for my sisters. We still had the slop jar over in the corner and that stovepipe hole over us boys' bed.

The next morning at breakfast, Mama said Daddy was going to be leaving for Wilmington in a little while and if I was going with him, I'd better get ready.

Mama, I've about got all my things packed in the suitcase except what I'm going to be wearing.

What you going to wear, son?

I thought I'd wear me a pair of dress pants, my best shirt and my sport coat.

Well, that'll look good, honey. You go on, wash up and get ready.

I washed up real good, got dressed and told Mama I was ready to go. She said, Come here, son. I've got something for you.

I bet you got my money, Mama.

Yeah, but I got something else.

What?

You just come over here and pull up your shirt.

I didn't know what Mama had in mind. She used to make me pull up my shirt when she was going to switch me across my back. 'Course them little switches she used didn't ever hurt that much. I pulled up my shirt and Mama put a wide cloth belt around my waist and tied it in the back.

Mama, what's that?

It's a money belt.

What's it for?

We're going to put your money in it.

Why? I've got a billfold.

If somebody picks your pocket or tries to rob you, they won't get your money because it'll be hid in this money belt.

I didn't know there was such a thing.

Well, son, there's a lot of things out there where you're going that you don't know about. You just always be careful and remember what you been taught.

I will, Mama.

Come here, son, and let me hug you.

Aw, Mama.

Don't you *aw Mama* me, boy.

Mama gave me a big hug and told me to go get in the truck. Daddy was ready to go.

Before I got in the truck, I turned around and looked at Mama and my brothers and sisters standing on the porch. My baby brother Denny, who wasn't quite three, was standing beside Mama, holding on to her leg. Mama motioned for me to go on. I put my suitcase in the back of the pickup and got up front with Daddy. He backed out of the yard and started down the dirt road. Before we got to the curve, I looked out the back window. Mama and my brothers and sisters were still standing on the porch. I waved and they all waved back.

I had a big lump in my throat and my eyes were wet. We went on around the curve. Daddy said something, I didn't know what. I just stared out the window on my side.

When we were about halfway to Wilmington, I pulled up my shirt and looked in the money belt. There was three hundred fifty dollars in it. Mama was right, I sure didn't want no robber to get my money. It had been too hard to come by.

When we got close to town, Daddy turned off on another road and stopped.

Daddy, why did you turn this way?

To take the shortcut around the edge of town. I'm going to your Grandma Harrell's house on Mercer Avenue.

I was hoping you'd take me by a bank downtown.

You can walk the rest of the way. It's not that far.

It's almost two miles.

You've walked further than that before.

I know, but I got my money and between here and the bank is the roughest part of town.

I got to get going.

Will you leave my suitcase with Grandma Harrell? I'll get it later.

I'll leave it with her.

Daddy drove off and left me standing beside the road. I watched him disappear around the curve. I thought I'd just stand there beside the road a while. Maybe he'd come back and take me downtown. He didn't.

I got back on the road that went downtown and started walking. After I'd walked about a half-mile, a car pulled up beside me. The man driving said, Hey, young man.

Hey, mister.

Where you going?

I'm going downtown.

You want a ride?

I'd just as soon walk.

You looking for a job?

Why, you got one?

We're still hiring at the shipyard.

Why'd you stop and ask me if I wanted a job?

I could tell by the way you was walking that you'd be a good worker.

Well, mister, I thank you, but I'm not ready for a job yet.

Okay, son, suit yourself.

I thought maybe I'd done wrong not taking that man's offer of a ride and a job, but I had things to do first. Besides, the last thing Mama told me was to be careful and that's what I was going to do.

I kept on walking towards downtown. There were people hanging around the street corners that kept looking at me like I didn't belong. I was beginning to think so, too. I looked straight ahead and kept on walking. In less than an hour I was downtown. There were a lot of cars driving around and people were walking everywhere. I wasn't as scared then. Nobody was staring at me.

A big building on the corner of Front and Chestnut Streets had a sign that read Morris Plan Bank. I went inside and walked up to the teller lady.

Hey, young man.

Hey, ma'am, my name's R.C. Fowler. I got some money I want to put in the bank.

Well now, son, you see that man behind the desk across the lobby? You just go right over there and he'll be glad to help you.

I thanked the woman and walked over to the man behind the desk. He looked up and said, What can I do for you?

Sir, that teller lady said I ought to talk to you. I've got some money I want to put in this bank.

You have?

Yes, sir.

Just have a seat and we'll see if we can help you.

I sat down and the man got out some papers and said, Now, young man, just how much money you want to put in our bank and what kind of account do you want?

I was thinking about putting about three hundred dollars in a savings account.

That's a lot of money for someone your age.

Well, I'm seventeen and I've got the money.

Okay, let's see it.

How much interest does this bank pay?

We're paying two percent on passbook savings.

That don't sound like much. That's only six dollars a year on my three hundred dollars.

Look at it this way, son. If you don't put it in savings, it's not going to earn anything. Besides, you can draw it out anytime you want.

Do I get something that says I got money in the bank?

Yes, you get a passbook with the amount stamped in it. You got the money with you?

Yeah, I got it. It's wrapped around my waist.

What you mean?

Well, Mama wanted me to put it in a money belt, and I got it on.

Where'd you get this money, young man?

I earned it. I sold off my acre of tobacco. That's how I got the money.

You been farming, huh?

You could say that. Is it all right if I pull up my shirt here in the bank? The money's under my shirt.

Yeah, go ahead.

I gave the bank man my money. He filled out some papers and gave me the passbook.

When I left the bank I walked down Front Street until I came to a bus stop. I knew I was supposed to catch a bus that said East Wilmington. I stood there at the bus stop along with some other people. I'd rode a school bus for eight years, and one of them years I drove it, but I'd never rode on a city bus. I didn't know if you were supposed to pay when you got on or when you started to get off.

It wasn't long before the bus came and people started to get on. Everybody got on but me. The driver held the door open and looked at me. I turned and walked away. The bus pulled off. I thought I'd just walk. It was only forty blocks.

I walked down Market Street until I got to Mercer Avenue. Then I walked down Mercer until I got to Aunt Ree's house. She was Mama's sister and one of my favorite aunts. I knocked on the door and Aunt Ree opened it.

Well, bless my soul, honey. Come on in. I've been wondering when you were going to be coming to town. I knew you'd been wanting to get here and get a job.

Yeah, I have, Aunt Ree.

Like I said before, you can stay with us until you decide to go somewhere else.

That's what I was hoping. I remember when we had the egg hunt last Easter, you told me I could stay with you when I finished school and came to town.

And I meant what I said. Now, come on back and I'll show you where you can sleep.

We walked to the kitchen and Aunt Ree opened a door that went to her back porch. It was a small porch closed in with windows, and there was a door that opened to the back yard. Aunt Ree pointed to a narrow bed next to a wringer washing machine and said I could sleep there.

Aunt Ree, I'll pay you for my room and board.

You can just pay me five dollars a week, if that's okay.

That's fine.

Don't worry about the washing machine. I won't be using it when you're sleeping.

Aunt Ree, I'm going down to Grandma Harrell's house and get my suitcase. I'll be right back.

Okay. I'll get the bed all made up while you're gone.

Grandma's house was only about two blocks down the street. I walked to her house, got my suitcase and came back to Aunt Ree's. I got settled in and went to bed early. When I woke up the next morning, I didn't hear anybody stirring around. I thought I'd just lay there a while. I got to thinking that something just didn't seem right. There weren't any mules whinnying or no cow lowing to be milked and fed, and there weren't any roosters crowing. About the only sound was a car going by now and then.

Things weren't as busy at Aunt Ree's as they were at home. Aunt Ree and Uncle Bud had two girls. They were a lot younger than me, and they didn't make as much noise as us six children did at home. After breakfast, I told Aunt Ree I was going downtown and see if I could find me a job.

Where you going to start looking, R.C.?

Mama wanted me to try and get on with the Atlantic Coast Line. I'm going to try there first.

I think that's a good place to work.

I hope so, Aunt Ree. I'm going to catch the bus downtown. I'll see you later.

I walked to Market Street and waited at the bus stop. When the bus came, I got on behind another man. He put a dime in the slot, went towards the back and sat down. I did the same thing. I noticed when somebody wanted to get off, they reached up and pulled on a cord that was overhead. When I got to the street where the Coast Line office was, I pulled the cord.

I got off and walked over to the Atlantic Coast Line office. I told the lady behind the desk I wanted to apply for a job. She said, Good, we're hiring right now. Just have a seat over by that desk and fill out this application. I filled out the papers and told her she could get up with me at the telephone number on the application.

I walked around town a while. Then I went in a drugstore and wandered around. I was listening to what people ordered and seeing what they got. A young girl ordered a milkshake. It looked like she was really enjoying it. I ordered a milkshake. The girl behind the counter asked, What flavor?

What kind you got?

We got vanilla, chocolate and strawberry.

I'll take vanilla.

She made the milkshake. I paid her, sat there on the stool and sucked it up through a straw. I kept glancing around, but it didn't look like nobody was staring at me. It looked like I was getting on to city life pretty good.

I walked around town some more, then went down to the river and watched the tugboats coming and going. I thought to myself, well, this is all right but something just don't feel right. I'm not working. I've got to get me a job soon.

I caught the bus and went back to Aunt Ree's. She asked how things went. I said, They went all right. I put in an application for a job at the Coast Line. Aunt Ree, can I tell you something?

Sure, son, what is it?

I put your telephone number on the application so they could get up with me if I got the job.

There's nothing wrong with that.

Only one thing, Aunt Ree.

What's that?

Well, I ain't never talked on a telephone.

You haven't?

No.

There ain't nothing to it, son.

If they call for me, will you talk to them a little first?

Yeah, I'll do that.

In a few days somebody from the Coast Line called and asked to speak to me. Aunt Ree talked to them a little, and then she handed me the phone. I said, Hello.

I'm calling to inform you that we have a position for you.

You do? What is it?

It's called traveling auditor. When can you start?

I can start anytime.

Come on down to our office in the morning and we'll go over your duties.

I'll be there.

I told Aunt Ree, Looks like I got me a job.

That sounds good.

I bet Mama's going to be proud of me.

I know she will, son. You can hang up the phone now.

Oh.

Next morning, I was at the Coast Line office when they opened. I told the lady behind the desk why I was there. She called a man over and introduced us. His name was Walter. Me and Walter talked a few minutes and then we went to a long building that faced Front Street. It must've been two blocks long. There was a covered walkway over Front Street that connected the main office with the other Coast Line buildings.

Walter showed me all around. He said my job would be to pick up invoices from one place and take them to another. Then he showed me a little wagon I'd be using to haul them around.

Walter, you mean my job's going to be pulling that little red wagon all around these buildings?

Yes. That's right.

That don't seem like much of a job to me.

Well, it's important that the invoices get picked up and delivered. You pick up the ones in the *out* basket, take them where they're supposed to go, and put them in the *in* basket.

I don't like the idea of pulling a toy wagon around.

Well, that's the best way to get them from place to place.

I thought when they said traveling auditor, it'd be different than this.

You want the job or not?

Yeah, I want it.

I went to work hauling papers around in the wagon from one office to another. It was kind of embarrassing, but I guessed it was a start. Besides, I was doing what Mama wanted me to do, working inside.

Everybody in the offices was real nice, except for one man, Mr. Barns. He worked by himself up in a tower. Every time I took something to him, I had to walk up a spiral staircase to get to his office. He was hard to get along with. Seemed like I couldn't do anything to suit him. I didn't like him.

There was this young girl that kinda took a liking to me. It seemed like she was always around. Her name was Barbara. She was real nice and friendly, but I still liked Cassie. 'Course, I hadn't seen her since school was out.

After I'd worked at the Coast Line about a week, I told Aunt Ree, I don't know if I'm going to work there much longer.

Why not, R.C.?

Well, it don't seem like much of a job. And I don't like pulling that little red wagon.

I'm sure it's not like farming.

I know. I could always look back at the end of the day and see what I'd done.

Just try and stick with it. Maybe things'll get better.

&

I'd been working at the Coast Line for nearly six weeks and things hadn't gotten any better. I still didn't like pulling that wagon around, and Mr. Barns, up in the tower, was still ornery as ever. That girl, Barbara, seemed to be everywhere I went. It seemed she wanted me to take her on a date. I'd never been on a date. 'Course, there was that time I rode Old Nell to the church and walked Cassie home. I'd have to think about this dating business. I didn't know exactly what to do on a date and I didn't want to mess up.

A few days later after work, me and Barbara went to a picture show. She lived downtown and after the show was over, I walked her home. On the way, we talked some and I told her I'd been thinking about quitting my job.

You have? Why's that?

I just don't like it.

Why not?

First of all, it don't seem like a real job and I don't like working inside. Another thing, that Mr. Barns up in the tower is getting on my nerves. I'm about ready to tell him off.

Now, don't do that. He's an important person with the Coast Line. That's why he's up in the tower by himself.

I don't care how important he is. I don't like him. He's ill as a hornet all the time.

That's just his way.

I don't care. Tomorrow I'm going to tell them I quit.

Don't do that.

I've made up my mind.

Now, you just can't say I quit.

How come? Who says?

You have to write a letter of resignation.

I'm not writing no letter. I'm just going to tell them that I quit and I want my money. Then I'm just going to walk out.

You've made up your mind, haven't you?

That's right.

R.C., I'll write a letter of resignation for you, but I hate to see you go.

You can write it if you want to. I'm leaving.

After I walked Barbara home, I caught the bus to Mercer Avenue. When I got to Aunt Ree's, I told her I'd made up my mind to quit my job.

I hate to hear that.

Aunt Ree, that job's just not for me.

What are you planning on doing, son?

Well, I've been watching them ships come and go up and down the river and I've been thinking about joining the Merchant Marines. At least that way I'll have a real job and I can travel around the world.

Do you know how to go about joining up?

Yeah, I been talking to some of them sailors down at the docks. All I have to do is go to the U.S. Custom House and sign up at the Coast Guard office. They'll give me the papers. Then I can go to Norfolk, join the union, get me a ship and ship out.

Sounds like you been checking things out.

Yeah, pretty much.

Well, R.C., if you've made up your mind, I've got a friend that lives on the outskirts of Norfolk. I'll write a letter for you to give to her. You can stay there until you get a ship.

That sounds good, Aunt Ree.

Barbara met me the next morning when I got to the Coast Line building. She said, R.C., here's your letter of resignation. I typed it last night.

Thank you, Barbara. I appreciate it.

I still wish you wouldn't go.

I'm going.

R.C., you know I like you.

I like you too, but I got my mind set on another girl.

I thought you must've. Are you going around and tell everybody goodbye?

Everybody except Mr. Barns.

You ought to go by and at least let him know you're leaving.

I might.

I turned in my resignation and then went around and told everybody except Mr. Barns good-bye. When I walked by the spiral staircase that led to his office, Barbara was waiting there.

Now, it's not going to hurt you to tell Mr. Barns goodbye.

All right, Barbara.

I walked up the stairs to Mr. Barns' office.

Hey, Mr. Barns.

Hey, boy.

Mr. Barns, my name's not boy, it's R.C. You know that.

You got something for me, boy?

No, I was going to tell you goodbye. But I'm going to tell you something else now.

What's that, boy?

Well, I want you to take that part of my job that was up here in this tower and stick it you know where.

Boy, you're an insolent thing. I'm going to put you on report.

Well now, Mr. Barns, when you stick that job where I told you, be sure and save some room for that report.

I started back down the winding stairs. I could hear old man Barns sputtering back up there in his office. When I got to the bottom of the stairs, Barbara was standing there.

Did you tell Mr. Barns goodbye?

Yeah, I told him.

Now that was the right thing to do. I know you feel better.

I feel real good.

I told Barbara goodbye and walked around to the Customs House. I got my seamen's papers, and then I went to the Army-Navy surplus store and bought me a duffel bag and some clothes like I'd seen some of them Merchant seamen wear.

I caught the bus, went back to Aunt Ree's, and told her I was going to catch the bus the next day for Norfolk, Virginia. She said she'd write the letter for me to give to her friend. That night, I packed my things in the duffel bag and put some money in the money belt Mama'd given me. I went to bed early.

I lay awake for a while thinking about the trip. The farthest I'd ever been away from Wilmington was Fayetteville and that was only ninety-six miles. I wasn't too worried about the trip. I'd probably like seeing the different places on the way to Norfolk. Besides, I'd left the farm to be on my own, and I guessed that traveling around was part of being on your own.

I'd told Aunt Ree I was worried that when I got on the ship I wouldn't know what to do. She said that somebody would for sure explain to me what I was supposed to do and for me not to worry. I was a good worker, she said, and everything would be all right.

Next morning after breakfast, I told Aunt Ree I guessed I'd be going. She said, Now son, have you got everything packed?

Yeah, I've got it all in the duffel bag.

What about your money?

I got what I'm going to carry in my money belt, and it's tied around my waist.

You're not taking all your money, are you?

No, I'm leaving most of it in the bank.

That's good, R.C. Now give me a hug.

I hugged Aunt Ree, slung the bag over my shoulder, walked out to the street and looked back. She was still standing on the porch.

Aunt Ree, tell Mama where I'm going and that I'll write her as soon as I can. When I get back, I'll head right home to the country to see everybody.

I'll tell them, hon. Write me soon.

I caught the bus downtown, got off at the station and bought a ticket to Norfolk. The ticket man said the bus would get to Norfolk about the edge of dark. I waited about two hours before they began loading. Then I got on and sat next to the window. I liked looking at the countryside as the bus rolled along. I stared out the window so much that my neck started to hurt, so I decided to close my eyes and maybe go to sleep. I closed my eyes all right, but I didn't go to sleep right off for wondering what lay ahead.

There I was on a bus going to Norfolk, Virginia, leaving all my family and friends and everybody I knew behind. I was headed for a strange city in a strange state. When I got there, I was going to try and get on a ship and go I didn't know where. I wished that I knew somebody in Norfolk. Maybe I'd meet some nice people. I felt my shirt pocket to make sure I still had the letter to give to Aunt Ree's lady friend.

I fell asleep. When I woke up, it was dark and the bus was pulling into the station at Norfolk.

I got my duffel bag, went inside, and showed the letter that Aunt Ree'd given me to one of the people that worked there. I asked him if he could tell me how to get to that address. He said it was way on the outskirts of town and that I should just go to the trolley stop at the next corner. The trolley I needed would be along soon.

It wasn't long before the trolley came. I got on and showed the operator the address where I wanted to go. He said he'd let me off there. I paid him and found me a seat. It was big dark by then. I looked out the window and wondered what Aunt Ree's friend would think about me showing up that time of night.

I put my duffel bag next to the window, propped my chin on it and looked at the lights outside. At first there were a lot of lights. Then it got to where there was just a light every now and then. After about a half-hour the operator stopped the trolley, looked back and said, Young man, this is where you wanted to get off.

I got off and the trolley pulled away. I stood there in the dark looking at a house across the tracks. The porch light was on and I could see the address on the porch post. I slung the duffel bag across my shoulder, walked up to the house and rang the doorbell. A lady came to the door.

Hey, ma'am. My name's R.C. Fowler. My Aunt Ree, who lives in Wilmington, North Carolina, told me to give you this letter and I might be able to spend the night here.

Let me see the letter, young man.

I gave her the letter. When she finished reading it, she gave it back and said, Son, I'm real sorry, but I can't let you spend the night because my husband's out of town for a few days. I'm afraid it might not look right. I'm real sorry.

That's all right, ma'am. I understand.

Are you hungry, son?

Not that much.

I could fix you a sandwich.

No, I'll just get me something when I get back to the bus station.

Are you going to spend the night there?

Yeah, I'll just sleep on one of them benches.

I hate for you to do that.

Oh, it's not so bad. I've slept on benches before. How do I get back to town?

That trolley you took out here will be back before long. Just get on it, it'll take you right back into town.

I'll do that. Bye, ma'am, I'm sorry to have bothered you.

I'm real sorry.

That's okay.

I caught the trolley back to downtown Norfolk, walked around to the bus station and got something to eat. I laid down on one of the benches. I hadn't been laying there long when a sailor came up and asked, Are you going to sleep there tonight?

That's what I had in mind.

You're not going to get much sleep there on that bench.

I'll be all right.

You in the Merchant Marines?

I got my papers, but I haven't been on a ship yet. I hope to get signed on to one tomorrow.

What's your name?

It's R.C.

My name's John. I've got a room at the hotel around the corner. You can share the room with me until morning if you want.

I thought about going around to that hotel, but I decided against it. I ain't never stayed in one.

Well, R.C., get your duffel bag and come with me. It'll be a lot better sleeping than that bench.

I walked with John around to the hotel. We went up two flights of stairs to his room. It was bigger than my bedroom on the farm. It had one big bed. I'd never slept with nobody but my brothers, but I guessed it would be all right. I took my clothes off except my shorts, undershirt, and money belt and got in bed. John got in bed, too. I told him I'd be leaving early so I could be at the union hiring hall first thing.

We hadn't been laying in bed long before John put his arm across my waist. Well, I didn't like that at all. I grabbed his arm with both hands and flung him off the bed. I got up, started putting on my clothes and looked over at him. He was still laying over against the wall. He looked dazed. He said, What'd you do that for?

Because you put your arm across my waist and I didn't like it.

I wasn't after your money. I saw that money belt when you took your clothes off.

Well, I don't know what you was after, but you just lay right where you are until I get out of here.

How'd you get so strong?

That's none of your business. You just better not get up before I leave.

I got my duffel bag, walked out in the hall and looked back. The sailor was still laying against the wall. I left the hotel, and on the way to the bus station I heard somebody call out, Hey, sailor. I stopped. There was a woman standing in an alley. I asked her, Are you talking to me, lady?

I sure am. Do you want to have a good time?

What are you talking about?

You know what I mean.

I didn't know what she meant. I adjusted the duffel bag on my shoulder and walked on. I got back to the station and spent the rest of the night there. When morning came, I ate some breakfast and found out where the union hiring hall was. It wasn't too far, so I walked. When I got inside the hall, the room was filled with merchant seamen. Most of them were looking at a big blackboard that listed the names of ships, their destinations and what crew they needed.

I walked over to the board and saw one Liberty ship was going to Trieste, Italy. I thought, boy, I'd sure like to get on it. Maybe I'd meet up with Sam. He was still in Trieste. I looked under where it said *crew needed* and saw *ordinary seamen.* Just then a woman working behind the counter said, Hey Johnny, if you're thinking about signing on, come over here.

Johnny? Ma'am, my name's not Johnny, it's R.C.

I was just teasing. I knew a Johnny one time, he was cute and he had curly hair like yours. What can I do for you?

I saw on the board that one of them ships needs an ordinary seaman. I'd like to hire on.

You look kind of young. You got your papers?

Yes, ma'am, I got them.

I showed her my seaman's papers. She looked them over and said, You've got the right documents. We'll just get you signed up. You know this ship's going across the Atlantic, all the way to Trieste, Italy.

Yeah, I saw that on the board.

The lady gave me some papers and an address where I could catch a small boat that would take me to the ship. I thanked her and left. When I got outside, there were some taxicabs waiting. I asked one of the drivers if he could take me to where I was supposed to meet the boat. He said he could. I threw my duffel bag in the back seat and crawled in.

After we got to the dock, I paid the driver and stood there a while wondering what to do. The lady at the union hall had said a boat to take me to the ship would be by soon. I sat down on the dock and let my feet hang off the edge. There was a ladder going down into the water. I guessed that was how I'd get on the boat.

I sat there looking out over the Chesapeake Bay. Several ships were anchored there and I wondered which one I'd be on. The lady at the union hall had said the name of my ship was the Charles G. Coutant, but I couldn't make out any names from the dock.

I hadn't been waiting long before a small boat pulled up. The operator asked if I was waiting to go to the Coutant. I told him I was, and he said to get in. I got in and the boat started out into the bay. I'd never been on a boat before. I stood up so I could see better, and the spray from the waves splashed my face. I liked the feel of it.

In a little while we pulled up alongside a Liberty ship. I knew that a lot of Liberty ships had been built in Wilmington and that Daddy had helped build some of them, but I'd never seen one. I was surprised how big it was. The boat operator said, Okay, young man. This is your ship.

Am I supposed to climb up that ladder hanging over the side?

Yes, you are. It's called a pilot ladder.

I took my duffel bag and grabbed hold of the ladder. When I got both feet on it, the small boat pulled off. I looked up and saw a young man about my age looking down. I said, Hey, up there.

He said, Hey, down there. I started climbing the ladder. It was about twenty feet up. When I got to the top, the young man reached over and helped me with my duffel bag.

I climbed over the gunnel and dropped to the deck. The fellow that had helped me said, Well, it looks like you made it all right. My name's Brett. What's yours?

It's R.C. Thanks for giving me a hand.

Oh, that's okay. Where you from?

I'm from a little farm in Pender County, but I was born in Wilmington, North Carolina.

Yeah? I'm from Carolina, too. My hometown's Smithfield. It's just a couple of hours' drive from Wilmington.

Well, at least we're from the same state.

Yeah, we just might become friends.

I'd like that.

R.C., what are you signed on as?

I'm signed on as an ordinary seaman.

I am, too. Come on, I'll show you the fo'c's'le.

What's that?

Well, on board a ship, a room's called a *fo'c's'le*, and that's what they call the room where we're going to be staying. It's short for forecastle.

Brett, how long you been on board?

Just two days on this ship. But I've been on other ships.

You have?

Yeah. I've been over to France and all around.

Boy, that's something.

Brett showed me my quarters. After I put my things away, we walked around the ship and looked it over real good. There were five big cargo holds that were real deep. We were looking down in one when all of a sudden Brett grabbed me around my waist and said, R.C., what would you do if I picked you up and threw you in that hold?

I figured he was just kidding, but if me and him was going to be friends, I might just better set him straight. I pulled his arms from around me, picked him by the waist and held him over the edge of the cargo hold. He started hollering, Pull me up! Pull me back up! For God's sake, don't drop me!

Well now, who was going to throw who down in that hold?

For God's sake, pull me up. I was only kidding.

I pulled Brett up and sat him back on deck. He was a little shaky.

I wasn't going to drop you, Brett. I just don't like to be bullied.

I'm sorry. How'd you get to be so strong?

It's a long story.

Well, I'll tell you one thing, we're going to be friends for life.

That sounds good to me.

Come on, let's go see the first mate. You've got to check in, show him the papers where you signed on and all. R.C., you scared the hell out of me.

I met the first mate and he seemed real nice. He told me to check in with the purser. He was the one who took care of that part of the ship's business.

I thanked him and said I'd like to ask him a question.

What's that?

Sir, is this ship really going to Trieste, Italy?

Yes, it is. But first we have to go to Galveston and Mobile to take on wheat. After we're loaded, we'll set course for Trieste.

I got a cousin in the Army and he's over in Trieste.

Oh yeah?

Yes, sir. We grew up on a farm close by one another.

You grew up on a farm, huh?

Yes, sir.

How long you been off the farm?

About six weeks, sir.

Well, I think you're going to work out okay. Brett, take R.C. on by the purser's office.

That night me and Brett lay in our bunks and talked 'til real late. Brett told me about his trips to France and other places, and how he'd hung around the drugstore in Smithfield and about his girlfriends. He even told me about seeing Ava Gardner, the movie star, in person. She was from Smithfield, too. Looked like I'd done found me a good friend. When I fell asleep, he was still talking.

Next day, about eleven-thirty, the first mate came around and told me to follow him. We went out on deck and walked over to a barrel that was filled with some kind of oil. He said, R.C., today I want you to start fish-oiling the deck. The oil's in the barrel, and there's the mop and bucket.

I ain't never done that before, sir.

There's nothing to it. All you do is dip out a bucket of oil, stick the mop in the bucket and start mopping.

I can do that all right. What's it for?

It helps keep the deck from rusting. Now, you'll work from twelve to four. Then a crewman from the next watch will take over.

Okay, sir. When do you think we'll be pulling out?

We don't call it *pulling out*, we call it *weighing anchor*. And we'll be weighing anchor as soon as we get a bo'sun's mate signed on. That'll give us a full crew.

The mate left and I started fish-oiling the deck. It wasn't hard work. By the time my watch ended at four o'clock, I'd oiled the whole deck. I'd used all the oil in the barrel. After I'd finished, I leaned over the gunnel and watched the ships out in the bay. The mate came by with a crewman from the four-to-eight watch. He looked at what I'd done and said, R.C., you've fish-oiled the whole deck!

Yes, sir. That's what I thought you told me to do.

Well, for God's sake. I didn't mean for you to do it in four hours. It's usually a two-day job.

I'm sorry. I didn't know, sir.

That's all right, just slow it down a little. Now I've got to find something for the next watch to do.

I went back to my quarters and told Brett what had happened. He laughed and said, R.C., you don't have to work that hard, you're not on the farm now. We went out on deck, leaned over the gunnel and talked. While we were talking, we noticed a small boat coming our way.

I told Brett, That looks like the boat that brought me yesterday. I wonder if it's bringing the bo'sun's mate?

If it is, we'll be shipping out soon.

That's right. We just might weigh anchor in the morning.

Yeah. That's what I meant, weigh anchor.

Brett, you sure you shipped out before?

Why'd you ask that?

Well, you said you just turned eighteen. I'll be eighteen in about three months and I just don't see how you could've been all them places you said, young as you are.

R.C., I'm going to tell you the truth. This is the first ship I've ever been on. I got here just two days before you.

That's okay. I didn't believe you anyway.

The boat that we'd been looking at came alongside and a man climbed up the pilot ladder. We helped get his gear on board. I asked him if he was the bo'sun's mate. He said he was. I told Brett, It looks like we'll be weighing anchor for sure in the morning.

Next morning, the bo'sun said we'd be weighing anchor right away. Brett and me were told to string out a fire hose and wash the mud off the chain and anchor as it came up. When the anchor was up and secured, the ship started moving. At first the whole ship vibrated, but pretty soon it smoothed out. The captain swung the ship around and headed out of the bay for the Atlantic.

In less than three hours we were out of sight of land. It was a strange feeling. I'd never been where I couldn't see land before. Our bo'sun kept us busy battening down the hatches, coiling rope and getting things shipshape. He said that night we'd start our regular twelve-to-four watch, so we'd better get some rest.

Me and Brett turned in right after supper. Before I went to sleep, I thought about how different my bunk was from the bed I'd slept in back on the farm. At least my bed back home stayed still. I guessed I'd get used to the pitching and rolling and the creaking sounds. I hoped I'd do all right on my watch come midnight.

At eleven-thirty the standby crewman on the eight-to-twelve watch opened our door and called out, Rise and shine for the maritime. There were three of us deck crew on our watch. I got up, put my clothes on and looked out the porthole. It was a cloudy night. It wasn't raining yet, but the wind was blowing right much. The waves were higher than when I went to bed.

We had a few minutes before we had to go to our stations. Each of us would steer the ship for an hour and twenty minutes, then spend the same time on lookout in the bow and on standby. The crewman on standby had to make coffee for the next watch and make sure they were up and ready in time.

My first duty that night was in the wheelhouse. It was a big room with lots of glass on the highest part of the ship. Sometimes it was called the pilothouse or the bridge. You could see pretty much all around. There was a big wheel with spokes on it called the helm or the wheel.

When I got to the wheelhouse, I reported to the mate on duty. He was the one that showed me around the second day I was on board. I said, Sir, I'm Fowler. I'm here to stand my watch at the wheel.

Oh yeah, Fowler. R.C., isn't it?

Yes, sir.

I remember you all right. You're the one that fish-oiled the whole deck in one four-hour watch.

Yes, sir, I guess I did. But I've slowed it down some.

Well, R.C., you'll find your watch at the wheel won't be as hard as fish-oiling the deck.

It wasn't so bad.

Okay, now take the wheel and hold a steady course.

Yes, sir.

I went over and told the helmsman, whose name was Joe, that I was there to relieve him. He said, You're right on time. The course is one-eight-zero. I repeated the heading because I'd been told to do that. I asked Joe if he knew what our location was.

Yeah, I heard the mate say we were two hundred miles off the coast of North Carolina.

What about that? That's my home state.

Yeah? I'm from New York.

Are you from New York, New York?

Yes I am. How'd you guess that?

I didn't know, I was just wondering. I had some dealings with some people from New York, New York.

Yeah, what?

When I was on the farm, we shipped some vegetables there one time.

Youse did? I love vegetables.

I'll bet.

Joe left. I thought to myself, damn Yankees.

I took the wheel. There was a big compass with an amber light that made the dark room seem a little more friendly. I was a little nervous at first, but I soon got used to steering. Sometimes I had to hold a little left rudder and sometimes a little right. I guessed it was the current.

After a while, I settled down and wasn't so nervous. I began to think about my home back on the farm. I wished Mama could see me out here in the Atlantic Ocean at the helm of this big ship. She'd probably worry at first, but then I bet she'd smile. If I could talk to her, I'd say, Mama, now just you don't worry about your curly-haired first-born 'cause he's going to be all right. And I'd tell her, I understand now why you always kept us busy and taught us that hard work, honor and fairness go hand-in-hand with truthfulness and responsibility.

🍂

I thought, I just bet if Mama knew I was out here in this big ocean, she'd start to sing one of her favorite hymns. In my mind, I could hear the words so clear,

> *Jesus, Savior, pilot me,*
> *over life's tempestuous sea.*
> *Unknown waves before me roll,*

hiding rocks and treacherous shoals.
Chart and compass come from thee,
Jesus, Savior, pilot me.

I knew that when I was growing up back on the farm Mama had tried to prepare me to meet the world when I left home. I felt like I was pretty well prepared and was just going to try and do the best I could.

Another thing, if I could talk to her, I'd tell Mama I'd always remember our humble home, our struggle to survive, and most of all, the closeness of our family. As I listened to the pounding of the waves against the ship on that moonless night, it seemed I could hear my mama singing another one of her favorite songs, one that she sang so often as me and my brothers and sisters were getting our homework by the kerosene lamp.

Precious mem'ries, how they linger,
How they ever flood my soul.
In the stillness of the midnight,
precious, sacred scenes unfold.

Just then, I felt those memories would not only linger, but would always guide my way.

The first mate came into the pilothouse, walked over, looked at the compass and said, Real good, Fowler, you just keep holding a steady course.

I'm going to try, sir.

Author in 1947 after leaving the Merchant Marine

About the Author

R.C. Fowler lives in Wilmington, North Carolina, the town where he was born. He and his wife have four children and three grandchildren. After spending more than fifty years in the real estate industry, he has more or less retired. He fulfilled his childhood dream of becoming a licensed pilot, and flew his own plane for both business and pleasure. The author enjoys playing the guitar, gardening, and taking weekly rides through the countryside, but his favorite pastime is spending time with his family.

Author today